JAMAICA

STRUGGLE IN THE PERIPHERY

JAMAICA

STRUGGLE IN THE PERIPHERY

Michael Manley

To David,
with thanks
for a fascinating
discussion!
Michael

Published by Third World Media Limited in association with
Writers and Readers Publishing Cooperative Society Limited.

Writers and Readers Publishing Cooperative Society Ltd.
144 Camden High Street, London NW1 0NE England

Published by Third World Media Limited in association with
Writers and Readers Publishing Cooperative Society Limited.

Cover Design Chris Hyde

Typeset by Shanta Thawani
Printed in Great Britain at the University Press, Oxford

ISBN Case 0 906 495 970

ISBN Paper 0 906 495 989

CONTENTS

THE LIBRARY OF THE THIRD WORLD

With this book, the Library of the Third World launches its participation in the effort to establish a more balanced world information and communication order. The Library will use the media of books, monographs, films, video and sound recordings in a comprehensive and multilingual programme which will provide for the Third World an opportunity—

— to publish the thoughts, opinions and experiences of those statesmen, scientists, scholars and artists who are striving for a fundamental restructuring of the prevailing political, social and economic order to make it just and equitable;

— to reflect the tradition and heritage as well as the movement and change evident in the culture of Third World countries;

— to present the results of research into subjects affecting the well being and happiness of people in the Third World.

The Library has been sponsored jointly by Third World Media Limited and South Publications Limited and has its Headquarters in London.

General Editor: Altaf Gauhar

ACKNOWLEDGEMENTS

Where the book is concerned, I owe so many people so much it is hard to know where to begin.

My wife, Beverley, has been by my side through every aspect of the struggle which the book describes. In addition she has helped in the manuscript with criticism, encouragement, typing and proofreading. Above all, her faith in the enterprise seems never to have wavered.

I am grateful to P.J. Patterson, D.K. Duncan, Rex Nettleford, Omar Davis, Paul Robertson, Arnold Bertram and Edwin Jones who all read the manuscript and made innumerable suggestions which are incorporated.

Colin Campbell, Carl and Monica Campbell and Arnold Bertram all helped with the research. Corina Meeks, Judy Wedderburn, Easton Lee, Jean Wilson and Karlene Kirlew combined proofreading with constructive comment.

Paul Robertson, Arnold Bertram and Monica Campbell are responsible for the research which made the notes appended to the work possible. I appreciate the painstaking work which this entailed. It was Paul who had the idea which led to us doing it that way.

Madge and Carmen Smith, Urla Junor, Glynne Ewart, Christine Cummings, Yvonne Lawrence, Bridget Keating, Dorothy Hollingsworth, Cynthia Thomas and Marva Roberts shared the typing while Rosie MacDonald photocopied their efforts. To them all, my heartfelt thanks.

Most of all I am grateful to the Third World Foundation for making this book possible and to Lisa Appignanesi of Writers and Readers for all her editorial work.

DEDICATION

To the memory of seven hundred and fifty people who died so needlessly, many in the first flower of youth.

PREFACE

This book attempts neither history nor autobiography. Even history that is written from a particular point of view must seek to convey an impression of the total experience. Autobiography expresses a point of view of necessity and is under no further obligation.

I am writing these reflections because an episode in history coincided with a particular aspect of my experience in a country which is a microcosm of the Third World.

Jamaica lies at this moment almost at the centre between the lowest point of departure and the highest point of present attainment in the Third World experience. Consequently, it is more representative of its kind than most. Between 1972 and 1980, it was the scene of some of the more controversial events of its colourful history. But the book is not intended as a chronicle of those events for their own sake, nor of the part that I played in them. Rather, it is intended as a reflection, after the event, upon the controversy which surrounded the events.

There is a sense in which the book is both a comment upon and a mirror of a dialectical process. Latin America and the Caribbean today are in the grip of that process. Forces contend for change while other forces defend the *status quo*. Through it all, the great imponderable, the factor half visible, half unseen, is US power. The history of this hemisphere is the story of the interaction between those forces. Events in the history of the nine years with which the book deals, and my own experience of it, enter the book only to the extent that they throw light upon the interaction between those same forces in Jamaica in that period.

There is much that happened during that time which I have not included. The omissions are not because the events themselves were unimportant. Things like an attempted army coup in 1980; the general style and behaviour of the major daily newspaper, *The Gleaner;* strange events with which Jamaicans would be familiar such as the Moonex affair, the Robinson 'spy' case, the attacks on and activities of the Cuban Ambassador, Ulysses Estrada, the use in parliament by the Opposition of doctored tapes of a speech I made to the National Executive of the PNP; the role of the Police Federation before the 1980 election — all added up to an extraordinary sequence. Some still contend that these things happened spontaneously. Others, including myself, find this difficult, if not impossible, to believe. The events appear to be more consistent with an orchestrated plan to bring a society to the very verge of chaos and paralysis. They certainly add up to a pattern of action completely outside anything consistent with the democratic process.

As to whether the events were orchestrated inside Jamaica alone or together with outside forces remains equally controversial. No 'smoking gun' has been found which establishes by irrefutable evidence whose were the hands involved. But then by definition, destabilisation is not intended to be discovered in that sense. In the meantime I have deliberately avoided making a list of innumerable strange events, in investigative journalism style, within the body of the book. This would amount to a multiplication of detail without contributing anything new to the analysis.

I will always be grateful that my colleagues, the Comrades of the People's National Party, my constituents in East Central Kingston and supporters in the wider society gave me the chance to be involved at the level where I sought to make my contribution. I am equally grateful that so many seem to wish me to continue.

I am most grateful of all to the men and women who built the People's National Party, which I have been privileged to lead since 1969, with their love, commitment, sacrifice, stamina and above all, their courage.

Needless to say, many people were involved in running the government, its many agencies and the Party during those hectic years. My failure to mention them all by name is in no way a reflection on the value of their service. It is strictly a consequence of the purpose of this book which is to indicate a dilemma, and not primarily to give a detailed record of the events of a period.

There is a sense in which this book is dedicated to all of these people past and present and to the things which we are striving to accomplish. There is another sense in which the book is a declaration of faith in the objectives which we have set ourselves, born as they are in the inspiration which we have derived from the work of the pioneers of Jamaican liberation: Nanny, Sam Sharpe, Paul Bogle, George William Gordon, Marcus Garvey, Alexander Bustamante and Norman Manley.

I write from the position of electoral defeat but not from the perspective of failure. Many battles can be lost in a struggle and they are defeats. Failure occurs only when the struggle is abandoned. In the broad sweep of history, our struggle is still in its infancy. It is only because I am convinced that this is so that I have found it both possible and necessary to commit these reflections to paper.

THE SETTING

1
THE CARIBBEAN DILEMMA

On December 2, 1823, an American President, James Monroe, was addressing the Congress of the United States of America. His message was to become one of the most famous documents in modern history. The President was concerned, as he had good cause to be in those days, with the threat of European intervention in American affairs. In particular, he feared for the new Republic, born in years of struggle a short two generations ago. It had already been the scene of a British invasion in which its capital, Washington, was burned to the ground. The President spoke of foreign relations and of the still considerable Spanish Colonial Empire elsewhere on the American continent.

... the American continent, by the free and independent condition which they have assumed and maintained, are henceforth not to be considered as subject for future colonisation by any European power. We owe it, therefore, to candour and to the amicable relations existing between the United States and those powers, to declare that we should consider any attempt on their part to extend their political system to any portion of this hemisphere as dangerous to our peace and safety. With the existing colonies and dependencies of any European power, we have not interfered and shall not interfere. But with the Governments who have declared their independence, we have, on great consideration and just principles, acknowledged, we could not view any inter-position for the purpose of oppressing them, or controlling in any other manner their destiny, by any European power, in any other light than as the manifestation of an unfriendly disposition towards the United States.

This speech, largely unnoticed at the time came to provide the excuse for the assertion of US power in the Americas. It became the point of reference, politically and intellectually, for the dominant view in US policy-making concerning the Western hemisphere. Beginning as a 'hands-off' directed against the European imperialist powers, it soon became a 'hands-on', justifying US interference in any and everything not to her liking in either the North or the South of the continent.

One part of our story begins right here with Monroe's speech and what it came to mean in later US hemispheric policy.

Of course, stories never begin at a single point. They begin at many points and the story itself consists of the interweaving of strands that flow like tributaries to make the main course of a particular river of history. The other part of the story began nearly one hundred and forty-five years later on November 10, 1968.

A man who was to be named a national hero of his country; who, more than any other, could claim to be the father of its independence; who had been its elected head of government for seven and one-half years and the leader of its parliamentary opposition for much longer than that, was making his last address to the annual conference of the political party that he had formed thirty-one years before and led ever since. He was speaking in Kingston, the capital of Jamaica which was then in its seventh year of independence. His name was Norman Washington Manley.

To thunderous cheers he said:

I say that the mission of my generation was to win self-government for Jamaica; to win political power which is the final power for the black masses of my country from which I spring. I am proud to stand here today and say to you who fought that fight with me, say with gladness and pride: mission accomplished for my generation![1]

But even as he was bidding farewell he knew that political independence for a small island in the Caribbean was only a beginning. Once achieved, the real struggles would lie ahead, struggles with the problems of economic development, with social injustice, above all with the implications of President Monroe's words.

Thirty years before, during 1938, a group of patriotic Jamaicans had approached Norman Manley to persuade him to help them form and, in due course, head a political party.

It was a time of turmoil throughout the Caribbean. Men of widely differing backgrounds and reflecting considerable differences in ideology were united in the view that Jamaica should become an independent nation. They were conscious of the great struggles of liberation which had marked Caribbean and Latin American history beginning with the Haitian Revolution led by Toussaint L'Ouverture.[2] They were convinced that the road to independence would be difficult and would require political organisation.

Some were patriots in the pure sense of men and women who resented being ruled by another people of another race from a centre of power four thousand miles away. Others were reformers who were appalled by Jamaica's class system, its extremes of wealth and poverty, its racial discrimination, its lack of social mobility and its exclusion from the political process of more than 90% of the population. Still others were ideologues who shared the patriotic and reformist zeal of their colleagues but went further to reject the whole plantation system which operated as an extension of European capitalism and left Jamaica suspended just about half-way between feudalism and capitalism. It was the patriotism that united them.

They turned to a man who had become a legend in his lifetime. He was a little bit like a figure of romantic literature: still the most complete schoolboy athlete the island had ever produced; Rhodes Scholar; World War I artillery man and hero with the British Army; the advocate who never lost a murder case; and with it all, a man of established patriotic credentials and socialist outlook.[3] On September 18, 1938, they formed their political organisation, launched it formally and named it the People's National Party. It was dedicated to self-government, independence, the reform of the political system and the reorganisation of the economy — indeed, the whole way of life of Jamaica.

Two years later, it was to declare itself a socialist organisation. During the next thirty years, it worked for independence and succeeded. It worked for a federation of the British Caribbean territories and failed.[4] It was to spend only seven and one-half years in power (prior to independence), yet it was to exert an extraordinary and unending influence over the course of events in the island and throughout the Caribbean. For thirty years, Norman Manley was to dominate his party and, along with his cousin, William Alexander Bustamante,[5] influence every aspect of the life of Jamaica. Together they were to have a profound influence on the course of the wider history of the English-speaking Caribbean.

In 1968 Manley was seventy-five and, with only a year to live, he had decided the time had come to retire. Some 15,000 members of his People's National Party were gathered. Each year, for the last thirty years, he had spoken on this occasion. Each speech — reflecting his philosophy, his analysis of the times — had been of the stuff of which historical drama is made. This was no exception. It was a charged occasion full of sadness and yet with that sense of inevitability and resignation that attaches to a farewell. Norman Washington Manley was making his last major political statement. Having proclaimed the accomplishment of the political mission of his generation he went on to ask:

> And what is the mission of this generation, the generation that succeeds me now that I quit my leadership? It is to be founded on the work of those who went before. It is to be made up by the use of your political power, of tackling the job of reconstructing the social and economic society and life of Jamaica.[6]

Like many of the great leaders of his time, Manley was becoming increasingly aware of the limitations upon political power and freedom that are imposed by economic structures. Those who knew him at that stage of his life were deeply conscious of his increasing preoccupation with the connection between the world's economic structure and the social and economic deformity of countries like Jamaica.

One by one, the great figures of the liberation process of the 1940s and 1950s were coming to realise that political freedom could become a sham.[7] This would surely happen if it did not rest upon the capacity to determine the course of economic development within the boundaries of the new nations. Each one was learning that its flag of freedom was only a symbol of new opportunities and not, by itself, evidence of real change. Those who wished to work for change would have to contend with more than poverty and entrenched oligarchies. Particularly if they were located in the Western hemisphere, they would also have to contend with American power and the reality of the most formidable hegemony in history.

The Monroe Doctrine, as the message of 1823 became known, really made three points. It said to the European powers, then in the full flood of their imperialist expansion: hands off as far as the American continent is concerned. It said to those powers which had existing colonies: we will not interfere. And it said that the independence of those areas which had already secured it should be maintained. Originally the work of John Quincy Adams, then Secretary of State, the Doctrine was a blend of national self-interest, a realistic recognition of the *status quo* and a declaration of economic intent. In fact, Adams wrote frankly at the time that the US intended to guarantee its 'commercial interests'. But it was hardly in a position to take on the world and so it indicated its acceptance of the *status quo*. Yet beneath these political considerations lurked the ambition of a nation which already regarded itself as a trader.

The Doctrine is also interesting from another point of view. It is one of the earliest and most explicit statements of hegemonic intent, later to become the 'sphere of influence politics' of the twentieth century. Although the Doctrine speaks of the acceptance of the *status quo* and indicates an intention not to interfere, there were countless interventions by the United States in the affairs of its neighbours to the south during the rest of the nineteenth and twentieth centuries: Mexico in 1848 and 1916; Columbia in 1903, ending with the creation of Panama by force to provide a political basis for the control of the intended Panama Canal; Panama itself, dealt with in 1915, 1918, 1921 and 1963; Nicaragua on innumerable occasions between 1848 and 1934 and more recently; Haiti in 1915; Honduras at least four times in this century, between 1912 and 1925; the overthrow of the Arbenz Government in Guatemala in 1954 as a climax to many acts of earlier interference; the Dominican Republic in 1960. It is a long and often bloody history. The Bay of Pigs in Cuba in 1961 is the one defeat suffered by US power in the western hemisphere.

Then came Chile and the Allende tragedy in 1973.[8] This marked the start of a new twist to the business of intervention. No US Marines ever landed, as they had in the Dominican Republic a mere decade before. The removal of the unacceptably progressive regime was not contrived through an army coup, at least not at first. Instead, the Central Intelligence Agency was to be the main instrument. The technique was first used against Mossadegh, the popularly

elected and progressive Prime Minister of Iran in 1953.
Mossadegh was destabilised and overthrown with ridiculous
ease. The Shah was installed on the Peacock Throne.

With the Iranian experience behind it, the CIA penetrated
the very fabric of Chilean life and helped bring the society to
the brink of anarchy. General Pinochet and the Chilean Army
overthrew and killed Allende, the people's elect, to 'restore
order'. But it was the CIA and its *agents provocateurs*, working
with the local vested interests, who had spread such terror and
confusion that the society was in fact grinding to a halt, thus
setting the stage for Pinochet's *coup de grâce*. Further
refinements in the techniques of intervention were to come;
but the new pattern was set.

As the years rolled by after 1823, US investment grew
throughout Latin America. As investments grew so did trade.
Statistical data for the 19th century are hard to come by.
However, there are interesting figures available for the 20th
century that illustrate dramatically the growth of the United
States' interest and stake in the world economy. For example,
America's share in exports of manufactured goods worldwide
rose from some 11% in 1899 to over 20% in 1967. In this
period, Britain's share, 33% in 1899, had fallen to 12% by 1967.

Of even greater relevance to the understanding of US
foreign policy are figures relating to foreign investment. In
1914 the USA had attained a modest 6% of all foreign
investment in the world. By 1960 the citizens of the USA
owned 59% of all foreign investment worldwide. Not
surprisingly, Britain's share, a whopping 50% in 1914, had
fallen to 24.5% by 1960. By 1975 the total US investment
abroad was $133.2 billion. In 1950 it had been $11.8 billion. In a
single generation it had increased by 1,029%.

Other figures tell yet another aspect of the story. Various
companies operating in Latin America on the basis of private
US overseas investment disposed of 93% of their production
with the local markets that play host to the particular
companies. Then again, between 1965 and 1980, 52% of all
profits of the US subsidiaries operating in Latin America were
repatriated to the United States. This means that for every
dollar of net profit earned by a global corporation subsidiary,
52 cents left the country, even though 78% of the investment
funds used to generate that dollar came from local sources.
Between 1960 and 1970, US-based corporations financed 83%

of Latin American investments locally, either from re-invested earnings, or from local Latin American savings. Therefore, only about 17% of US investment during the period represented a transfer of capital from rich countries to poor.

By 1896, President Grover Cleveland watched askance as civil authority collapsed in Cuba, his closest overseas neighbour. The Cubans were nearing the end of their long and bitter struggle for independence; the Spanish were barely retaining control in the major cities. The island was in chaos. Cleveland's reflections are symptomatic of the evolution of US thinking since 1823, matching the changed circumstances on the continent.

Speaking of the extent of United States financial exposure in Cuba, Cleveland remarked:

> Our actual pecuniary interest in it is second only to that of the people and Government of Spain . . . Besides this large pecuniary stake in the fortunes of Cuba, the United States finds itself inextricably involved in the present contest in other ways, both vexatious and costly.

This reflection led the President to the following conclusion:

> When the inability of Spain to deal successfully with the insurrection has become manifest ... a situation will be presented in which our obligations to the sovereignty of Spain will be superseded by higher obligations which we can hardly hesitate to recognise and discharge ...

A mere two years later, William McKinley, who succeeded Cleveland as President, was to intervene to bring the 'hopeless struggle' to an end. Unquestionably, McKinley was motivated by concern for the 'pecuniary interest' which had exercised Cleveland's mind. By 1902, the notorious Platt Amendment[9] had conferred a right of continuous American intervention in Cuban fiscal sovereignty.

In 1906 Cuba was the subject of armed intervention to protect American property interests. It was Haiti's turn in 1915. By now those 'commercial interests' which had concerned Quincy Adams were the explicit motive force behind US action in the hemisphere. Arbenz of Guatemala, Juan Bosch of the Dominican Republic, Salvador Allende of Chile, were all to become men famed in history, not for what they accomplished but because they were crushed for daring to challenge this 'pecuniary interest' which had excited Cleveland's attention and driven McKinley to act.

While the whole of Latin America was becoming an extension of US economic power and cultural influence, European imperialism was reaching new heights throughout Africa and Asia. By the end of the 19th century, it was beginning to occur to the great European imperial powers that it might be simpler to slice the cake by a process of negotiation rather than as a consequence of war. In 1894, with inspired foresight, the German Chancellor, Otto Von Bismarck, invited some 14 European countries to a conference in Berlin. Here, with the sole exception of Switzerland, Europe made the partition of Africa peacefully around the conference table. They did their job so thoroughly that by 1900 it is estimated that only one-tenth of Africa was left unapportioned. In a moment of unselfconscious revelation, Gladstone, Prime Minister of Britain, delighted with the success of the conference and confident of Britain's continuing leadership in a world dominated by imperialism, welcomed Germany to the imperial group with the following words:

> If Germany is to become a colonising power, all I can say is, 'God speed her'. She becomes an ally and partner in the execution of the great purpose of Providence for the advancement of mankind.

Providence apart, these empires were exploited for their natural resources and for their primary products. Where the products did not exist they were planted or developed. Caribbean sugar cane, Ghanaian cocoa, East African sisal and coffee, Rhodesian copper, Malaysian rubber were all grown or mined or tapped to supply the raw materials for the expanding industries which followed in the wake of the industrial revolution. Much of the finance which fuelled the spectacular growth of European industry was accumulated from the surpluses created by the production of the empires.

But even as the empires were expanding and the systems of economic exploitation being perfected, the contradictions were growing. Throughout the Caribbean, Africa, Asia and the Pacific, people wearied of poverty and became defiant of alien authorities. Slave uprisings were already rocking the Caribbean while the Monroe Doctrine was taking shape in Washington.[10] The Spanish empire in Central and South America was under constant attack and in steady retreat. Elsewhere, the empires were coming to the end of the phase of expansion and comparative stability. However, it was not until the 1930s that systematic opposition to external domination became a significant new force in world history.

Between 1945 and 1970, virtually the entire colonial world was to rise up, demand and secure political independence. Within the space of five years some one and a half billion people, all colonised, all the abject objects of imperial domination and exploitation up to 1945, were to become free. Flags of independence were to rise in more than 100 national capitals. Some won their freedom in bloody wars, as in Kenya and Malaysia; some through extraordinary acts of moral mobilisation, like the civil disobedience movement of Gandhi in India; some through explosions of worker protest followed by systematic political organisation, as in the Caribbean. Suddenly, liberation had become a more significant political force than domination.

In all these countries the first energies were directed towards political independence. There was a general awareness of exploitation of national economies but the more urgent psychological impulse reflected the urge to freedom and the need to escape degradation. Every new independence experience was accompanied by excitement and hope. But the liberated spirit cannot exist on a diet of freedom alone. The great imperialisms had left behind societies where the majority lived in abysmal poverty with little education, inadequate health services and squalid housing. Independence had not been won for bread alone; but bread in the sense of the hope and the reality of material betterment, was always the largest part of the equation. Independence had to be followed by material progress for that majority who had never known it, indeed could never know it, while part of the colonial experience.

In due course, thinking in newly independent countries would shift in focus. The earliest preoccupations were with political forms and relationships. Some countries, like those of the English-speaking Caribbean, adopted British parliamentary and party political forms. They were to become the strongholds of what the political thinkers of the West describe as 'plural democracy' — except for the Marxists who substitute the word 'bourgeois' for 'plural'. Whatever the political forms and economic circumstances, these countries came, in due course, to be known as the Third World.

No one is absolutely sure about the origins of the term

'Third World'. However, the phrase must be understood in three senses.

Historically, 'Third World' is intended to describe that group of nations now numbering some 117 who were former colonies or dependencies of the great empires of the 19th and 20th centuries. The term is intended to convey a sequence. The industrial powers of the West in the northern hemisphere are seen as the 'First' major phenomenon in the modern historical process. 'Second' refers to the Socialist group of countries headed by the Soviet Union following the October Revolution in 1917 and the establishment of the Comecon Group of countries under communist leadership after 1945. 'Third' is intended to identify the rest who only emerged as a group with any self-consciousness in the 1950s after the first great phase of liberation successes. These countries constitute the 'periphery', the South, completely dependent on the North, the 'centre' of power, for technology, finance and markets.

The term also identifies a political grouping because there is a general feeling of common antecedents. In addition, there is the need to be identified as a political force capable of making itself heard above the din created by the power struggle between the first and the second groups, East and West.

Finally, 'Third World' is a statement of economic intent because there is a growing awareness within the group that the world's economic structure was established by the imperial powers and works substantially to the advantage of those who enjoy industrial power, technological superiority, and market and financial control. The members of the Third World are uniformly conscious of the fact that one of their hopes for a better share of the world's prosperity lies in their capacity to change this system and make it more equitable.

By the time Norman Manley came to make his speech in 1968 and talked of economic independence as a task of the generation of leadership that was to succeed him, he did so against the background of a growing recognition that political independence confers no magic of its own other than the benefits to the national psyche. He, the most rational of patriots, as far back as 1961 had come to realise that no national aspirations were likely to be realised in Jamaica or elsewhere in the Third World unless and until their economies could be modified and restructured. They had to be restructured to ensure that Jamaica produced more of what it needed for itself;

that its exports represented a rational disposal of productive surplus to finance the purchase of those things which it chose to import from abroad. He recognised that it had to deal with transport and communications and shipping; that it had to keep as much of its raw materials at home for processing as technically feasible and financially possible.

He was also recognising that there is a direct connection between the structure and nature of a colonial economy and the structure and nature of colonial society. So he spoke of social reform meaning by that the reshaping of the social relationships. But he implied, also, the need to reorganise opportunity and redistribute wealth. He was setting out a historical charge, knowing full well that any strategy of economic independence might run foul of the forces that had not hesitated to remove Arbenz in Guatemala and Bosch in the Dominican Republic. He reflected upon the fact that local oligarchies which had felt threatened by policies of change had made common cause with the instruments of US power in securing the removal of both those figures.

The powers which built the empires when they conceded political independence did not lie idle. As quickly as the tide of imperialism in its implicit, political form retreated, just so quickly did it put in place new institutions which would ensure the survival of the economic system which it had created. The International Monetary Fund (IMF) and the International Bank for Reconstruction and Development (IBRD) were established immediately after World War II. The IMF was created ostensibly to manage the world's monetary system. The World Bank, as the IBRD was popularly known, was to provide development capital for the less developed countries from the surpluses of the more advanced economies, but by working with favoured private capital and facilitating the flow of private investment. Both bodies were dominated by the United States from the outset.

They created the framework within which new economies resting on fragile foundations, dominated by foreign ownership, locked into a world system hostile to change, were to seek the goal of 'development'.

For several years, the political voice of imperialism was silent. Why should it speak since the armies had come home? Even the political aspects of the Monroe Doctrine seemed to be collecting dust, though the 'pecuniary interest' did not lack for defenders among successive US administrations.

Then suddenly, twelve years after Manley's call for economic independence, Ronald Reagan, the President of the United States was to give the Monroe Doctrine a new twist. Speaking to the Canadian parliament on March 12, 1981, he said:

> On this side of the Atlantic we must stand together for the integrity of our hemisphere, for the inviolability of its nations, for the defence against imported terrorism and for the rights of all our citizens to be free from the provocations triggered from outside our sphere for malevolent purposes.

At that particular moment Reagan was referring to the struggle in El Salvador. He was invoking a fear of the same power, Russia, which had prompted his predecessor's remarks in 1823, but he was adding a new political twist. He was implying that the threat was now ideological as much as national. Years of silence on the matter were being replaced by a clearly stated political and ideological justification. Not for Reagan the simple, explicit action based on 'pecuniary interests'. He was, at least by implication, clothing action based upon those interests in the garb of ideology.

The assertions of hegemonic powers are the same whatever the language that describes them. Manley's call for economic independence would demand unflagging spirits in the years to come. Clearly, the citadel of economic power was not going to lack for equally resolute defenders.

2
THE OTHER SIDE OF THE MOON

To the heirs of President Monroe, Jamaica is an extended beach, a tourist paradise. Tourism is in the business of transient pleasure, of escape. The last things a tourist wants to know about are the poverty and the problems which lie behind the luxury hotels and the bright, white-sand beaches. In any event, the tourist has inflation, international tensions and his own urban ghettoes to fret about when he is at home.

Ninety miles to the south of Cuba and 75 minutes by jet to the south-east of Miami, two and a quarter million people occupy an island 144 miles long and 49 miles wide, making up 4,000 odd square miles. Largely mountainous, with its highest peak some 7,400 feet, Jamaica is widely regarded as one of the most beautiful islands in the world. Its Blue Mountain Range produces one of the great luxury coffees of our time, and its rugged grandeur combines visual excitement with a sense of permanence and strength. As one travels westward from this great range one never fails to be surprised by the sheer beauty of Jamaican scenery. In the north and middle of the island is a parish named St. Ann which reminds the English of the soft, green, rolling contours of the Surrey Downs. More to the west the same traveller may be reminded of the steeper contours of Sussex. Beaches abound with their coral sands, startlingly white in the tropical sun. There are roads leading from the mountains down to the coast where thick, almost forest-like foliage suddenly opens to reveal the sea seeming to stand before one's eyes like some great wall tapestry. At the bottom are pale greens shading through turquoise and emerald to the deepest sapphire as the eye travels across the deepening ocean-bed, tilted upward by the optical illusion of the car's passage down the mountainside. For range of visual spectacle, it cannot be surpassed in the tropics. This is the very stuff of which tourist dreams are made; this is the bright, green side of the tourist moon!

The other side is the poverty which still plagues the majority of Jamaicans.

It is customary for commentators with a superficial view to describe Jamaica as 'rich in natural resources'. By this they mean that it has fertile plains and a lot of people who have survived by a combination of resilience and courage; a people quick to laugh, as the tourist is told, but equally quick to anger, as he sometimes discovers to his surprise. It does have one of the world's largest proven reserves of bauxite, the ore from which aluminium is made. However, it also has 80% of its land surface in slopes too steep for modern agricultural implements except after huge investment in terracing.

Its political history is marked by six major dates. In 1494, Christopher Columbus came upon an island inhabited by peace-loving Arawak Indians. He named it Jamaica and claimed it for the Spanish Crown whose property it remained for the next 161 years. It was partially settled by the Spanish. Then, in 1655, the British under Penn and Venables surprised the local garrison one night. Thereafter, it became one of the finest jewels in the British Crown.

The British lost no time in putting their conquest to work. Settlers arrived closely followed by their families and soon established a thriving sugar industry. African slaves supplied the labour, and for nearly 200 years the island played its part in providing the financial basis for the industrial revolution. This period was marked by successive slave rebellions. There was the legendary woman Nanny, who defeated the British time and again with her successful guerrilla tactics, leading her followers to believe that she was blessed with magical powers.

There was Cudjoe,[1] who was to fight the British to a standstill and eventually win a formal treaty of recognition. The British recognised the runaway slaves who formed Cudjoe's and, earlier, Nanny's armies as free people. Two areas of freedom were established — one in the east and one in the west of the island, high up in the mountains which they had held against all comers. In return, however, Cudjoe undertook not to provide a haven for escaped slaves. Here was one of the first acts of neo-colonial accommodation. Some would have it, of course, that Cudjoe was merely a realist.

Slave uprisings continued from time to time, and finally, in

1831, there was the biggest revolt of all, led by a slave, who was also a Baptist Deacon, named Sam Sharpe.[2] The whole north-west of the island was alight in a battle that shook the local settlers and slave owners to their core. Sharpe refused to recant, and immortalised the cause of all slaves with the simple pronouncement as they prepared the scaffold from which they would hang him: 'I would rather die on yon gallows than live a slave.'

By the 1830s slavery had become an expensive proposition. At that time, it behoved the slave owner to keep up the strength of his property — which meant feeding. Then there was the business of putting down the slave uprisings. Sam Sharpe's rebellion coincided with new forces contending in the British parliament. To some of these, slavery was an economic anachronism, an inefficient survival that had no real place in a world whose shape was being determined by the industrial revolution. To still others, slavery was morally repugnant. And then again, there was that difficult business of the slave uprisings. By 1838 slavery was abolished in Jamaica, to be succeeded by wage labour which, in the absence of trade unions or political rights, was to prove to be a cheaper method of production.

The abolition of slavery was accompanied by the first rush to the hills as the former slaves claimed parcels of land in the high mountains. This established a peasant class; but such were the rigours of agriculture on the mountain slopes that it was not long before poverty drove most of the former slaves back to the sugar estates in search of work, and the pittance which was offered as a wage. Meantime, the population grew and pressure upon the land with it.

So we come to the fourth chronological milestone. It was known as the Morant Bay Uprising of 1865. It was led by another Baptist Deacon named Paul Bogle,[3] son of a freed slave. Bogle took up the cry of the landless, urging the powers-that-be to cede lands, particularly in the eastern end of the island which was his home. He was supported by a Jamaican legislator of mixed blood and strong conscience named William Gordon. The uprising followed a march upon the court house of the capital city of the eastern parish of St. Thomas where there was a brief but violent passage of arms. The insurgents lost. In due course Bogle and Gordon were hanged. But Bogle's act was to have far-reaching effects which extended over the next hundred years.

Up to that time Jamaica, like its sister island Barbados, was a strange constitutional creation. There was a local legislature, called the House of Assembly, and people of property were free to elect representatives.[4] This assembly had certain powers although its authority was entirely subject to the will of the British Crown exercised from Whitehall in London. The assembly was a place where the local plantocracy and, to some extent, the rising middle class of professionals and sugar estate managers could express their views and propose how the colony might best be administered. Their powers were limited but then so were their needs since their interests were firmly bound to the British Raj. They were the elite class created by colonialism, enjoying extraordinary privileges in return for running the island which was an extension of Britain's economic interests. Here was a perfect 'marriage of convenience'.

After the abolition of slavery, the marriage seemed destined for a comfortable middle period. The only indigenous peoples of Jamaica, the Arawak Indians, had been quickly wiped out. The population was made up of people recently transplanted from somewhere else. The sugar estates and the trading houses were owned and run by the descendants of English settlers. The labour force on the estates and the docks and in the homes was supplied by descendants of the slaves who were themselves transplants, via the middle passage and the slave ships, from Africa.

Between these poles was a convenient middle class, originally the offspring of the mating between white plantation owners and black female slaves who would have resisted at the cost of their lives. This residue of mixed blood had provided the book-keepers and the house-keepers of the system. Ambitious for their children, they had sacrificed to ensure that education would maintain the upward momentum through the second and third generations of free people.

Here, then, was a unique social mix: the slave owner was white, and culturally and psychologically still an Englishman. He was keenly aware of the advantages of the system. Then there was the slave who had been the object of the most sustained act of cultural destruction known to modern history. The break-up of slave families and the banning of African traditions are all well documented now and understood to be part of the ruthless and systematic attempt to wipe out the sense of heritage by blotting out cultural memory.

In between lay the middle class, insecure in its origins and blinded by its determination to escape from the African, slave side of its roots and heritage. Constantly knocking at the door of social and economic acceptance, it was a class driven by the desire to get inside the citadel of privilege represented by the plantation owners, the big merchants and their families.

As the generations passed, these main categories evolved into a highly complex class structure in which elements interacted with each other and with the basic groups in often unpredictable ways. The hillside peasants lived side by side with medium sized farmers. The first regarded themselves as working class and the latter as middle class. Yet both would often combine in hostility towards the agricultural labourer and sugar estate owner alike. The urban middle class aspired to the standards of the big business group. But white collar workers increasingly gravitated to the unions in search of collective advantage. Of middle class origin, they began to develop dual characteristics. In this they joined the hillside peasant who had long since become a sugar estate worker for half of each year. Indentured Indian labour was introduced in the 19th century and formed an enclave on the sugar estates. Indian, Chinese, Jewish and Lebanese traders all came, settled and added to the mix.

However, in 1865 it was the occupants of the citadel and those knocking at the gates who enjoyed a measure of representative government and who were shaken to their foundations by Paul Bogle's uprising. In an act almost unique in modern history they petitioned the Crown to take away their slender legislative powers. Her Majesty, Queen Victoria, graciously consented and so Jamaica stepped down from her tiny constitutional pedestal to become that most abject of constitutional creatures — the Crown Colony.

For the next half-century, the island pottered along producing sugar and enjoying cycles of prosperity and misfortune in accordance with the state of the sugar market. Then in the 1920s arose the first of the founders of modern Jamaica. Pulling together in his person and vision all that was implied in the struggles of Nanny, Cudjoe, Sam Sharpe and Paul Bogle, Marcus Mosiah Garvey[5] began his lonely protest against virtually everything in Jamaican society. At the same time, he became the first and greatest of the voices calling the black man to ethnic, political and economic redemption.

Garvey never himself witnessed any changes in the structure of power or modifications in the anatomy of injustice in Jamaica. But he sowed seeds. He was to become the most significant of the black voices in the United States, demanding equality and justice. He was, in many senses, the ideological precursor of Paul Robeson and Malcolm X. But more than any other man's, his was the voice that stirred the slumbering giant of Africa to its first political awakenings. Kwame Nkrumah of Ghana, Azikwe of Nigeria, Kenneth Kaunda of Zambia, Julius Nyerere of Tanzania, Malcolm X himself and Paul Robeson, all have testified to the impact of Garvey upon their thinking. He was last in Jamaica in 1935. He had founded the Negro Improvement Association in Jamaica in 1914, moving to the United States in 1916 where he had talked of the mass exodus of the black man to his original homeland. Finally, hounded and framed by the powers that be, he died in England in 1940, with no part of his vision yet discernible in the everyday experience of black people.

Nineteen thirty-eight is the next date. That year witnessed the culmination in Jamaica of labour unrest which had started in Trinidad in 1937 and spread throughout the English-speaking Caribbean islands. Labourers were protesting against their terrible wages and working conditions. For a century they had endured brutal working hours and the lack of any form of security or protection on sugar estates, banana plantations, the docks and just about everywhere else which depended upon the labour of black hands for economic effectiveness. By the time the dust had settled in Jamaica, William Alexander Bustamante had formed a trade union that bore his name and was to be the major vehicle of mass protest at the time. His cousin, Norman Washington Manley, had founded the first political organisation — the People's National Party (PNP) — to the end that they win freedom and democracy for all.

Within two years the PNP was to declare itself socialist and Bustamante was to emerge as a union activist but political conservative — bitterly opposed to socialism.

Manley was very much the product of Fabian socialist tradition. Bustamante was like a charismatic George Meany. In the polarisation of their political outlook was born the modern Jamaican political system. Manley fought for universal adult suffrage and self-government, while Bustamante fought for higher wages for workers. In a typically British experiment, a new constitution based on universal adult suffrage, but giving only limited powers to the legislators who would be elected, was granted in 1944. In 1943, Bustamante formed a political party based on his mass trade union that he called the Jamaica Labour Party, somewhat ironically, as it turned out to be the main vehicle of conservative politics in Jamaica. Somewhat more logically the PNP, formed five years earlier, was to become the party standing for more or less radical change from time to time.

Interestingly enough, neither leader was populist in the strict sense of that word. Bustamante had the style of a populist, but ran three extremely cautious governments. He was much admired by the conservatives of the society for the care with which he avoided committing public funds to programmes which would help the poor and his own popularity. Manley's two governments were more audacious, committed as they were to broadening educational opportunity and relieving unemployment. But the main efforts were directed towards the modernisation of the country's institutions, as the way was prepared for independence.

The populist label was later to be attached to our first government between 1972 and 1976 — perhaps because of the sheer extent of our popularity. It is true that we invested substantial sums in social programmes and in fighting poverty. But the profound need to relieve hopelessness and create fundamental change was for us an extension of a philosophical position, not simply an attempt to win popularity and power. Historians will have to determine the question of whether the label was a correct one.

The two parties were to share power between 1944 and 1962, when Jamaica finally attained its full and sovereign independence. This was a period full of strange historical twists. Although Manley's PNP had fought for the vote for all, it was Bustamante's JLP which won the first election. The PNP spoke of organisation, management of the economy and self-government as the necessary preconditions of progress. These were intellectual formulations that were swept aside by the simple appeal of 'bread and butter' which was the Bustamante platform. In that first contest in 1944 the JLP won in a landslide. It is not difficult to reason why.

Where imperialism has intruded upon an indigenous people with their own cultural background and sense of historical continuity, it is the loss of freedom that usually dominates consciousness. Throughout Africa and India, the first preoccupation of a conquered indigenous people was how to recover that which they had lost. Only later did economic issues or questions of workers' rights become of central concern. But the Caribbean is the home of the transplant. Nobody is indigenous in the longer historical sense. Everybody came or was brought to do the job at hand. Hence, one discovers a Caribbean idiosyncracy. The first energies of the broad masses were directed towards bread and butter issues. The institution that first caught the collective imagination was the trade union. The general acceptance of the primacy of the liberation struggle and the importance of political organisation directed towards political objectives came later. Only gradually did a sense of national and cultural identity begin to emerge — nurtured in part by the flowering of indigenous art in the 1930s — and make the limitations of trade union action apparent. Political organisation had to provide the framework for political education before the people were to understand the nature, purpose and possibilities of political power. But in due course this happened, and so the PNP had its turn at power in 1955, where it remained until independence in 1962.

This came after a period between 1958 and 1961 when Jamaica was part of a federal experiment.[8] The period involved an important but unsuccessful attempt to form a federation of the 13 English-speaking Caribbean islands. The Federation of the West Indies was created out of two impulses. On the British side was the impatience with dealing with so many small principalities and powers across the many islands of the archipelago. On the Caribbean side was the view, largely restricted to the intelligentsia of the middle class, that the Caribbean islands would be stronger and have a more meaningful voice in the world if they combined.

At the time when the federation was formed in 1958, no island had attained independence. Some had internal self-government, like Jamaica, Trinidad and Tobago and Barbados. Others were still crown colonies. The plan was to create a federation which would stop short of independence to begin with. After the first five years it was to achieve full freedom with each island achieving independence as part of the new state.

However, Bustamante and the Jamaican people would have nothing of that. He began a campaign against federation on the grounds that the smaller islands of the east would be a burden upon the already bent backs of the Jamaican people. One must understand that large and small are relative terms. Jamaica is only two and a quarter million people, but Trinidad and Tobago is only just over one million, Barbados a quarter of a million and little Montserrat 60,000. Manley decided to hold a referendum to determine Jamaica's fate in the federation. He was overwhelmingly defeated, and so Jamaica proceeded to independence alone. On the 6th of August, 1962, the Union Jack was hauled down for the last time; the green, gold and black flag of Jamaica was raised. Having won a close general election which Manley called specially, Bustamante and the JLP prepared to take this young nation into its first ten years of independence.

Nanny, Sam Sharpe, Paul Bogle, George William Gordon, Marcus Mosiah Garvey, William Alexander Bustamante and Norman Washington Manley were all to be named National Heroes by the citizens of the fledgling nation. The designation 'National Hero' is the highest honour that can be bestowed and is reserved for people who have made an extraordinary contribution. The National Heroes together symbolise the critical elements of struggle in Jamaica's history. Nanny was the slave who took to arms and won freedom for the Maroons by black military prowess in the mountains of Jamaica. Sam Sharpe symbolised the unquenchable thirst for freedom of slaves after more than a century in bondage. Paul Bogle died for the right of the people to own land and George William Gordon joined him on the gallows symbolising the capacity of men to champion worthy causes at the behest of conscience alone. Marcus Mosiah Garvey was the messenger of black equality and racial pride. William Alexander Bustamante symbolised the struggle of the workers for recognition at the work place, while Norman Manley was the great patriot and political thinker, the symbol of Jamaica's nationalism, the intellectual who understood the nature of political power and who, together with his cousin, established the modern political system.

3
THE THIRD PATH

To understand today's politics one must always begin with yesterday's economics. The islands of the Caribbean are perhaps the most perfect examples in today's world of the effect of colonial economics. This is so because, more than would be true of any part of the Third World, the Caribbean was entirely a product of the colonial process. If you think of Africa, memory reverberates with the history of the Ashanti and the Zulu and the Hausa civilisations. Imperialism imposed its power upon a people who were there first and who had already evolved their own indigenous culture, values and economic systems.

Serious study of the economic history of the Third World, which is most vividly illustrated in the Caribbean, must begin with an understanding of three facts. There never was any attempt to produce what was needed but only to produce what someone else needed. Trade did not involve a calculated exchange involving surpluses but the importation of virtually everything that was needed and the export of virtually everything that was produced. Finally, the surplus which a group normally uses to increase its production was largely exported in the form of profit to the centre of colonial power. Hence, at every single level of importance, the natural economic process was diverted, thwarted, frustrated and ultimately destroyed. These propositions need restating not because they are original, but because they are basic to any understanding of the contemporary issues of Caribbean politics.

The normal process by which a community of persons develops into a society and eventually into a nation is clear and straightforward. The group produces as much as it can of its needs. As these needs grow more sophisticated and complex it produces some of what it needs, concentrating on things that it does well or which do well naturally in the particular environment. The surplus is then available for trade so that other needs or merely desires can be satisfied from the surplus of a neighbouring or even distant group. Thus the two basic legs of the economic process are: firstly, the production of what you need, and secondly, the production of a surplus for trade.

In the meantime the group is growing both in numbers and in needs. Hence it becomes necessary to produce another kind of surplus and that is the surplus for investment. This is the surplus which involves doing without something that you have produced so that you can develop the capacity to produce more on a permanent basis. For example, one could grow corn and set aside enough to replant to maintain the same level of production. But one can also set aside even more than that so as to increase the amount of acreage that is under corn.

These basic principles apply in even the most modern and sophisticated societies. Individuals and groups are all involved in the business of production, savings and surpluses. The surpluses are exchanged for the satisfaction of other needs. So too with the nations to which the groups belong.

The Caribbean is unique in that its indigenous peoples, the Carib and Arawak Indians, did not survive the colonial presence. From Trinidad and Tobago along the great curve of the archipelago and to the northernmost tip of Cuba one witnesses a set of peoples, societies, cultures that were created exclusively within the colonial matrix and each of which is a pure product of a colonial process. English, Spanish, French and Dutch settlers were transported to the islands, their destination determined by whoever had won the last European war and secured or lost one or more of the islands as a sideshow to the European power struggle. In all of the islands the settlers quickly concluded that the tropics are more pleasant if somebody else does the work. In due course the various coasts of Africa were plundered for slaves. And so emerged the first and hopefully the last region of the world to be populated entirely by plantation owners and their slaves. There was a small infrastructure of agricultural supervision, on the one hand, and the merchants who supplied the needs of the population, on the other.

Sugar was king. The typical Caribbean island consisted of extensive sugar estates with occasional side excursions into the

growing of things like coffee and cocoa. The slaves did the
work. The more pliant became supervisors. However,
supervising was carried out in the main by the bastard but free
offspring of the slave owners who, with little work to do, had a
lot of time to breed with the more attractive slave girls.
Needless to say, the owner had the power to ensure
compliance. This was to be the source of the middle class of the
19th century. Racially, socially, and economically insecure, it
was a class suspended between its divergent roots, but
struggling to escape from the stigma of the one into the status
of the other. The entire production of the island would be
geared to exporting sugar and other crops which were in much
demand on the fashionable tables of Britain and Europe. Little
or no attention was given to the production of the
commodities which the island's population needed. Virtually
all of this was imported and, of course, imported from Britain
or Europe. Hence we saw for the first time the development of
economies that were entirely peripheral to something outside
their home shores and geographical boundaries.

When the great explosions of 1937 and 1938 occurred and
the nationalist movements which they spawned began to take
root, the thinkers of the region began to wrestle with these
problems. What was the way forward? To go forward you had
to recognise the depth of the trap in which you were caught.
Hence, 'forward' became not so much a matter of marching on
level ground, but had to begin with the question how to climb
up out of a trap which was part hole and part maze. There were
some levels at which the problem could present itself in
relatively simple terms.

Obviously to have entire island economies resting on sugar,
coffee, cocoa and bananas was untenable. The simplest
common-sense would show that you had to begin to
supplement this with a manufacturing capability. But here was
the rub. Where was the capital to come from with which to
build the factories? Living standards were already so low that
to ask for some great act of popular national sacrifice would
involve a contradiction in terms. In 1935 11% were
unemployed and 50% underemployed; 92% of those who
worked earned less than 25 shillings a week.[1] There was no
room for sacrifice! The irresistible impulse was for the masses,
so long deprived of anything more thàn the barest subsistence,
to have more and have more now. The profits from the

agricultural enterprises, such as they were, were still directed abroad because they were still largely under foreign ownership. In any case, by the 1940s these Caribbean plantation economies had become dilapidated and ill-equipped. By now they represented a comparatively slender economic base. Meantime the populations had grown over the generations in the context of the distorted economic process which the system produced. Hence, there was always unemployment. Clearly, manufacturing had to become a part of the economy. But there was no money available locally because the bulk of the profits over the years had gone back to Britain. So it seemed that the only way to finance the building of factories and the diversification of these stunted economies was through the harnessing of overseas capital.

To begin with, the lid of the trap was the fact that the bulk of the productive capacity was owned abroad and hence the bulk of the surplus ended up abroad each year. Now the trap was going to perpetuate itself. With no easy means of capital accumulation available within the economy one would be forced to return to the same source for capital to establish factories. These would be built, once again, on the basis that the value of the surplus which they created would end up abroad. Unjust as it must seem, from one point of view and within the framework of one analysis, it appeared that there could be no other answer. Thus was born that concept of post-colonial economic development which has become known as the 'Puerto Rican Model'.

Simply stated, the model calls for diversification of the economy through the development of a manufacturing sector. This manufacturing sector is designed in the first instance to produce goods which have hitherto been imported from one of the industrial countries. This is called the import substitution process. The capital and know-how are invited from abroad. The advantage which is offered to this capital is the comparatively low wage rates which the local labour force will require. Visiting owners of capital demand and must receive absolute security for their investment, the guarantee of the right to ship all of their profits out and usually, in addition, a guarantee of being able to ship out their profits at a rate that pays off the original investment in a comparatively short period of time.

Of course there are benefits. The host country becomes

exposed to higher levels of technology. New investment does occur, creating new jobs and requiring the training of the local workforce. New investments are accompanied by inflows of foreign exchange which ease balance of payments difficulties. All this, by providing temporary relief, tends to mask the real problem. Yet it does represent one set of logical responses to objective conditions.

To understand the full implications of the Puerto Rican Model, one must see it in its political and economic setting. Itself a Caribbean territory, Puerto Rico was one of the very few outright US dependencies anywhere. Roughly Jamaica's size, it suffered all of Jamaica's problems as both entered the post-World War II era. It was a part of the general movement of the time away from out and out colonial status. However, under an able leader, Munoz Marin, the country worked out a special relationship with the United States called Common-wealth Status. Under this arrangement the US would undertake central services such as security, customs and the like. The costs of these would be borne by the federal authorities in Washington. Puerto Rico would also benefit from a number of social security arrangements.

In economic matters, Puerto Rican products would be treated as if originating on the mainland, with free and unlimited access to US markets. In the political sphere, Puerto Ricans would enjoy the right to form political parties, freedom of speech and the other traditional rights guaranteed by the rule of law. On the other hand, the country would not be independent, would have no foreign policy or defence capability of its own, and of course, no costs to bear in those areas. It was, and is, a classic, Western plural democracy shorn of its sovereignty which, in fact, the majority of its people have not claimed in the last two generations.

Thus Puerto Rico started out on the model which bears its name with two clear advantages. Many of the normal overheads of running a modern state were absorbed by the US. More critically, the US market was accessible to the Puerto Rican economy.

It is in this political, administrative and economic environment that the policy of 'industrialisation by invitation' was to be implemented. Foreign capital was to be the engine. Naturally it would come from the US. Hence the model started with a third advantage. This was the most important of all, though not necessarily the easiest to detect. Implied in the arrangement was a built-in opportunity for the further promotion of those 'commercial interests' of the US which had first excited Quincy Adams' attention. Furthermore, the model was completely consistent with those US interests which determined the motivation and course of her hegemonic policies. Once on the Puerto Rican Model path, you were assured of US approval. Stray from it and questions would inevitably be raised.

Norman Manley came to the conclusion by about 1950 that industrialisation involving foreign investment would have to play a vital part in Jamaica's economic development. The St. Lucian Nobel Prize-winning economist, Arthur Lewis, played a significant part in promoting the idea in his mind.[3] Indeed it was the PNP which, from opposition, had moved the resolution in the House of Representatives in 1950 which led to the creation of an Industrial Development Corporation by the JLP government of the time. This was to be the main instrument for the invitation of foreign capital to Jamaica.

Experiments along Puerto Rican lines have all benefited from special circumstances. For example, Taiwan and South Korea have had authoritarian regimes which have held the union movement at bay. This has preserved the wage-productivity differential between the host country and the metropolitan source of capital which is a feature upon which the model depends if capital is to move. Even in Puerto Rico itself, the success of the model is questionable. Literally millions of Puerto Ricans migrated to the US. Capital has poured in from the mainland for more than 30 years and still unemployment today is admitted to be 25%, with other estimates ranging up to 40%. A letter from the island's governor, Carlos Romero Barcelo, to President Reagan of the US complained about cuts in aid. According to the Governor, 2 million out of 3.2 million Puerto Ricans — 62.5% — depend on food stamps! Food aid is US $1.5 billion a year. Romero asserted that the cuts would cause serious migration and unrest.

At the same time, 80% of the Puerto Rican economy is owned by US multinationals. Foreign capital controls 90% of the assets in manufacture, 70% in banking and finance and 90% in land, sea and air transport. This represents a drain of $2,216,200,000 in net profits and dividends annually. It is estimated that the total has been $40 billion since 1940. Twenty-four United States chain-stores are responsible for 90% of all sales in Puerto Rico.

Evolving along with this economic pattern were different types of political experience. The English-speaking Caribbean countries all experimented to a certain degree with representative government. Certainly in the Caribbean it was typical of British colonialism that there was some attempt to export the home political model. Hence, there was no real contradiction between the small number of persons who would have been entitled to vote in Jamaica in the middle of the 19th century by comparison with England herself. At that point in history, only a small percentage of the English had the right to vote. However, although Britain's political system still rested on a class basis, the base was widening because the industrial revolution was expanding the numbers who satisfied the property criteria for voting rights. In Jamaica in 1863, there was no expansion. The plantocracy and merchant class provided 1,798 voters in a population of 441,264!

In the meantime, the 'mother of parliaments' was already established as the senior institution of representative politics in the world. Whatever its shortcomings, the British political system demonstrated a persuasive power representing itself as the best of which man is capable. In the English-speaking Caribbean, this was to become increasingly accepted as axiomatic.

The British educational system which dominated the school life of a country like Jamaica was designed to create a small Jamaican elite with the basic ideas of the British political system ingrained in its attitudes. It is interesting to observe that virtually without exception every single popular, nationalist leader who emerged throughout the English-speaking Caribbean in the 1940s was committed to a plural democratic system exactly replicating the current British version as it had evolved by the early twentieth century.

But not all imperialism was British imperialism; and although colonial economies are common to all areas of the Caribbean, the political processes with which they were associated were strikingly different. To the north of Jamaica in the island of Cuba, the experience was of another order. There the Spanish held sway until the end of the 19th century. A long war of liberation raged throughout the latter half of the 19th century following on the earlier and successful struggle on the mainland under the leadership of the great liberator, Simon Bolivar. In the end, at the moment when the local patriots, inspired by the teachings of Jose Marti and led by indigenous military leaders were on the verge of victory, the US intervened.[5] President William McKinley ordered the US Army into Cuba, and by these means imposed a new form of external domination which would not be expressed by political control. Instead it would work through the guarantee of certain economic rights and privileges for US investment. Once again an external intervention was to impose an artificial element upon the economic process which would distort its natural evolution.

From the early twentieth century up to 1959, Cuba witnessed an enormous expansion in US investment. Vast profits were exported from Cuba annually, thereby perpetuating the traditional consequences of the colonial process. There evolved a totally corrupt, brutal and tyrannical political system. By the time of the rule of the notorious Fulgencio Batista in 1952, Cuba had become a land dominated by a secret service that was among the most vicious in Latin America. Those who expressed opposition or championed the rights of the people faced the prospect of being dragged from their homes in the middle of the night. Thereafter they often disappeared. Such democratic political activity as existed did so in the certain knowledge of its own futility. Nowhere did the historical experience sustain hope in a democratic solution to the questions of power and national decision-making.

It is against this background that the Cuban Revolution became a historical inevitability, foreshadowing similar processes for similar reasons in countries like Nicaragua and El Salvador. By 1959 the Cuban Revolution had triumphed and the decade of the 1960s was to witness two contrasting political experiences in Jamaica and Cuba.

During the years of the Batista reign of terror and the long struggle of the Cuban Revolution, Jamaica was proceeding on a comparatively trauma-free path. Between 1945 and independence we established, in quick succession, a genuinely representative parliament elected on the basis of universal suffrage; internal self-government in which the elected representatives of the people became responsible for the conduct of all except Defence and Foreign Affairs; a full-fledged system of Cabinet government; and, finally, full independence in August of 1962.

During the period of internal self-government we began to lay the foundations of the Puerto Rican Model. In 1952, the Industrial Development Corporation was established, its primary focus on the attraction of overseas investment. Laws guaranteeing the special status and rights of the foreign investor were passed. At the same time we also established the legal framework for land reform, although not much land actually changed hands; and began to experiment with the widening of the education system by the allocation of two thousand free places in the secondary schools open to the children of the poor by yearly competition.

In terms of all the classic indicators of economic success one might have been tempted to feel that the model was working. In the first ten years of independence the gross national product grew at an annual rate of 6.5 per cent per annum in real terms. Something in the region of 115 new factories were established, mostly of the import substitution variety. It is estimated that they provided 15,467 new jobs and involved an investment of 70 million dollars.[6]

A major supplier of bauxite, Jamaica increased its production from 7,495,000 tons a year in 1962 to 12,784,000 tons in 1973. Within that period new investment in the alumina industry was $560 million and production increased from 655,000 tons to 2,054,000 tons. Total new investment in the period was $629.4 million of which some 80 per cent originated in the USA. The number of hotel beds available to the tourist industry grew from 7,471 to 17,944. On every side the Puerto Rican model was working to the extent that 'working' can be measured statistically.

But the social experience was quite different. Perhaps the most important test of the effectiveness of a society — its economy, political system, culture and social institutions — is its ability to find useful employment under tolerable conditions for the great majority of its members. It is true that 'useful' and 'tolerable' are relative categories. However, society is well able to define for itself what is acceptable at any point in time. In 1962, Jamaica was deeply concerned about an unemployment rate of 12%; by 1972 this figure was 24% with the rate for youth and women in excess of 30%.[7] In the field of education, only 15% of the children who left primary school at

the age of 15 or 16 were able to secure a single day's instruction
of any kind, academic or practical, thereafter. A very small
proportion of children benefited from any early childhood
education and most began their educational experience at age 6
or more likely 7 in the public primary system. In short, we were
neither able to find work for our people nor able to train our
people for work.

It is estimated that 40% of the adult population was
functionally illiterate.[8] Child malnutrition ran at over 30%.[9]
According to estimates Jamaica needed to build at least 15,000
houses a year if it were to overtake any kind of minimum
expectation on the part of its new families and make a token
dent in the backlog of need. By 1972, we were building little
more than two thousand a year. But there were deeper
consequences still.

One has to remember that colonialism created a small
plantocracy with all the features of an oligarchy to which was
attached a slightly larger but wholly dependent middle class.
Later in the 19th century, the merchant side of the economy
added a new dimension to the power structure without altering
its essential character. Now the Puerto Rican model was to do
the same. In the 1950s and 60s the new manufacturing sector
was to take on some of the features of obligarchic control and
privilege. However, it was nationalistic and the best of the
group were genuinely patriotic. The people who serviced this
new sector represented new entrants to the middle class. The
class became larger as a consequence, but not so large as to
represent a major source of stability and power through their
sheer numbers. As oligarchy and middle class grew, the total
population was growing faster still. The workers who found
employment in the new factories soon attained previously
unheard of levels of wages and working conditions. But in the
meantime, the great majority of the population was left further
and further behind.

As late as 1972, it was common for workers who could not
benefit from direct representation and contract negoiation by
the union movement, to be forced to work 13, 14 and 15 hours
a day at $5 a day and without hope of legal redress. The gap
between rich and poor, 'have' and 'have not', grew wider and
wider, while the economic indicators told their positive story.

Where poverty is shared it may be endured. Where poverty
is mocked by extravagance it becomes the condition within

which resentment smoulders. Where there is general hope of relief from poverty it will be endured with fortitude as people patiently await their turn for better things to come. However, if it is clear that the great majority will never have the better things that are so visibly there for the few, deep and dangerous divisions and frustrations emerge in the society. It is not surprising that in the decade of the 60s Jamaica had two uprisings and at least two serious riots.[10] The Jamaica experience is a complex one which needs careful examination. Few societies coming to independence in the 20th century could be more attuned to the Puerto Rican model. The country benefited from a stable political system founded upon two parties that were quickly becoming traditional. Power changed hands peacefully on a number of occasions and the general political environment was one in which the overseas investor could feel completely at home. There was a powerful, sophisticated trade union movement. Unfortunately, it was split almost in two. Those who were members of the union Bustamante had formed, supported his conservative brand of politics. The rest were mainly in the PNP-affiliated National Workers Union, or members of the few other smaller unions, which tended to support the more progressive politics of Manley. But apart from this split the union movement had a good record of honouring contracts even if the contracts themselves were negotiated in a tough manner. Certainly, the unions were very similar to the kinds of organisations with which the foreign investor dealt habitually at home. Furthermore, Jamaica had not come new to the Puerto Rican Model upon attaining independence in 1962. By 1972 we were more than twenty years into the experience of the model with tragically inadequate social results.

But even if the social benefits of the model were negligible and the consequences divisive, one needs to ask whether the model at least achieved its economic objective. Here the experience is instructive.

At a superficial glance it appeared that Jamaica was beginning to deal with one aspect of its economic problems: the relationship between production for one's own needs by comparison with imports. One could now buy toothpaste, clothes and shoes which were made in Jamaica and be tempted to feel that this was the beginning of a solution. A closer look revealed, however, that a new contradiction was emerging.

When a foreign investor is invited to take the risk of going into a strange country, he understandably seeks an area that involves the lowest risk and the least effort. Hence, many of the foreign-financed factories that were springing up were, in fact, following the line of least resistance. The easiest way to make money quickly and securely was to import raw materials or components which could then be turned into finished goods and supplied to the local market. This placed no strain on research facilities and called for no investment for the development of local sources of inputs. As a consequence the new factories tended to import nearly everything that they used.

The establishment of a whole new manufacturing capability must either replace imports or create exports. Only marginally is it likely to be directed at a completely new home market which it 'creates'.

Therefore as the years pass, the economics of the model should assist the country to become less dependent on import and strengthen the export situation. But in the Jamaican case, from about 1953, when Jamaica began to apply the model, to 1968, imports rose from $86.6 million to $416.8 million. Exports rose in the same period from $71.9 million to only $325.4 million.

When the model began, the value of exports was already a dangerously low 83% of imports. Fifteen years later, far from improving, the situation had worsened. By 1968 exports had fallen from 83% to 78% of imports. The trade gap was widening. Raw materials, which should not create an increasing drain on foreign exchange, were doing exactly that. Thirty per cent of earned foreign exchange was devoted to raw materials in 1953. It had crept up to thirty-two per cent by 1968. This was happening while the trade gap was steadily widening. Raw materials were increasing because the new factories were dependent on outside inputs.

Hence, the strategy was not reducing Jamaica's dependence on outside sources for its needs but increasing it. At least in the days of the early plantation system most of the inputs into the growing of sugar cane were local. Sugar machinery had to be imported because Jamaica has neither iron nor coal upon which to base a steel industry. But we were spawning a new kind of economic activity which imported not only the machinery but the raw materials as well.

Thus behind the glittering indicators of success lay stark facts. Unemployment was increasing. Social services reflected little improvement. The degree of economic dependence was actually increasing rather than decreasing. Finally, the traditional problem of exporting surplus to foreign owners remained unchanged because the new industries were also foreign.

While all this was happening in Jamaica, another model was evolving in Cuba, a model based on revolution. By 1960 revolutionary turmoil was over and a basis for stability existed once again. During the early 1960s, the new regime took over its foreign enterprises, became the object of a punitive economic blockade by the United States, fought off a counter-revolutionary invasion at the Bay of Pigs, became the beneficiary of aid from the Soviet Union and set out to consolidate the revolution. During the period there was no question of political elections or plural democratic activity. Under the leadership of an increasingly consolidated Communist Party the country was mobilised for production and for the development of a major defence capability. With Soviet aid the best army in Latin America was developed even as successive attempts by the CIA to destabilise the revolution and kill its leader were continually frustrated.[11]

The Cuban model was developed along strict Marxist-Leninist lines. The concept of the dictatorship of the proletariat cannot be challenged. Minority views and particularly those opposed to the revolution are simply not allowed. A vigorous democratic process exists, but only within the revolution: there are no political rights outside it. Of course, welfare advantages are universal. It must also be said that of all the countries that have undergone revolution, Cuba remains one of the most humane in its application of the revolutionary process.[12]

The economic side of the model rests upon two foundations: planning which is centralised and absolute and insistence upon fundamentals. Every person has absolute rights to employment and to health care. Every child has an equal right to education. Planning begins with these as given.

In economic terms Cuba did not achieve anything that could remotely match the Jamaica success story as measured by growth statistics. From 1960 to 1972 the Cuban economy grew at only 2.85% per annum as against Jamaica's 6.5%. There were successes: sugar production increased substantially as did electric power generation and cement production. Footwear trebled. Textiles doubled as did oil refining.

But when we look at it from the point of view of social indicators we find a dramatic reversal of the Jamaican experience. Over the period unemployment fell from 30% to 0% by 1962. The number of school places almost trebled and by 1972 the school population was three million out of a population of nine million.

Even in housing, which the Cubans regarded as an area of failure, they were out-performing Jamaica marginally. At the end of the period Cuba was building workers' housing units at the rate of 16,000 a year for its population, by comparison with Jamaica's 2,000 a year. Hospital beds had increased from 28,536 to 46,402 in 1974. Nothing comparable was happening in Jamaica. Clearly, on the basis of a less successful economic performance as measured by the classic indicators, Cuba had achieved a considerable social transformation in a remarkably short period of time. She had done so against the disadvantage of the US blockade but with the advantage of substantial Soviet aid.

Jamaica's political conditions were as stubbornly a part of objective reality as Cuba's although they were absolutely different. The question was: did Jamaica have no options between the experience of the Puerto Rico Model and the Cuban Revolution, both of which were unfolding in an atmosphere of increasing dependence on foreign powers?

In 1969, Norman Manley retired as leader of the PNP and of the opposition in parliament. I was elected leader of the Party in March of that year. Suddenly we were the new generation of which Manley had spoken. Exactly three years later, the PNP won a landslide victory in the general election of February, 1972. Before our eyes were these two models — Puerto Rico and Cuba. Surely there was another path, a third path, a Jamaican way rooted in our political experience and values, capable of providing an economic base to our political independence and capable of some measure of social justice for the people. We were to spend the next eight and a half years in our periphery exploring that third path.

4
DEFINING A DOMESTIC POLICY

The judgments of history must be shared between intentions and results. In our search for another way we began with clear intentions. Like all governments our achievements were often wide of the mark. When a government attempts to change things it runs into unforeseen factors. Sometimes these originate outside the particular country and are due to causes that are beyond control. Sometimes the intentions themselves create unforeseen consequences. Hence, for a variety of reasons all governments spend a fair amount of time upon the action which they originally intended and a lot of time reacting to circumstances that they did not predict. But it is proper to begin with intentions.

We began and ended with four basic commitments, each of which bears a relationship to and reinforces the other three. Firstly, we wanted to create an economy that would be more independent of foreign control and more responsive to the needs of the majority of the people at home. Secondly, we wanted to work for an egalitarian society both in terms of opportunity and also in the deeper sense of a society in which people felt that they were of equal worth and value. Thirdly, we wanted to develop a truly democratic society in which democracy was more than the attempt to manipulate votes every five years. Finally, we wanted to help, indeed accelerate the process by which Jamaicans were retracing the steps of their history. We were convinced that it was only through the rediscovery of our heritage that we would evolve a culture that reflected the best in ourselves because it expressed pride in what we were and where we came from. The largest of all our roots, Africa, had symbolised only the stigma of slavery. It, too, had to become the source of ancestral pride.

A more democratic society will lead, in due course, to a more

equal society with a greater degree of popular control over the
economy. Simultaneously a more equal society can only be
achieved through a profound democratisation of institutions
at every level and through genuine popular control of and
sharing in the economy. But for all of this to happen a people
must begin with a sense of self-worth. Art, music, dance must
all spring from a common root, founded in the experience of
the people. Experience must reflect ethnic pride. None of
these aims was new in itself. Each had been pursued at different
times by different governments. But this was the first time a
government would pursue all four simultaneously and in the
face of the opportunity which independence alone can provide.

These intentions must be seen against the background of
Jamaica in 1972 which had a dependent economy: in the sense
of having to import its needs, and in terms of ownership.
Foreign interests owned 100 per cent of the bauxite and
alumina industry,[1] more than half of the sugar industry and
much more than half of the tourist industry, to say nothing of a
substantial proportion of the new manufacturing industry that
had resulted from the Puerto Rican Model. Land ownership
can best be described by the statistics: 2.2% of farms occupied
63.1% of arable acres, while 97.8% of farms shared 36.9% of
arable land.

In spite of a well established two-party democratic system,
the society was still firmly elitist and those elements of the
economy which were in local hands were controlled by a tight
oligarchy.

The trade union movement had made massive gains, but the
majority of the working class was still wholly excluded from
those benefits. Even in 1972 it was common for a person to
work for upwards of a quarter of a century with a particular
employer and to be fired without cause with a total
compensation of two weeks' wages. No laws provided for a
universal minimum rate or for standard maximum hours of
work.[2] If a firm went into liquidation, its workers stood at the
bottom of the line of all creditors, behind banks, financial
institutions, trading companies and just about everything else
when it came to discharging financial obligations. Although
both political parties depended heavily on trade union
support, neither had ever attempted a real assault upon these
injustices. This is not to say that nothing had been done.
Minimum wages for certain industries were controlled by law

and a form of contributory pension scheme had been introduced. These efforts, however, had been desultory and piecemeal and had never been the result of a clear commitment to the creation of a general legal framework within which social justice might be pursued as a fundamental objective.

Some of the responses which we were to explore in the next eight years and eight months were part of an original body of intentions; others developed logically from these as our experience of the problems grew. Perhaps the best way to understand both the intentions and the subsequent policies which developed is to divide them into the three categories of the economic, the social and the political.

In the economic field we were determined to make the process of the production and distribution of goods less dependent on external factors and local oligarchic control. This intention was clear and unequivocal and never wavered. It implied many things. The most important of these was to begin to develop what economists call 'internal linkages'. By this they mean the development of your own sources of raw material and other kinds of inputs wherever possible. It means carrying out, yourself, as many of the functions between production and the ultimate market-place as possible. The first group are known as 'backward linkages' and the second as 'forward linkages'. To give a practical example: if producing cardboard boxes, you can simply import cardboard and the necessary glues and put them together locally. They will then sail in ships owned by someone else, insured by a foreign company and finally be delivered to a foreign country. Alternatively, one could explore local raw materials and develop a glue industry of one's own and, in the longer term, develop one's own paper and cardboard industry. This will involve in turn developing forests as the basis of a pulp and paper industry, saw mills, transport and so on forwards and backwards. Each new link in the chain means more jobs, more local production, less dependence on outside sources. At the same time you can set up a local marketing organisation to make arrangements for foreign sales and even work to develop one's own shipping line so that some day the profits from shipping the cardboard boxes will accrue to you. The search for linkages represented a high priority.

We were determined to try to put the whole question of foreign investment on some kind of rational basis. Make no mistake about it: we wanted foreign investment, and in the end this was one of the areas in which we failed most completely. But we were not willing to continue the approach to foreign investment of the Puerto Rican Model type, where foreign investment is seen as the main engine of development with all policy being made to revolve around the entrenching of that element. We saw foreign capital as part of but not the whole of the development process. In fact in the end we worked out a foreign investment code that spelled out in the clearest possible terms the rights and privileges which would be enjoyed by the foreign investor — and they were considerable; but it also sought to spell out the mutuality of the relationship which we envisaged. It called for good corporate citizenship on the part of the investors; required respect for local conditions and traditions and made it clear that we, as the host country, would wish foreign investments to be consistent with our own national development plans.

A third priority was the intention to enlarge the public sector, particularly in strategic areas of the economy. We planned to nationalise public utilities and the foreign companies which still owned the lion's share of the sugar industry. We intended to commit public funds to investment in agro-industrial enterprises. In the field of finance we regarded the creation of a commercial banking sector in public ownership as a priority. We conceived of this as operating alongside a section of the banking system which would remain in private hands. Thus we were to acquire one major commercial bank and create another, the Workers' Bank, for the explicit purpose of increasing the proportion of financial institutions under public control and sensitive to priorities of public policy. There were already a publicly owned Development Bank and Mortgage Bank along with a Small Business Loan institution. The acquisition of Barclay's of England in Jamaica in 1975 was the first nationalisation of a private, commercial banking institution.

There were certain aspects of distribution which we felt should be under public control. The first of these involved the marketing of sugar. There was already a Sugar Industry Authority in place and we planned to expand its functions so as to bring all sugar marketing under public control. Again, this would be the deliberate result of the general intention to make strategic areas of the economy subject to direct public control.

Later, we were to create a State Trading Corporation which took over the function of the importation of basic necessities such as staple foods, drugs, timber for the construction industry and the like.

We were to embark upon the first major land reform programme in Jamaican history. We intended to experiment with the establishment of various types of co-operative farming. In a further attempt to widen popular participation in the economy, we were greatly to expand the assistance offered to small business enterprises, and we built a number of small business complexes which provided factory space in a centralised location for aspiring small businessmen.

Throughout all of this the common threads of purpose were: reducing dependence of the economy as a whole, reducing dependence on foreign ownership, reducing the degree of control of the local oligarchy, widening the degree of social control over the economy through direct state activity and widening the participation of the people at large in beneficial economic activity. We were clear that we would never expropriate property, but would make acquisition in the public interest on a basis of fair compensation.

We also had a firm and unwavering commitment to the preservation and development of a strong private sector. We did not believe in a pure free enterprise model of economic development and, consequently, saw the private sector as having a particular place and filling a particular role. But we did want that place to be permanent, and the role to be dynamic. Communicating this intention was another matter. But that was the intention. In fact, we were to bend over backward time and time again to help the private sector and to reassure its members of the sincerity of our commitment to their role. However, we were to discover that a certain type of private sector man approaches society on an all-or-nothing basis. There must either be the appearance of a complete commitment to their kind of system or they become suspicious and uncooperative. The economy was to suffer considerably from the refusal of this element in the private sector to take advantage of the many incentives offered to stimulate increased production.

We were, from the outset, committed to the development of worker participation. We believed in the right of workers to develop committees at the shop floor level which would participate with supervision in determining methods of improving productivity and discipline. We were committed to worker participation in major decision-making through representatives on Boards of Directors. We wanted to develop models of worker participation in ownership. Nor was it our feeling that these models should be restricted to the private sector. We did much over the period to ensure that worker participation was introduced into publicly owned enterprises where, not surprisingly, more practical success was actually achieved.

Needless to say, we attached great importance to the distribution of wealth. Quite apart from access to the economy through land reform, farmer co-operatives, small business development and worker participation, we were determined to take direct steps to achieve a more equitable distribution of the existing wealth. The disparity between visible wealth and taxes actually paid in Jamaica was as notorious as it was startling. We attempted to find answers to our own variant of what is a fairly international scandal in tax avoidance and downright tax evasion with our own form of wealth taxes. It was later claimed that the hostility which the established interests displayed towards the government was caused by ideology and socialist rhetoric. In fact, the first signs of hostility were apparent with the introduction of wealth taxes[3] which were levied on actual property owned, instead of that mercurial category known as income.

I have saved for the last because it had, in many ways, the greatest strategic significance, our intentions with respect to the bauxite and alumina industry. By 1972 Jamaica was mining 12 million tons of bauxite a year and using more than 5 million tons of this to produce some $2\frac{1}{2}$ million tons of alumina a year. This US$550 million investment provided employment for 9,719 people. As a point of comparison, sugar and its allied cane farming activities were providing employment for some 60,000 people at this time. Apart from the employment and the capital inflows which the investment had provided during the construction period, together with the paltry revenue of US$25 million a year, Jamaica had little to show for all of this.

The first Bustamante government in the period 1944 to 1954 had agreed that our bauxite could be shipped out for a royalty of some ten cents a ton. Norman Manley's pre-independence government of 1955 to 1962 had increased this fourteen-fold by negotiating a new royalty and tax arrangement at $1.40 a ton. Even so, the total return to Jamaica for this production, which made Jamaica the second largest bauxite/alumina producer in the world, exceeded only by Australia, was providing Jamaica with less than US$30 million a year. Nor did we have any additional foreign exchange benefit other than the money to pay wages and other local inputs because the alumina operation was part of an integrated multinational economic activity. There was no market value to the export of bauxite/alumina which could be brought to account in a national bank and form a part of our foreign reserves. Jamaica's total benefit consisted of the royalties and taxes and the money for wages and other local inputs.

Obviously, this was a grossly unsatisfactory state of affairs. We were determined to pursue the two broad objectives of national participation and control on the one hand, and equitable returns to the nation on the other. We intended to proceed cautiously because bauxite was our largest invest-ment, our greatest potential national asset, but also a highly sensitive investment for two very obvious reasons. The entire investment was North American and the bulk of that US owned. The Kaiser Aluminium & Chemical Corporation, the Reynolds Metal Company, the Aluminium Company of America and the Anaconda Corporation all had major shares in this activity. The Aluminium Company of Canada owned two of the island's five alumina plants. In addition, alumina is high on the list of metals categorised as strategic from the point of view of US defence capability.

We were to spend more than a year studying the world aluminium industry from the vantage point of government, with all that this implies for access to sensitive information. In the end we concluded that across-the-board nationalisation would not be an appropriate strategy. Two factors were specially in our mind in coming to this conclusion. Firstly, within the Jamaican Constitution the government could only acquire productive assets at current market value. Compen-sation on that basis to the Jamaica bauxite/alumina industry would have put us in an impossible financial situation for the foreseeable future. To the hostility which the act would generate would have been added an impossible financial burden. Secondly, we did not have the technical expertise necessary for managing the highly complex processes involved in the alumina plant. Finally, we well understood the difference between bauxite and, say, oil. From the point of view of the bargaining position of the owner of the resource, oil is a 'hard' product. Exploration costs may be high and risky, but demand is eternally expanding, since economic progress and energy are absolutely linked. By contrast, bauxite is a 'soft' product in the sense that there are huge, accessible deposits in many parts of the world. Aluminium fights other metals and new synthetics for markets every inch of the way. Even now when the comparatively appropriate pricing of oil makes it more vulnerable to competition from other sources, the knowledge that the world supply of oil has not much longer to last gives it a special premium value. In any event oil is the base for the vast and expanding world of synthetics.

In the end we settled for six specific objectives. Firstly, we intended to renegotiate the tax and royalty arrangement to try to get a bigger return. We were also determined to invest the word 'return' with a dynamic significance. World inflation means that value, as measured by the price of metals like alumina, rises as the years pass. Although there are times of recession the general trend is upward. Any taxation arrangement worked out at a particular point of time is likely to be soon out of date because one is not dealing with a self-contained, locally based enterprise making its profits locally and subjecting that profit to tax. Because the local operation is only a part of a highly complex integrated international activity, one is dealing with national values at all stages. If one assumes a particular value for bauxite/alumina at a particular point of time and bases the national tax upon that, a problem will arise shortly when those national values are out of date. The host country will then be receiving revenue based on out-of-date factors but will, in the meantime, be buying goods on the world market that reflect the new inflationary prices. Ironically, these goods will even include finished products which originated in the raw material of the host country. We intended, therefore, to find a way to tie our taxation to an index that would reflect these inflationary factors.

Our second objective was to devise means by which Jamaica could participate nationally in the ownership and control of the industry. Therefore, we wanted to develop local managerial and technical skills as rapidly as possible and to secure for Jamaica a role in the marketing of bauxite and alumina. This was critical because Jamaica could never pretend to some measure of economic independence when the marketing of our most strategic resource was exclusively in the hands of foreign multinational corporations and entirely subject to their interests. This led, in turn, to our objective of diversifying the marketing outlets of the industry.

Bearing all this in mind, our awareness of the comparative 'softness' of bauxite as a subject for international negotiation confirmed the need for an international bauxite producers body. Long before OPEC had demonstrated its bargaining muscle in 1973 my union experience in negotiating for bauxite workers had led me to a rudimentary grasp of the nature of producers' international corporations. In due course we had learned that a bauxite strike in Jamaica was only marginally effective because the corporation could accelerate its operation in Guyana or Surinam to compensate for the lost production. This had led us to the formation of the Caribbean Bauxite and Metal Workers Federation,[4] of which I was the first president, and which brought together all the bauxite and alumina workers of the Caribbean Basin. We fared noticeably better in negotiation in the post-Bauxite and Metal Workers Federation period because we were able to co-ordinate our negotiating strategies.

Early in the 1960s we had proposed to a number of governments that, in the protection of their national interests, they ought to explore the possibility of an international association of bauxite producers. If given the chance, we intended to act. Since the corporations could play off one producer against another, should any try to secure more equitable participation in the benefits of the industry, it seemed critical to us to get all the producers together so that we could all act in concert in the protection of our national interests. Hence, the sixth objective was the formation and development of an international bauxite and alumina producers' body.[5]

But, while we were tackling basic aspects of Jamaica's neo-colonial economy, there was much else to do. Our social objectives can be broadly outlined under two categories: the law and the service sector.

The state of the laws in Jamaica reflected a collective failure to make law itself the foundation of social justice. For example, the basic act determining relationships between worker and

employer from the legal point of view had been established
more than a hundred years earlier, and had benefited from no
significant amendment since. Appropriately enough it had
been called the Master and Servants Law. It is astonishing to
reflect that during twenty-six years of representative
government, ten of them as an independent nation, in a
political system heavily influenced if not dominated by the
trade union movement, we had found it possible to leave this
law untouched. It is as if the fact of the trade union movement
had led to some strange, perhaps unconscious assumption that
such matters could be left to the unions and need not concern
the law-makers. This was, of course, very convenient for the
employing classes since the people who actually sold their
labour to survive as domestic helpers or by working in small
business establishments in the nooks and crannies of the
economy, represented the majority of the workforce of the
country.

No legislation spoke to the rights of women either in respect
of their employment or generally. Enforcing maintenance
orders against wayward fathers was a difficult and humiliating
business to be pursued in open courts more adjusted to
criminal proceedings.

Inevitably in a society where unemployment is endemic and
economic insecurity a part of the natural order of things,
concubinage is more common than marriage. The majority of
Jamaica's children were literally and legally bastards. The
distinction was reflected in the law and resulted in a
disenfranchisement from first class citizenship for the majority
of the Jamaican people.

What is remarkable about all of this is the extent to which it
reflected the deeply ingrained elitist assumptions upon which
the society was based. The plantation system, slavery,
colonialism and more recently the neo-colonialist emphasis of
our basic development strategy had all served to reinforce and
perpetuate an unspoken assumption about the social order.
This assumption had not yet yielded to either traditional party
politics or trade union activity. The assumption was that the
majority of the Jamaican people, held to be equal in the
constitution, were not equal in law, in opportunity nor, most
profoundly, in the unspoken and unwritten assumptions
which underlay the social order.

We did not believe that we could change the unwritten

assumptions overnight. We knew that equality of opportunity arises far down the line of a development strategy aimed at that objective, pursued relentlessly and acted upon effectively. But the laws could be dealt with very quickly. We were to do just that.

The other area lay in the strategy for the services. Firstly, there was the matter of education. We were to decide early that the state should undertake all the expenses of tuition right up to university level.

Then we wanted to tackle the two weakest areas of the system: the pre-primary or basic period, and the post-primary secondary period. We planned to commit considerable resources to the enlargement of these two sectors: without education in the four to six age group, the child embarked on its primary experience at a great disadvantage. Equally a failure to reinforce the primary period with some sort of secondary training put the child at an impossible disadvantage on entering the labour market.

There was also the question of curricular content. We were determined to shift the emphasis away from the academic/ classical emphasis bequeathed by colonialism, to a system better geared to the needs of a developing economy. This meant a far greater emphasis on technical and trade training which we sought to achieve by an experimental expansion of the secondary system. We tried to reintroduce an agricultural element into the school system by a regular programme of attaching farming areas to schools in rural Jamaica. We insisted upon increasing emphasis upon work/study methods in teaching, so as to develop an understanding of the working environment which each child was preparing to enter. Finally we wished to develop a more positive and natural view of work itself in a society whose experience still tended to a negative perception of work as something unpleasant that is imposed by an alien authority.

In all of this, like every other Third World government, we were struggling to find a means to make education a positive contributor to development. It is astonishing the extent to which the education systems of post-colonial societies are actually counter-productive unless radically reorganised.

In health, we recognised the classic problem of the poor developing society. Even where the hospital services have become relatively sophisticated, the hospitals themselves are

too few and far between. The professionals in the sense of
doctors and dentists are hopelessly outnumbered by the
patients in need of care. Like so many others before us have
done, we decided to go for a system of clinics and for the
development of a para-medical system which would bring
preventative medicine and the treatment of simple ailments to
the people in the countryside.

Finally, and significantly, there was our view of
employment. We felt that each citizen had an inherent right to
employment and it was the state's duty to provide this to the
limit of its means. All the governments of Jamaica before us
had recognized this to some extent and had made token
gestures in the field of unemployment relief. But we were the
first government to try to organise massive work programmes
for unemployment relief as a positive social duty.

Then there were the political objectives. From the start one
of our deepest concerns was how to mobilise the people for the
kind of effort which alone could make Jamaica prosperous,
permit all its people to share in that prosperity and create a
genuinely independent nation. The Puerto Rican Model could
guarantee the first in a superficial sense, but at the price of the
two last. But could the people be led to struggle to achieve the
last two as a natural part of the first? Could they be inspired to
sacrifice some of the immediate prosperity for a minority so
that everyone might work for and share in slower but more
dependable economic progress? In short, could they, who had
always struggled to survive individually and as families, come
to commit themselves to a struggle in which it was the larger,
more abstract, more remote thing, the nation, which we were
striving to build?

Our competitive two-party democracy was the instrument
least likely to achieve such a situation. We wrestled with this
contradiction between our needs and our political instrument.
It struck us, as it had others before, that a way had to be found
to de-tribalise politics. With nothing to which a political
commitment could be made in earlier times, people tended to
form blind attachments to one or other party. It became 'my
party', right or wrong. People were literally happy if things
went badly for the country under the 'other' party, since that
indicated a victory for 'their' party at the next election.

This pattern was further entrenched with a spoils system.
On both sides scarce benefits like relief jobs and houses would

go to strong party supporters. The ties of loyalty were thus drawn tighter by clientelism. In the end, supporters of the two parties tended to become more like members of opposing armies than citizens with different views about their country. The consequences are serious because the climate in which to mobilise people behind national objectives is thus extremely difficult to create. Opposition is said to be vital to the functioning of a developed, plural democracy. But mobilisation is the key to development, if not survival, in a poor Third World country. Jamaicans are expert at providing opposition and well nigh incapable of uniting behind national goals.

When we came to office, Jamaica had become a house divided in the fullest sense of the biblical phrase. Could a way be found to create a kind of participatory democracy in which groups could be invited to help examine issues and so influence policy? Would this lead to involvement on a national level?

We were determined to try, and tried to the end. The phrase 'politics of participation' came to summarise what we attempted. It was tried at every sort of level. Indeed, in the end, private sector, union, technocrats and the political directorate were joined in an economic commission which dealt with such sensitive matters that its members had to take the oath of secrecy.

The politics of participation could be promoted by involving existing institutions and organisations in planning. But obviously the concept called for more basic political engineering. It called for the democratisation of the whole society. This could not be achieved overnight, perhaps not in a generation; but the road was clear. Wherever else we may have faltered, this path was pursued constantly and even successfully at times. That the process was eventually overwhelmed by the contradictory and often openly conflicting interests of the society, frustrated by political habit and finally distrusted by some of our own party members, is another matter.

A logical corollary of this analysis is the question of democracy itself. The politics of participation may or may not be relevant to the development of patriotic attitudes. But the superficiality of democratic processes which begin and end with elections is obvious. It is also dangerous, because the system can quickly become despised as an illusion. We were determined to deepen the democratic process in Jamaica.

Firstly, there was the structure of the democracy itself. For years we had endured an insane local government system. Reasonably enough the island was divided into fourteen parishes, each with its own popularly elected Local Government Authority. All the elements of genuine, democratic, representative local government were present. What was missing, however, was the power to act. Although the areas of responsibility of the local government were as clearly defined as one could hope to see, the power to act was absent. No Local Government Authority could take any action without the permission of a minister of the central government. This anachronism had arisen for the quaintest of reasons. Originally, Jamaica's colonial constitution had reserved all power to a government acting on behalf of the British authorities in Whitehall. Hence both central and local governments had areas of responsibility but could only act with the British government's permission. When this state of affairs was corrected at the level of the central government with the attainment of internal self-government and later independence, either old habits died hard or the legislators simply forgot. Whatever the cause, the Local Government Authorities remained as before: representative, responsible but powerless. For them, colonialism remained unchanged except that the permission to act had to be sought in Kingston instead of London.

This to us was symptomatic of a deeper problem in our democracy, a problem which we shared and still largely share with many other so-called democracies.

We dismiss as self-evident nonsense the notion that a society is democratic merely because people vote every five years and are free to exercise that vote in a choice between different political parties or different individual candidates. We see this as a starting point and even a critical element in the democratic process but our experience has shown us that democracy that is limited to that act of periodic choice can quickly become a form of legitimised dictatorship subject to recall every so often. It is true that the knowledge that one is subject to recall has a restraining influence on the use of power. On the other hand, such are the manipulative powers that are available to those who govern that there is always the temptation to act in an undemocratic and authoritarian manner with the belief that one can escape the consequences later with the help of a good media campaign.

More fundamental, however, is the problem arising from being excluded and eventually alienated from the decision-making process. The truth of the matter is that the ordinary citizen of the typical plural democracy has little sense of participation in or influence over affairs. Consequently, to that citizen politics does not represent a series of activities in which he can participate; but rather appears as something carried out by others in his name but not necessarily, in his view, on his behalf. We felt and still feel that this problem gets worse and worse as society becomes more complex and its economic process more dominated by advanced technology. We were convinced that you have to work at democracy; that you have to build democracy in terms of a substructure which underpins the institution of parliament and the divisions of government through which the political system acts. The parliamentary system can be like a building without a foundation. The political parties cannot be a complete foundation because they divide the society in too many ways at too many levels. Something else is needed to give the system lasting foundations grounded in the daily experience of the people.

Local government was one area which could be remedied. But we felt that one must penetrate the life of the society even more deeply and intimately than is possible through the Local Government Authority representing anything from one to two hundred thousand members of a parish; or, in the case of Kingston, representing three quarters of a million people. So we were to create community councils which brought together groups of people small enough to identify themselves as a community and with shared relationships, problems and aspirations.

Similarly we were convinced that democracy organised outside the workplace and firmly banished from it is a dangerous illusion paid for in strikes, uncertain productivity, hostility and general tension. Thus we attempted to introduce a worker participation programme. This met with little success, probably because the whole system began to buckle under the strains of the post-1973 economic crisis. As inflation began to gallop, workers became understandably preoccupied with the business of protecting their standard of living for which they had fought in negotiations, strikes and arbitrations for years and which was now being trampled before their very eyes. In addition, many union leaders were suspicious of the process, doubtless fearing that worker participation might undermine their personal power. There were some successes however, and these could be seen to produce the first beginnings of a change in worker attitudes.

Perhaps the most fundamental thing that we were to try in this attempt to deepen the democratic process was to be found in the school system. In a highly controversial programme which met with widely varying degrees of co-operation from the teaching profession, we set out to introduce an element of democratic participation by students in the running of schools. This took the form of elected class committees and, for older students, a right of election of representatives to committees who would sit with the school principals in an advisory capacity. It seemed strange to us that we were committed to the evolution of a democratic society, yet devoted no part of the education of children to preparing them for this experience.

Finally, we were to reorganise the boards which manage schools. Representatives of students, parents, the ancillary staff and the outside community all took their places beside the traditional members. Previously these had been chosen exclusively for their supposed expertise.

Of all the things which we set out to do on the home front, the most controversial was to do with ideology. The People's National Party had been declared a socialist party in 1940. It had been torn apart by an internal struggle which finally led to the expulsion of some of its leadership in early 1952 on grounds that they had set up Marxist cells within the organisation. From 1952 to 1972 the party had paid lip-service to ideology but had never really grappled with its implications. After losing power in 1962, the party had again become a battle-ground over the question of the platform with which to face the elections of 1967. In the end Norman Manley had thrown the weight of his prestige behind a radical policy reflecting a number of strongly socialist proposals, but this had not been associated with an attempt to discuss socialism as an ideology, to re-examine it in the light of contemporary circumstances and to seek to determine a shared interpretation by the members of the party. There was a sense in which the party was socialist because it never said that it was not; had fought an election on a strongly socialist programme as recently as 1967;[6] but had not since 1952 ever made socialism the subject of an explicit, internal dialogue.

We had two choices. We could have left the current situation where it was. Alternatively, we could decide that it was time to deal with the matter afresh in the light of international circumstances, the internal dynamics of Jamaican society and our own composition and structure as a political organisation.

I have always had a profound distrust of the use of political labels that are not themselves subject to careful analysis and definition. On the other hand I am convinced that no society can achieve greatness except within the framework of a set of ideals, assumptions and ideas about economic and political organisation which command the clear and committed support of an effective majority of the population. Two of the world's societies that have been most clearly organised along lines that reflect a particular ideology and that have tried to be faithful to that ideology over an extended period are the United States and the Soviet Union. In each there is a substantial, working majority of the people genuinely committed to a set of ideals, assumptions and ideas about economic and political organisation. Each represents the most formidable force known to human history. The US has accomplishments in the economic field that are staggering and only latterly matched by the Japanese. The Soviet Union has achieved a degree of equitable distribution of the benefits of economic activity which, taking into account levels of production, is the most remarkable in human history. Each has achieved its goal while maintaining incredible military strength. It is significant that the Japanese, who are beginning to surpass the United States as a productive society, also represent a national group with a highly developed sense of social method.

For all these reasons, I was and remain convinced that Jamaica cannot conquer its problems and become a genuinely effective society if it cannot define for itself a set of ideals, assumptions and methods of working that are appropriate to itself. Obviously, this is a profoundly difficult undertaking. As of 1972 what were Jamaica's ideals? Mostly they reflected an acute dichotomy between the rhetoric of certain classic, liberal ideals and existing practices.

What were the assumptions? We claimed to be democratic and for equality but were still profoundly elitist. We were for democracy but were in a society where the masses, workers, students and women were largely without access to any form of meaningful decision-making. We assumed that we were for justice for the workers because our leaders said so, but we had never taken the trouble to adjust our laws to reflect the assumption.

What was our working method? We had some vague notion about developing our economy with foreign capital, and simultaneously claimed that we became politically independent so that we would be genuinely independent. We had a view of ourselves as being a part of the Western capitalist system but had an entrepreneurial class most of whose members had little of the initiative and sense of risk-taking adventure that characterises those who must drive all successful experiments in that economic model. Nor had we given thought to the fact that the more deeply we explored that system, the more deeply were we dividing the society between haves and have-nots; and excluding a mounting percentage of our people from economic opportunity.

It seems to me that an over-crowded island facing unimaginable problems of development has two choices. It can be completely neo-colonial in the sense of not pretending to itself that independence is more than a cosmetic exercise. It must suppress the rhetoric of social justice and equality; say simply and clearly that it is too small to be viable, that the process of political independence is part of an exercise in psychological therapy and nothing more. It must offer itself as an area for exploitation on the terms that are demanded by those who have capital to export, seeking at best to maximise the benefits that come to its people by a sort of cautious cunning. It is a way. We do not believe it is ultimately a way for the Jamaican people. In that event, another way must be found.

Therefore, we decided that our ideology of socialism should not remain gathering dust on the shelves of history and in the failing memories of our membership. Rather, we decided that ideology must be a principal element in national development. So we took our socialism off the shelf, dusted it off, and embarked upon a major exercise in analysis, self-examination and evaluation of our times and our circumstances. We set out to clarify our ideology to ourselves to mobilise the country around a set of ideas, assumptions and methods which could be contained in and be the expression of that ideology. That it would be controversial came as no surprise.

That we lost an election eventually under the banner of that ideology is not a reflection upon the ideology but upon us who were its exponents, and upon the circumstances in which and the methods by which we tried to apply it. That it remains the best hope for a country like ours, even placed as we are geographically, remains our firm conviction. Needless to say, the most difficult factor to be overcome in its application is to be found in our geographical location so close to the United States of America. That difficulty was never a conclusive argument against trying. Indeed, it is causes that justify all struggle and all real causes are difficult.

5
A FOREIGN POLICY FOR
THE PERIPHERY

One half of the driving force behind developments in Jamaica after 1972 came from the changes which brought first unease, then resistance and finally total opposition from the local vested interests. The other half came from our foreign policy.

In 1962, Bustamante had celebrated our independence by inviting the United States government to establish a military base in Jamaica. That was how much political freedom meant to the half of the people in whose name he could honestly speak. Mercifully, the Americans declined the offer: whether with thanks is not clear. Until 1972 our foreign policy consisted of cosmetic gestures to the Third World whilst in reality being numbered among the favoured faithful of the First World.

We had a clear choice to make: did we believe in the world as we found it, favouring a close, subservient alliance with the US? Or did we make common cause with the Non-Aligned Movement and work for changes in the world's economic system in a principled way? Whilst making it clear that we were not part of any anti-US hate campaign, indeed that we wished to remain friendly, we placed ourselves firmly in the camp of the non-aligned and for the first time began to hammer out a foreign policy for the periphery.

By 1972, the Non-Aligned Movement was beginning to make itself felt. It was growing in membership and was beginning to grapple seriously with world economic and political issues. The UN system had created a forum through which the smaller countries of the world could make themselves heard and even felt. This was true to the extent that a well publicised, moral international issue has to be dealt with by the world's power brokers even if it is eventually ignored. In spite of these gains, however, the world was still dominated by

the East/West, USSR/USA, communism/ capitalism polarisation. Issues of poverty, the nature of the world's economic
system, even human rights were all caught up in the magnetic
field of the East/West power struggle. Poverty was not, indeed
is still not, an affront to the social conscience of the entire
international community. For many it is recognised only to the
extent that it is supposed to provide a breeding ground for
communism. Gross abuses of human rights in particular
countries were, and still are, largely disregarded by the other
members of the camp to which they belong.

Jamaica is a part of the West geographically, historically,
economically, by political tradition and by cultural penetra-
tion. What does being a part of the West imply? Primarily, it
implies dependence and the occupying of a minor, peripheral
status in the total Western system. When you are a part of that
structure, things are geared to the achievement of a particular
result. The result is the entrenchment and spread of the free
enterprise system. The nature of a postcolonial economy
presupposes a heavy reliance on private, foreign investment
capital. This is a self-perpetuating arrangement in which
capital is invested to the extent that an attractive climate is
preserved. If there is the slightest doubt about the present
atmosphere or future intentions of a particular society the
capital, understandably, does not come. Even the aid that is
provided, either bilaterally by a particular government among
the industrial nations, or through the multilateral institutions
has tended to reflect this working bias. Until very recently aid
tended to be concentrated in those areas which would provide
the infrastructure necessary to the kind of environment in
which private investment capital could do its business
successfully. It was easy to get loans for highway systems and
to build schools for the training of the workforce. None of this
was bad in itself but interesting when contrasted with the
difficulty in obtaining assistance for certain kinds of
agriculture or housing development. This has changed to some
extent in recent years with the development of multilateral
institutional support for this kind of programme.

Until recently, however, there was little hope that assistance
could be found for the expansion of the state sector of an
economy or even for the development of co-operative
enterprises. The finance that was available was of two kinds:
economic infrastructure through multilateral or bilateral

public sources; and private investment.

By 1972, there was little in the Jamaican experience to suggest that this concept of economic development could ever lift the majority of the Jamaican people out of the trap of poverty and into any form of broadly shared prosperity and social justice. But this was not all. The industrialised countries had created and dominated the world economy. They had created it during the period of politically apparent imperialism, particularly between 1850 and 1950. They had subsequently secured its survival by the dominant place occupied by those financial institutions and multinational corporations which had entrenched themselves in every corner of the globe. They had rationalised and justified the system by the development of an economic philosophy. They had then proceeded to invest that philosophy with the characteristics of permanent revealed truth. The word was spread by the electronic media, the press and all the paraphernalia of modern communications. The propaganda was never-ending.

The world economy, of course, continued to work beautifully for the industrial powers. The terms of trade as between capital and manufactured goods on the one hand, and primary products, crops and raw materials on the other, could be depended upon. It worked in favour of the industrialised powers and against the interests of the newly independent, developing countries. Jamaica's experience in colonialism was multiplied a hundred-fold throughout the developing world. As time passed it would cost more and more to buy machinery, or tractors or automobiles by comparison with the prices fetched for sugar, cotton, sisal, coffee, copper and the rest.[2] More and more production of these primary commodities would be needed to maintain the same level of imports and hence the same standard of living. Since our people would share the same appetites and hopes and expectations with all other people, but with far more desperation than in the developed countries, something would have to be done to close the financial gap. And here we are not speaking of the financial gap between the living standard of the developing and the developed world. We are talking about closing the financial gap between the standard of living enjoyed in the developing country ten years ago, and the standard of living enjoyed ten years later in that same country, after the terms of trade had wreaked their havoc. Faced with this dilemma, many countries start processing their own commodities like cocoa, or raw materials like cotton. They promptly find that they run into high tariffs in developed countries. In other cases, freight rates increase differentially to make their products uncompetitive.[3] Therefore, attempts to beat the terms of trade are defeated by other devices.

Ironically, the standard response of the developed countries involved the customary cry about productivity and application. If only the Third World countries and their people would apply themselves to the business of production all would be well! The developed countries seemed to say: 'Look at us; look at what we did!' No one bothered to remember that the accomplishments of these countries, particularly in terms of the rate of investment in economic expansion, had been based upon two processes of exploitation. At first the capitalist system exploited its own workforce to create the surplus for the wealth of the owner and the expansion of the business. Later, in the imperialist phase, the colonies and their workers were exploited for the same reason. This provided cheap raw materials and basic goods. Finally, the surplus acquired through control of the overseas economies made it possible to maintain economic expansion and begin to share the wealth with the workers at the imperial centre.

Magically, Third World countries, starting with economies all askew because of their colonial experience, were able to duplicate this experience although the objective conditions on which it was based no longer existed.

In addition to the effect of the terms of trade, there exists a vast economic complex consisting of multinational corporations, financial institutions, systems of patents, trade marks, royalties, all of which serve to guarantee that financial, technological and even productive control remains in the hands of the developed countries. Hence, when a developing country seeks to apply itself with the required diligence to the building of a productive machine equal to the challenge of the times, it discovers that adequate money and needed technology come at a price. The price excludes national control. At every step of the way the system ensures that for every step forward in terms of increased economic potential there is one step sideways in terms of ownership and one step backwards in terms of dependence. Experience has shown that there is nothing that guarantees its own continuity like dependence just as there is nothing that reinforces its own authority like power. To them that have, even more shall be given.

One is often driven to wonder how the industrialised countries insulated themselves from criticism and political counter-attack for so long. One of the reasons, of course, is to be found in their capacity to control education and propaganda. Through the education system they were able to invest the reality of their own view of power with a corresponding moral authority by creating a philosphy in which profit was equated with virtue and virtue with personal application.

In time however, the counter-attack came. New thinkers began to challenge the system, questioning both its effectiveness and its fairness. First there was Marxism and the socialist and later communist movements. Then after World War II, even non-socialist elements began to criticise the economic order. New forms of management of the international economy were proposed.

Although the communist movement did not provide the main source from which alternative proposals for the world economy were coming, the establishment responded with a propaganda campaign which continues to the present. Proposals for change are labelled communistic. An historical coincidence between the emergence of plural democracy, the recognition of human rights and the underlining of personal liberty, on the one hand, and the capitalist system, on the other, is emphasised. It is implied that there is a natural link between these things and that to change any one of them is to undermine them all.

As the propaganda war continues, the communist label provides a convenient point of departure for the attack on any movement seeking to change things. Socialism is dealt with by a form of guilt by association. In the end, people in the West are put in a position where they are pressured to choose between one system or the other, between God and the Devil.

By all these means — economic, financial, technological, political and psychological — pressure is maintained on developing countries, particularly in the Western hemisphere, to choose. Not to be with the West is to be against 'God'. To be with the East would certainly reveal an alignment with the 'Devil'. As it happens, most Third World people do not wish

to be with either the West or East for a variety of reasons. To
have to be with one or the other might involve a surrender of
the very sovereignty which had been missing for so long and
struggled for so hard. All citizens of the Third World have
their experience to tell of the economic system of the industrial
contries that has exploited them historically and offers no
prospect of economic progress, equitably shared. On the other
hand, there is probably much in the newer, evolving socialist
bloc countries which does not appeal. For many, there is the
great unknown factor of the one-party state and the concept of
democratic centralism. Equally, the idea of an entirely
centrally planned and bureaucratic economy, overwhelmingly
under state ownership would not necessarily find welcoming
echoes in the cultural patterns and the historically conditioned
expectations of many Third World people.

The more I thought about it, the more I was convinced of
the necessity for the Third World to evolve its own paths to
salvation; paths that would reflect the cultural pattern and
historical experience, the need and the expectations of the
various people involved.[4] Certainly, it seemed like the ultimate
contradiction to be asked to believe that one's best interests
would be served by remaining unquestioningly part of the very
system that had conquered or captured us, traded us from time
to time and exploited us consistently. It was this system which
even now nurtured the very deformities from which we
continued to suffer.

To be part of an empire, as distinct from its centre, is to be
part of the periphery. Imperialism had made us all peripheral.
It may be true that before imperialism we did not amount to all
that much as measured by the values that European nations
proclaim. But little as we may have been, we were ourselves and
certainly not peripheral to an external, foreign system. Here,
of course, one does not speak of particular areas which may
have been suffering from recent conquest by a neighbouring
group as was often the case in Africa. Nor is there any
suggestion that what we now call the Third World was the
scene of some sort of idyllic, splendid, simple past, each of us in
a 'simple state of natural liberty'. Far from it. Rather the point
is that now some two-thirds of mankind have been reduced to a
peripheral status in political, economic and even social terms.
It is the degree, the scale, the ruthlessness, the completeness of
the exploitation which marks this imperialism, that sets this

process of domination apart from any that have preceded it.

Throughout the first years of independence, foreign policy had been understood by most Jamaicans as something that the big powers dealt with. Since there was nothing a small country could do about it, what would be the point of a foreign policy, the argument ran? By 1972, we had come to realise that foreign policy was at the very heart of the economic process. If there were to be significant change in favour of self-reliant development, there would clearly have to be a different world environment. I have often remarked that you cannot change Jamaica if you do not change the world. I have never meant by this anything so naive as to suggest that little Jamaica could change the world. Nor do I mean that Jamaica can avoid its responsibility to itself. We must use our resources intelligently and manage them effectively. No one owes us charity nor should we wish to take it were it available. On the other hand, the system works against countries like ours. Hence it is that international economic system which we must work to change.[5]

How to change it was and is the problem that confronts the whole Third World. There are more than 120 newly independent members of the group. Clearly, no one Third World country can hope to make any impact on the present situation. On the other hand, all the developing countries acting in concert represent a force which may be resented but cannot be ignored.

From the start, we were clear that Third World co-operation cannot begin and end with the declaration of political objectives and with the taking of resolutions to the United Nations. The reason for the identification of the Third World as a new force is to be found in economic experience. Therefore, the rationale of the Third World is the search for economic answers: How do we achieve economic development at a rate that keeps pace with the desperate need for better standards? How do we make such developments consistent and reliable in terms of growing economic performance? How do we ensure that this growing economy provides the basis for and the equitable sharing of benefits? And how do we ensure that our economies grow less and less dependent on external factors and more and more capable of response to internal, national development policies?

By 1972, our foreign policy had clarified three major

objectives: we would seek to avoid being sucked into the East/West polarisation and play our part in the building of a third, non-aligned political force; to do everything that lay within our power to encourage increasing attention by the Third World to questions of economic strategy and to the pursuit of policies that would strengthen our hand in negotiations with developed countries; press our colleagues to take advantage of every opportunity for economic co-operation amongst ourselves. These three objectives were the necessary preconditions for any attempt to find that 'third path'.

Our foreign policy was sometimes described as running in concentric circles. We believe that economic and political co-operation begins most logically and naturally amongst one's neighbours. Distances are short and the likelihood of a common understanding of issues and sharing of objectives most likely to occur. Hence, we looked at the experience of Jamaica at the time of the Federation and at attempts to build a form of economic co-operation through the development of the Caribbean Free Trade Area, CARIFTA. We were firm and enthusiastic supporters of this development and were determined to play our part in the deepening of the free trade area into an institution working for economic integration and political co-operation wherever feasible and possible. As a natural extension of our commitment to our English-speaking brothers and sisters in the Caribbean, we were determined to work to bridge the gap which separated the English-speaking nations from the rest. But our objectives here went far beyond cultural exchange. We were looking towards the time when the raw materials and energy from the different parts of the region would be brought together in new enterprises owned and controlled within the region; when commonly owned shipping lines would begin to move our products; when we could share the technology which each was struggling to develop.

Looking beyond the region we were aware of other natural areas of co-operation. The African, Caribbean and Pacific countries which had been parts of the various European empires would soon have new opportunities arising from the creation of the European Community. Jamaica would become a vigorous participant in the activities of the ACP Group[6] and a leader in negotiations with the European group.

From the ACP Group we moved into the wider circle which formed the Group of 77 and the Non-Aligned Movement itself. Our membership in the Group of 77 was automatic, but the degree of participation was our choice. The Third World spoke in the United Nations on economic matters through this Group. We chose to be active and to commit all the resources that we could spare to playing our part in the effort to make the Group coherent and effective in the forum. So, too, with the Non-Aligned Movement. There was to be no tokenism for us. The Non-Aligned Movement presented our best political hope for the development of a third force in world affairs.

In addition, there were two parallel areas. Our party, the People's National Party, had long been a member of the Socialist International. This is the body to which are affiliated the great democratic socialist, social democratic and labour parties of Europe, along with newer parties in Africa, the Caribbean, Latin America and Canada. We decided to activate our membership in this group so as to have the opportunity to speak up for the interests of the Third World. Here was an institution which had long tended to be a sort of reformist European Club — preoccupied with European interests on behalf of European trade union members and their allies amongst the middle class intelligensia and the like. We wished to discover whether they could be persuaded to support the just causes for which we intended to fight. In short, was socialism for export? Equally, we determined to be active members of the Commonwealth.[7] The Commonwealth Heads of Government Conference which met every two years and the Secretariat that services the group and its decisions in between, seemed to us to hold yet another kind of opportunity for pressing the Third World cause.

We always regarded the socialist bloc countries as potential allies in certain areas of our foreign policy objectives. These countries had always assisted liberation struggles. They represented a critical element in the balance of forces and could help neutralise the raw power of economic imperialism.

And finally, there was of course the United Nations itself. Not for us a dormant role upon the back benches of that body. We were not concerned about the criticism implied in the question; who is little Jamaica to think it can be heard in the UN? We were determined to be heard because we felt that we had something to say and that our responsibility was to say it in such a manner that others would be forced to listen rather than question the size of the country which spoke.

If all of this was to work we faced major difficulties. Unless one has come out of the cataclysm, or at least the catharsis, of a revolutionary process, new attitudes and new policies are hard to develop. One of the neater tricks of imperialism has been to persuade so many colonial people that imperialism was their great opportunity. The real difficulty, so the argument runs, results from our failure to take advantage of those opportunities, a failure that has resulted from laziness or other congenital disabilities. We had no illusions about the difficulty of taking Jamaica out of the traditional orbit and into a new path as a genuinely non-aligned country.

We had been taught to believe, and observation had confirmed, that the United States was the sun and England its moon. Of course there was an earlier time when England was the sun and the US didn't figure at all. But we were dealing with the present. Could we get the Jamaican people to understand that we are all planets and must work for an equitable cosmos?

We set ourselves targets. At the head of the list was disengagement from a slavish obedience to the US and the countries of the NATO alliance merely because we were weak and economically dependent. Some would argue that our policy should have been determined by that very dependence. To this we would reply that as long as we accept our dependence as a natural and permanent condition, so long will we continue to suffer all the disadvantages of that status. We were determined. We were sure that the break had to be made and that there is no 'correct' time for the decision to become independent. The Non-Aligned Movement seemed to us our natural and proper home, and that way we headed. Jamaica had joined the movement under our predecessors, but had never been active. It is the degree of activity which was to separate the present from the past.

Fresh from our own search for freedom, we determined to support all the genuine liberation struggles. One might ask, what is a liberation struggle? It is quite simply any situation where a group of people large enough to command attention determine for themselves that the conditions under which they live are oppressive and intolerable, can show rational cause why this is so, and proceed to struggle to remove the yoke that oppresses them. Our understanding of our own situation led us to the conclusion that ethics and self-interest combined to demand our support for the liberation movements of Southern Africa, of Latin America, of the Vietnamese people and others. The logical corollary of support for the liberation process is insistence upon the rights of small nations to the enjoyment of their sovereignty. This question does not involve empty rhetoric. It goes to the very heart of the future of mankind.

Our strong opposition to any infringement upon the sovereignty of a small nation and its rights was to lead us to the most controversial single aspect of our foreign policy. This was our friendship with and consistent defence of Cuba and her right to normal, unfettered membership of that part of the family of nations which occupies the western hemisphere. Many have thought that our Cuba policy was a quixotic mistake. Others interpreted it as implying secret, communist purposes. Still others have believed that I fell under the spell of Fidel Castro; that Jamaica became Moscow's cat's-paw through its relationship with Cuba. All of this, without exception, is poppycock.

For me the question of Cuba's relationship with the United States goes to the heart of the question of the kind of world Jamaica can occupy with pride, with independence and with success in the future. No such prospect exists for a country like Jamaica as long as it is possible for the United States to continue to bully, to ostracise, to exert pressure against, to blockade Cuba and to maintain an unwanted base on her sovereign territory. As far as I am concerned, Cuba represents a non-negotiable point of principle about the kind of world in which we live. It is not, let me add, the only such issue. The taking of American hostages in an Iranian Embassy is to me an equally non-negotiable and indefensible issue. If it comes to that, Jamaica was among the first countries of the United Nations to denounce the intervention in Afghanistan.

The Cuban issue is simply this: if the United States has the right to exert this pressure against Cuba, what are our rights as a sovereign nation? What is our security, should we ever do anything to cause the displeasure of the powers that be in the United States? So far as I am concerned, to back away from the principled and friendly relationship with Cuba was to admit failure at the start. That friendship was maintained in spite of the wide differences in political organisation and social and economic objectives between Cuba and ourselves.

To us, the challenge of foreign policy was to make the term, 'Third World' the badge of a cause rather than the description of a sad condition. It represented a positive assertion of a new sense of what international relations could be about.

Of course nation states act selfishly in defence of their own interests. But equally, a nation state can be guided by principles of justice and equitable co-operation comparable to those which we seek to develop among the members of a community. It is in this sense that the term 'Third World' was seen by us as representative of a new view of international policy. And most importantly 'Third World' meant to us the response to an economic challenge. Could poor countries develop such a sense of their common interests as to begin to work together to build new means of production, distribution, transport and exchange by their own efforts and through their own co-operation? It was of this that Julius Nyerere had spoken with his phrase 'Trade Union of the Poor'.[8] This was a pithy summary of the theme, and of the need for Third World countries to unite. All my active life had been spent among working people and was about that accession of strength, confidence and capacity for action that results when two or three, who are weak, are gathered together and by that act become strong.[9] Perhaps our foreign policy could best be described as an intention to gather two or three together so that they might be strong.

This foreign policy was not likely to please the US Establishment. In due course they were to make known the exact extent of that displeasure. In this they were not unlike the local oligarchy. They were to make a formidable combination.

Many have argued that this was predictable. Some sympathisers have contended that we should not have 'irritated the giant to the North', to use a phrase then much in vogue. In fact we worked sincerely to make it clear that we were not anti-American as such, but only firm in our support of particular principles and in our determination to work for them. We sought, constantly, to explain our position and to persuade Americans to accept it at its face value. We were scrupulous in our treatment of US investments and, apart from the major quarrel over bauxite taxes, maintained good relations with our many overseas investors. Equally, we never

failed to make it clear by word and deed that we had neither the
desire nor the intention to destroy our local business class. We
wished to reduce their power and make them share some of
their wealth within reason. We wished to make them a
legitimate part of a democratically controlled society rather
than its hidden, if not open, masters. But we neither wished nor
sought their demise.[10]

In short, we knew that change in politics is like motion in
physics, breeding its own opposite reaction, and sought to
ensure that the reaction would be rational. We worked to
secure that it would be a measured response to our real actions
and intentions rather than an hysterical reaction to imaginary
dangers. Time was to show how great that reaction would be
and how out of proportion to the actual degree of threat.

ACTION

6
CHANGE AND REPERCUSSIONS

We won the 1972 election comparatively unencumbered in so far as the specific pledges of a detailed, traditional election manifesto are concerned. From another point of view we were massively encumbered: by history, by need, by hope, and by a set of generalised expectations. We could not escape responsibility for the last. We campaigned on a slogan involving change and around the specific phrase 'Better Must Come'. There is a sense in which the phrase was ill-advised. In the absence of specifics, 'Better Must Come' is the kind of omnibus expression which invites every section of society to assume that better means better for them and for them in terms of their interests.

We won by a landslide. Fifty-six per cent of the population — the largest proportion achieved by either of the Jamaican political parties up to that time — voted for the change which we symbolised more than specifically promised.

It has been contended since that no government in Jamaican history has ever started with such goodwill. Needless to say, the assertion is made by our present critics. Our friends are more likely to say that no government started with such expectations to live up to. Some may even point out that the expectations were not entirely of our own making and that we had, in fact, tried to minimise them in the course of the campaign. In many ways, the expectations were a response to the widespread disillusionment which had been the end result of the first ten years of independence. But all that is for the historians. Of immediate concern are the questions: granted our intentions, what did we try to do, what did we accomplish and finally, what particular actions along the way engendered the hostility which would lead to the government's downfall?

Not everything that any government does is controversial.

The fact that we managed to build twice as many houses a year for low income groups as our predecessors and in spite of world economic conditions that bordered on chaos, was obviously not controversial.

There was little controversy when, in 1977, we introduced a scheme to establish a growing fund for housing construction through compulsory contributions. Workers and employers were to put up 2% each. When a group of houses was built, they were distributed by drawing lots among all contributors within a certain radius. The scheme was administered by a board drawn from the unions, employers' bodies and government. The National Housing Trust, as it was named, ws adapted from a Mexican model. In the three years up to 1980, it built 17,381 housing units.[1]

We were attracted to the scheme because it was an effective way of increasing the funds available for low and middle income housing. It also absorbed millions in cash which would otherwise be putting additional inflationary pressure into the economy. These were all economic factors. There was an added political implication which did not appeal to everyone. The drawing of lots for houses removed one substantial slice of a scarce benefit from the pork barrel. Our predecessors in office, the JLP, were savage when it came to distributing the couple of thousand houses they built each year. Only die-hard supporters came near the opportunity. We were under tremendous and constant pressure to retaliate now that our turn had come. The National Housing Trust was a good way of lifting the majority of the units to come on stream in the future, out of that whole syndrome. It was a correct decision for which we paid a high price in discontented cadres. Clientelism had become an entrenched part of the system and we were trying to break it down. The recollection sits in the memory with a certain wry irony compared with the propaganda campaign to portray us as corrupt victimisers.

The imagination that lay behind the expansion of the Port of Kingston to make us a major trans-shipment centre for containerised cargo caused no controversy, indeed was popular to the extent that it was noticed. The Free Zone for strictly export industry attached to the new container port was not even criticised by the communists! The expansion and modernisation of our airports; our new highway programmes which helped transform transport in the tourist areas; the huge increase in farmers' feeder roads, in rural electrification; in the provision of playing fields and community centres, seemed to be appreciated, particularly by those who used them. In fact, by the end, it was ironic to observe the people that benefited through the use of these things and still berated us for spending the money on them!

Similarly, the literacy campaign which we organised nationally and which cut functional illiteracy by half during our term, proved a successful instrument of mobilisation. Thousands volunteered as instructors and served without pay, some for years. More than 200,000 graduated with literate and numerate skills. Many ignored the call for help but equally, many responded. Few attacked it, certainly not openly.

We started to develop a system of comprehensive health care resting on a firm para-medical base. The plan which called for a network of primary care clinics was established, each feeding into comprehensive clinics and finally into a regional hospital. Despite the severe financial restrictions, this was put in place through most of the West of the island as the first phase of a national plan. Remarkable advances in general health and particularly in child nutrition were achieved. It is difficult to quarrel with better health, so the propaganda was reserved for 16 Cuban doctors who helped make the plan work.

However, most of what we did was controversial.

Jamaica was, and remains, a society full of contradictions. Both political parties were strongly union linked and historically union based. They had dominated the political development of the country. There had been great changes. Yet the patterns of the past persisted. All classes found a place, in varying degrees, in the political movements. Yet class divisions remained. There was an element of upward mobility but the newcomers to each class promptly volunteered to man the barricades which protected it. There was upward mobility but little downward empathy.

At the apex was the oligarchy, springing from the plantation owners and merchants of the earliest times but now including the financiers and industrialists. Attached to the oligarchy and largely sharing its views, was a traditional establishment of senior bureaucrats, managers and older professionals.

Oligarchy and establishment saw eye to eye on the natural order, often combining to manipulate the political leadership.

Where this proved difficult they would seek to frustrate it, prepared for quiet sabotage if this extreme were required. In times when the natural order was under threat, oligarchy and establishment merged and were indistinguishable in action. There were, of course, always notable individual exceptions.

The upper strata of the society, therefore, had a highly developed sense of privilege and a strong instinct for separation. To all who were below it was: 'Keep your distance', and 'Know your place'.

Not surprisingly these sharp, social attitudes had major economic consequences. Factory organisation was normally elitist with clearly drawn lines separating managers, administrators and upper level supervisors from the rest. Management with jacket off and dirty hands, together with the fellows on the shop floor, was rare. Social status implied access to wealth. It also depended upon wealth to make itself known. The older members of the upper groups accepted their wealth as a natural right. To the newcomers wealth was the passport to be displayed prominently at the barrier. Like all who are newly arrived, ostentation and extravagance were necessary. Without huge homes and flashy cars, the neighbours might not notice that one's time had come. Indeed, even the newcomers might themselves doubt whether it had happened.

There is nothing new in any of this. But it was acute in a society like Jamaica, its people unsure of their place in history, its newer classes unsure of their place in society. Only the oligarchy was sure of its right to rule. The difference here was that many of the Jamaican oligarchy had no deep conviction that this was their home, regardless of circumstances. Other oligarchies have stayed, perhaps fought, when change came; have learned to accommodate it, even to bear with it; but always have stayed. Colonial oligarchies love the colony as long as it is indisputably theirs. When this is in doubt, they revert to the metropolis, as if following a prior historical attachment. Rather than stay, they migrate. There were always exceptions, even notable ones, in every group at each level. But the broad tendencies were then and still remain singularly stubborn in Jamaica.

In this context, almost anything which was done to create a more equitable framework could lead to resistance. Battle lines would be drawn; the barricades would be manned.

The areas which had to be changed and which many would

seek to defend fell into four clear categories.

First there was the psychological area. — Who is a Jamaican? Are an upper class and a lower class Jamaican members of the same national family? Or are they merely heirs to a superior and an inferior legacy happening to occupy the same island? Only cultural strategies could affect these age-old difficulties. Secondly, there was the critical question in all elitist societies: where does real power reside? This group of problems would only yield to political engineering. Thirdly, there was the question of class status and differentiation. Here social initiatives were urgently needed. Finally, there was the matter of wealth and how it is shared. This, along with the vital task of expanding and simultaneously restructuring Jamaica's productive apparatus, was the area for new economic policies.

All this would come to a head in initiatives through which change was to be effected. Over it all hung the question: could Jamaica be a viable society in the future if the changes were not made?

To begin with we must understand the psychology of the transplanted society.[2] One needs to step back from Jamaican or indeed Caribbean society to understand how deeply it is still influenced by outside and particularly by North American values.[3] We all become so immersed in the habits of American culture that if we are not careful we mistake them for life itself. Our habits of dress, our sense of social hierarchy, our acceptance of monarchy can all be laid at the door of British colonialism and the skill with which empire fashions the mind of the governed. But America has never needed to precede its conquests by military action. Hollywood films, glossy magazines, canned television shows have all created a cultural invasion. This has proved more powerful than the attack of any army because it proceeds by stealth to occupy the corners of the mind and needs no fortress upon the ground to uphold its influence.

We had come a long way by 1972. Our institutions were developed; our artistic movement vigorous, and often original, But for the mass of the population, values were those disseminated through the stream of propaganda and entertainment that poured out of Washington, New York and California. In the end, it was difficult to tell where entertainment ended and propaganda began. Hence, expectations never flowed naturally from the unfolding of Jamaican experience. They were imported. America was so close that to many Jamaicans going shopping meant hopping on a plane to Miami; and those who could not afford the plane ticket lived for the day when they might.

The perception of values originally reflected the things that were taught in a secondary school system transplanted from Britain. To this had been added the expectations of the American consumer society. The first was ingrained because it had been a long time aplanting. The second drew its strength from a variety of factors. Jamaica is close to America. It is naturally appealing to present a view of society in which husband and wife each have their own car and can go about their more or less lawful business independently, beautifully dressed, finally meeting still smelling like roses to prepare for a night on the town. Who can quarrel with a new dress for Madam for every party?

In all of this what was the Jamaican identity? In a normal and healthy social process, culture is the mirror of reality and art a means of knowing what we are doing here. The arts can also show us what we should avoid and to what we can realistically aspire. But the first problem for the Caribbean is to find out who he or she is. The second is to separate dreams from possibilities. But before any of this can be done, the Caribbean needs to come to terms with its own history and to subject influences to microscopic examination. Until such a process begins, culture is not one's own and art tells us nothing about ourselves. Hence, we decided to challenge some of the more obviously irrelevant influences.

The previous government used to run an official beauty contest, the winner of which would proceed on a pilgrimage to London each year to compete in the Miss World contest. We felt that if ever there were an activity appropriate for private enterprise, this was it, and discontinued government support. The three-piece suit worn in the tropics is a valuable support for the heavy textile industries of the developed countries, but incredibly inappropriate for the tropics. We changed the rules and made tropical dress acceptable in protocol. Whereas our predecessors in office had banned much of the protest music of the ghetto, we opened the doors and, on the contrary, worked to assist in the promotion of the cultural energy of the ghetto as expressed in reggae music. Malcolm X was forbidden reading. We opened those doors also.

At the more fundamental level we were determined to foster a new cultural direction, drawing upon the work of the past since the 1930s but focusing specifically on the African root. Through all its institutions the government encouraged and supported local and indigenous expressions of culture in art, music, the dance.

To promote cultural cross-fertilisation, Third World countries were invited to send representative cultural shows to Jamaica. A multi-disciplinary, cultural training centre was built. Originally planned by the JLP, it brought under one roof training in painting, sculpture, music, dance, drama, ceramics and jewelcraft. Each school inspired and challenged the others. This was the internal process of cross-fertilisation. The annual Independence Festival, started by the former JLP administration, provided outlets for folk art and genuine community involvement. We made it more of a reflection of community self-expression. Reggae music, springing from the gut experience of the ghetto, was given maximum recognition and exposure. Indeed, a new Copyright Law to protect local artists was passed. It was not put into force because the CARICOM Secretariat was working to harmonise all the copyright legislation in the region. They had not finished their work when we left office.

There was a new upsurge of cultural expression. This was undoubtedly the product of the imagination and creativity of the Jamaican people; we claim only to have provided the environment, the support and the encouragement which helped it to full flower.

There was trouble about all of this and one could detect early a growing uneasiness in the establishment. Although to some it may have seemed peripheral, it represented a challenge to the established order of the mind. There was a constant tension which resulted from the battle between the traditional values of imperialism and a new and psychologically independent Jamaica struggling to find roots in past and present experience. This tension was present through all that was to follow. One would see the occasional letter to the press bemoaning the collapse of proper values. The breakdown of discipline was a constant cry. Some were quick to forget that discipline is a matter of degree. People have complained about discipline in Jamaica for the last 300 years, beginning with fractious slaves who refused to give a fair day's work in return for the contract by which they were owned. Equally forgotten were the riots of the 1960s in which discontent went beyond individual expression to collective action. Now, the problem was perceived in terms of these dangerous ideas about rights and freedom and African history. The old elite were sure that all this was undermining discipline. The Jamaica of nostalgic illusion was disappearing.

To a certain extent it was true that there were problems with discipline. The question is: what caused them? Discipline before, such as it was, had been the result of fear, of the power of sanction exercised by a minority backed by the external imperial force. Local instruments of enforcement were in place when the imperial authority withdrew. But on whose behalf was this authority exercised? At some point there had to be a change so that authority would seem to act in the name of all the people; in the interest, at least, of the great majority of the people; and through instruments which the people understood. Jamaica was in a state of flux because it was and is in transition. The growing pains are unmistakable and they include problems with discipline.

The establishment perceived the cultural problem as part of the political intention. However, objections were still relatively muted as if waiting for the political hand to be revealed. This is where the trouble really began. The combination of a new cultural emphasis together with experiments in democratic participation seemed part of a plan to change traditional, English-derived customs and ways of doing things. It is here that the controversy became vocal. This was so for two reasons.

We tackled the problems of the ingrained elitism of the society by devising policies and programmes to democratise the society. But every increase in the level of democratic participation is a challenge to the existing order and the method by which power is maintained and effective authority exercised. Therefore, the declaration of democratic intent has a revolutionary implication for the powers that be, whatever and whoever they may be. In addition, we had to contend with an opposition who had been reluctant to join issue with us in the cultural field. It is difficult to look at a 90% black population and disagree with the attempt to create an awareness of African culture and history. On the other hand, new political institutions are fair game and to the extent that

they are unfamiliar, can be easy targets. The JLP attacked
democratic changes from the start, charging Cuban influence.

We put a lot of effort into the establishment of community
councils. Participatory politics may be all very well at the top.
You can call in the leaders of institutions to help formulate
national policy and this is an advance. But this is a far cry from
creating a sense of participation in the mind of a small farmer
high up in the mountains, getting up at half past four each
morning to trudge the five miles to the fields where his yams
are growing. It also has little to do with the problems of the
community from which that farmer sets out each morning. As
like as not, this community has become like a house divided
against itself, constantly excited by the agents of the political
parties into hostility, disunity and contentiousness about
anything and everything.

We hoped that the community councils would create a new
arena for group co-operation and, consequently, a new focus
for a sense of communal reality. Here was the point where we
hoped the members of a community might bury the political
hatchet, at least as long as the council was in session, and regain
some sense of united purpose around shared objectives,
however limited in scope. In no time our worthy opposition
had leapt upon this simple act of indigenous social engineering
to proclaim it a copy of a Cuban model intended to undermine
and eventually destroy the Jamaican democracy. Those already
made uneasy by the cultural trends took note.

Even crime was to provide an area in which we experimented
with participation. No government has ever dealt with 24%
unemployment without serious crime. Like most crime,
Jamaica's had an economic base and a psychological
superstructure. At that time crime was bad and getting worse.
There were those who were poor and had nothing, those who
had little and resented it. Then there were those whose
resentment spilled over into the relations between the sexes.
Robbery with rape had become the new curse. Perhaps too
many ghetto youths had received too many blows from the
grandmother who sought to keep order amongst half-a-dozen
youths, deserted by their fathers and uncertain in their
relationship with their mothers. But the presumption of a
psychological cause was no help in this situation. In many cases
robbery was becoming associated with the mindless and
unnecessary killing of the people who were robbed. A mask to

prevent subsequent detection would have cost less than the
bullet which killed, but the bullet was preferred, presumably
because this also reflected some form of psychological
derangement present in the personality of the robber. This did
not help either.

The stealing was unacceptable but at least it had a basis in
logic. The society could deal with it without panic. The casual
killing and the rapes were something else. Half-way through
our first term of office, panic over crime loomed. We had put
money into the police, upgrading their equipment, salaries and
numbers. But it was obvious that no amount of money that we
could afford would create a police force that could really
control the situation.

More importantly, it seemed to us that a solution conceived
purely in terms of traditional law enforcement versus ghetto
discontent could not provide the whole answer. Part of the
answer had, of course, to come from new levels of economic
opportunity; from stable homes; from a new form of society in
which people could feel hope in the future because they
experienced involvement in the present. But how soon could
all that happen? In the meantime, the very hope of
improvement was being dashed to bits in the crime rate.

To us, the solution lay in the mobilisation of the people
themselves to help the security forces in the fight with crime.
There were two powerful justifications for this. Firstly,
volunteers for security duty could lead to an enormous
increase in the daily and particularly nightly outreach of the
security forces for a given security expenditure. More
importantly, the involvement of the people in the policing of
their own neighbourhoods and communities might change the
psychological environment in which the criminal plied his
trade. Many practical consequences could flow from this.
Crime detection was often frustrated by the fear of giving
evidence. A family which was part of the law enforcement
process would surely be less afraid to give evidence. The
criminal who saw life in terms of 'them and us' would find it
harder to believe this, if his father or brother were part of the
security forces. Most importantly, the community might be
led to feel that life itself involves group effort and community
co-operation. Accordingly, we formed a home guard and
invited the members of both parties and members of no party
to join.

We offered basic training in the use of small fire-arms and patrol duties. Home guard units were formed on the basis that they would operate only in their direct neighbourhood village or community. Arms would be kept in the police stations and issued to each patrol when going on duty. All patrols were to work under the direction of the regular police and to be accompanied by a representative of the regular police when going on duty.

Once again, we could rely upon our opposition. This, too, was represented as a Cuban/communist device. Incessant propaganda was maintained to the effect that the home guard was being established to replace the regular police force as the first step in an elaborate communist take-over. Again, this interpretation was not unnoticed.

Two features of our political development within the People's National Party were to prove unendingly controversial. Both involved a view of democracy. We had a view of the role of the party itself in decision-making. Traditional two-party democracies continue to wrestle with the question: what is the role of the party when the government which it has made possible is in office? Superficially, it would seem to be a ridiculous question about nothing. Surely, the party represents a group of people organised around common objectives who undertake to govern in a certain manner and contest an election on that basis. If the party wins, it forms the government and governs for the period of time prescribed in the particular system. During its term of office, it is more or less the same group of people who offered themselves to the electorate in the first place to run the country. It is to be assumed it is they who take the decisions of government during the term. Presumably they will do so by reference to their principles and ideals, if they have any; by their judgement of circumstances as they arise; by their memory of what they undertook to do when they fought the election; and by their awareness of the fact that they have to face the electorate again. But, of course, it is not that simple.

In the American system, the party really has little to do with policy since the whole apparatus is held together by habit, the spoils of office, the pressing of sectional interests and the hope of reward. In other systems, however, it can become a real problem because of a theory that a government once elected must represent all of the people since it has to govern all of the people. Within this argument, the government becomes a convenient prisoner of the interests of all the people, however much at variance these interests may be. The party is supposed to recede into the background as a latent force, not to be heard from again until the next election. This is justified on the grounds that they are a partisan force.

This may be very convenient for those who benefit from the *status quo*. But if every element in the *status quo* must be represented beneficially, regardless of the relative advantages they enjoy to begin with, it is difficult to see what can be changed without offence to the principle. Equally, the theory contains a temptation. The members of the party who have made it to the cabinet of the government can be led to believe that they are the sole repositories of wisdom since they alone have access to the official files.

Behind the whole fiction, of course, lies the equally convenient consideration that the quieter the rest of the party is kept, the more absolute and unquestioned is the power of the cabinet ministers and the less likely are they to be replaced if their performance is wanting. It is easy to see how governments in power quickly become estranged from the parties of which they are a part and whose collective efforts put them where they are.

Governments in power are subject to the laws of inertia as much as anything else. Indeed, we had watched the process of estrangement from the people overtake successive Jamaican administrations. We had seen the same thing happen over and over in British politics. We were determined that it would not happen to us. From the very outset we created a positive, participatory role for our party executive to which the government and individual cabinet ministers had to render account from time to time. In fact this was very good for both government and ministers, keeping them in touch with popular feeling and the daily experience of broad sections of the public. But all this was bitterly resented by the establishment. We were constantly lectured and upbraided for this gross breach of our constitutional 'duty'.

Obviously, the establishment knew well, and valued more, this theory of separation between government and party when in power. From their point of view they were quite right. As the administration unfolded, there were many instances where it was the determination of the party cadres which kept the government on course. It was often they who ensured that cabinet had the courage and the determination to act in the face of a cacophony of protest from the conservative press and from the major establishment institutions like the local Manufacturers' Association and the Chamber of Commerce. From the start the role of the party represented a battle-ground between the oligarchy and ourselves.

Among the things that caused political controversy, the most difficult to analyse and problematic to weigh was the question of political rhetoric. Terms such as 'rapacious capitalists'; the fact that our executive was called the 'politbureau' even though in accordance with Third World rather than Soviet practice, certainly played their part. Some have even gone so far as to suggest that the migration of wealthy Jamaicans can be traced to the political rhetoric of the time. This is not confirmed by the historical record, though I do not doubt that the rhetoric of the time — particularly from the extreme left of the party, since the right operated more in the corridors of power — added to the existing tension. There certainly were indiscretions from many quarters. Differences in perception concerning socialism, or simply about change, led to inconsistencies. In time, the overstatements were to abate somewhat, as idealism and impatience yielded some ground to experience. In the meantime, however, some of the rhetoric provided the enemies of the process with a convenient beating stick, a ready means of turning uncertainty into panic. And there is no doubt that the rhetoric heightened fear and was seized upon to excuse and justify opposition on other grounds.

But the real and abiding cause of the problem was to be found in what we were doing to alter the basic relationships in Jamaican society and to shift the centre of power away from the wealthy apex towards the democratic base.

Two things which began to bring matters to a head in the first term were education and taxes. Both were part of our social engineering. Education policies were vital if elitism were to yield. Taxes have to do with wealth. In 1973, we decided that the state would take over the expenses of all tuition costs throughout the secondary and tertiary educational systems. The government primary system had long since been organised on that basis. We could not afford to pay for everything, but tuition fees in the high schools and the university were substantial. At the same time, we reorganised the system by which primary school students could enter secondary schools. Previously, the state provided for some 2,000 free places each year that were competed for by some 40,000 to 50,000 eleven-year-olds. The other 7,000 or 8,000 places went to the children of the parents who could afford it. Now, the best 9,000 regardless of parental status would get into high schools.

At the same time, we decided to set up a system of national youth service in which high school graduates would be asked to do one or two years national service in some useful field, such as forestry, teaching, the literacy programme or some form of community activity. The youth service members would be paid an allowance, and would give this service a sort of investment in the society which had provided them substantial educational opportunity largely without charge. We also felt that this would be a means of developing a sense of patriotic service, community involvement and egalitarian spirit.

In the end, the national youth service proved extremely expensive and we were never able to operate it for all high school graduates, though we preserved a token service involving 2,000 to 3,000 a year. They made a significant contribution and it was a tragedy that subsequent economic pressure made it impossible to run the programme on a full-time basis.

The combination of free competition for secondary admission and required national service provoked the deepest alarm at the upper levels of the society. So great was parental concern that we had to set up public meetings with anxious mothers and fathers who seemed to feel that dangers hidden and unnamed were pressing in upon the world they knew. In a sense they were right. The prospect that money alone, however honestly earned, might not be able to secure the most privileged opportunities in education as a matter of right must have seemed revolutionary. The degree of panic, however, was instructive. There were still private schools in which education of an expensive kind was available. It was not as though all avenues were blocked. The truth is that the intense reaction reflected a feeling that a natural order was under attack.

Equally interesting was the reaction to national service. If this had taken the traditional form of a stint in the army, I believe the reaction would have been quite different and probably approving. This would have fitted in nicely with an authoritarian view of society; it would also have rested on a considerable precedent. Instead, national service was to involve a contribution to development and the improvement of community service. This was also seen to strike at the root of the notion of privilege.

Nothing that we did in our first term caused quite so great an upheaval as the announcement of the property tax. For years, income taxes had failed to make a dent on the distribution of wealth in Jamaica. Apart from wage and salary earners who were on a pay-as-you-earn system of deductions, we seemed incapable of developing the means to collect. Not surprisingly, those who had large incomes seemed to be infinitely resourceful when it came to hiding what they earned. The one thing that the wealthy could not do, however, was to hide their wealth, which could be seen in the splendid mansions that were built on almost non-existent incomes.

For years, property taxes in Jamaica had been based on what was known as the unimproved value system. That is to say, all land was taxed on the basis of a notional original value. If you improved the land agriculturally or by putting up structures on it, you were taxed nothing extra. This was a sound economic measure, designed to encourage the development of land and to make it relatively expensive to keep land undeveloped. If a means had been found to collect taxes on the incomes which resulted from the development of land, all would have been well. But nobody seemed to make any personal income worth mentioning from anything in Jamaica, so all was not well. We decided to tax people on the value of the property which they had developed or house they had built since we could think of no other means of starting a process of redistribution of wealth. Agriculture was made an exception and farmers paid little extra under the new arrangements.

The uproar cannot be imagined. Those who have subsequently claimed that the migration of the propertied classes from Jamaica was the result of political rhetoric will do well to go back to the facts. The exodus began with the property tax. In no time this was being represented as the thin end of the wedge for the expropriation of all property in terms of the strategy, real or imagined, of out and out communist governments. Touch a man's pocket book and you will pull the first trigger for his political acts! Property taxes were estimated to collect only twenty-five million dollars in the first year by comparison with income taxes in 1973 of $148.7 million. But the reaction went well beyond the scale of actual redistribution of wealth which had been contemplated. The property tax upset the wealthy by seeming to invade their right to proclaim their worth while hiding the source.

The labour legislation that we introduced struck at the root of the master and servant relationship on which the entire Jamaican economic system is based. Not for nothing had I had the privilege of working in the union movement for twenty years. I had learned in a thousand negotiations and on a hundred picket lines how heavily the system was biased in favour of the boss and against the workman. Only raw union strength stood between the individual worker and the almost unlimited legal power of his employer. It was idle even to pretend that Jamaica was a just society as long as this situation continued. As we had intended we introduced comprehensive labour legislation that would abolish the century-old Master and Servants Law. We put in its place a modern labour statute that defined the relationship, the rights and obligations of employer and worker in a manner both sensible and just.

The Labour Relations and Industrial Disputes Act tried to some extent to provide an alternative to strike and lock-out action. In cases of a dispute, either party could ask the Ministry of Labour to set up an arbitration tribunal with binding powers to decide upon the subject of a disagreement. The law made it an offence for any employer to refuse to recognise and deal with a union chosen in free democratic election by a group of workers. Individual workers who were dismissed had recourse to a tribunal to determine whether their dismissal was justified. If not, the tribunal had the power to award either compensation for the loss of job, or the reinstatement of the wrongfully dismissed workers.

Once the minister had intervened, neither worker nor employer, respectively, could strike or lock out, provided the minister acted in keeping with the law and set up a tribunal to hear and decide any dispute.

At a stroke, the idea of the master and servant was abolished. In its place was a law which defined worker and employer as being the necessary working parts of a principled, disciplined and logical productive relationship. Once this relationship is determined, by reference to comparative functions, and to no other consideration, you have laid the foundation of equality.

There was companion legislation dealing with the rights of redundant workers to severance pay. Workers in bankrupt organisations received priority treatment in the liquidation of assets. All these pursued the essential thesis along the corridors of the system. It was the basic act that was critical, and which put the final legal seal on the changes that were implied in the great upheaval of 1938. These had often been secured for particular workers where unions were particularly strong. But they had never been the subject of a universal sanction before, applying to all workers as a right.

There were other changes that caused mild concern. The legislation of equal pay for equal work on behalf of women upset employers and even the more chauvinistic male workers. The law which abolished the status of bastardy and the process of setting up the family court seemed to have been universally acclaimed. Less popular was the act requiring the registration of fathers.

It may be that no action in the social field had quite the impact of the Minimum Wage Law. This simply provided a basic rate below which no one could be asked to work; and for a maximum number of hours beyond which no one could be required to work without overtime payment. More than thirty years after the 1938 labour explosion and well into the collective history of the trade union movement, one wonders how it could have had such an impact. The difficulty was certainly not caused by the method of passing the law. This was a model of participatory democracy at work. A committee was established to examine the issue and held hearings for months in every corner of the island. Evidence was put before it by every imaginable employers', workers' and social organisation. In the end, the law itself was very simple. It provided only for the regulation of minimum wages and hours. Of course, it pegged hours at eight hours a day and forty hours a week, and probably trebled the lowest wage then to be found in small sweatshops or private homes. A significant story is told about Jamaica when it is realised that first law set the minimum wage at the equivalent of US$22.00 a week.

The impact of the law lies, I think, in what it did to alter the relationship between the classes. Traditionally, the home was the place where the advantages of class could be most effectively enjoyed. Here two situations existed. Many working wives were forced to employ help in the home so they could go to work themselves. Often employer and employee would have similar class backgrounds, and their relationships would benefit from a rational basis in mutual need. Then there was the situation where the household help assisted a wealthy housewife in enjoying the extended leisure that was her life. With heavy chronic unemployment, it was always easy to find a girl for the house or a boy for the yard and to treat them as a sort of convenient sub-species to be ordered around, capable of the most exhausting hours, and paid a pittance. Perhaps even more important than the comfortable life which hard-working, underpaid servants made possible, was the continual reminder of the advantages of class. This was particularly important to the *nouveaux riches* who had emerged through the Puerto Rican Model. To the socially insecure, nothing is more consoling than to have someone to bully. Suddenly, the Minimum Wage Law made a difference. It brought into the home, that final citadel, the changes that began with the work of the trade unions in major industries.

A constant irritant, rather than a focus for a power struggle, in all of this, were the government's attempts to relieve unemployment. For the first time extensive programmes were being designed for the purpose of doing something about the vast backlog of unemployment which we had been bequeathed by 300 years of colonialism assisted by 20 years of the Puerto Rican Model. Much of this was not directly productive work, but service work — like running daycare centres and basic schools; the massive literacy campaign; preparing the land to be attached to schools as part of our attempt to create an agricultural base to learning in the country.

Allowing for all of that, there was much in the programme that was wasteful and which angered not only the oligarchy but the middle classes and even parts of the trade union membership. To these people it seemed, understandably enough, as if taxes were being thrown away for many people to idle away hours which should be spent working. If the workers had been on relief and had been sitting at home drawing perhaps some lesser amount of money in unemployment assistance, it might have caused less difficulty. Instead, people were visibly on the streets and were supposed to be keeping them clean and were obviously not doing so. They were, it is true, working under harsh conditions for a pittance. Many were middle aged yet only in their first job! However, all this notwithstanding, the sight of persons apparently being paid to do nothing offended both the sense of order and the work ethic. We constantly tried to make the programme productive and to improve the level of discipline, but with only moderate success. It was not our finest hour!

Cultural and political developments, wealth taxes, and the use of law to define new social relationships all helped to create the sense and reality of class struggle in the society. Needless to say however, the most important arena in which the battle was being waged was the economy. We had three primary objectives. We were determined to enlarge the public sector and to create an economy broadly under social management while retaining a dynamic and expanded private sector. We were determined to start a serious process of land reform; and we were determined to develop the co-operative sector of the economy. Despite the resulting furore, much that we did was not actually controversial.

Bearing in mind the neo-colonial experience of the last twenty years, the economy was fragile and skewed. It had come to the end of a phase of expansion through alumina, tourism and pure import substitution in the main. These could not be the major source of development during the next few years. This had to come through the exploration of linkages, non-traditional agriculture, agro-industry and the like. To the extent that a framework existed, the interstices needed filling in. This was a task for economic planning.

There was general approval of this approach which led to a huge initial effort in domestic agriculture and the development of several agro-industrial enterprises to process.

We began with obvious things like taking over the public utilities, paying fair compensation after honourable negotiation. The public utilities as a group were partly foreign and partly locally owned and this seemed to cause hardly a ripple. Perhaps the business community was glad not to be involved in an activity where the price to be charged would be a constant source of trouble with the consumer!

We acquired nearly half the number of major hotels in Jamaica. Again this was not difficult at the time, presumably because a number of foreign operations decided to quit Jamaica after the world economic debacle dealt its blow to international tourism in 1974 and 1975.

A major reorganisation of the industry included worker training and popular education in the business of tourism as an industry. We set out to break the old elitist pattern in which tourist hotels were like enclaves, shut away from the local population by psychology as much as by price. In the summers, when the hotels have their slack periods, we organised holidays for Jamaican workers. Families from the bauxite or sugar industries or from government itself would get special rates, these in turn being subsidised by the employer. A janitor from the office of the prime minister might be on holiday with a manager of a commercial bank, a conjuncture unheard of before 1972. Today the beaches of the tourist areas serve both locals and guests. Time had been when you would not see a black skin for miles.

Throughout the period we went about quietly acquiring all the foreign-owned sugar estates, once more on the basis of negotiated compensation. Again the particular acquisitions raised hardly an eyebrow.

Hostility to the government began with our determination to acquire the sole cement factory. Presumably the acquisition of the public utilities could be passed off with a shrug as something that most countries had long since decided was sensible from a non-ideological perspective. Similarly the rescue operation in tourism and the repatriation of our sugar lands were digestible. But the cement plant was something else again. This was a monopoly that had made huge profits for years for its majority shareholders consisting of a group of Jamaican businessmen. They had been clever enough to get into the deal at the start, 20 years before, when the monopoly franchise was granted. We wanted the cement factory because it was strategic to the entire construction industry and in particular to the government's mass housing efforts. Here we were touching deeply vested interests. This was a sign that the government was willing to exercise judgements about the domain of the private sector by standards not determined by the private sector itself. Hence it became a battleground.

Our land programme also reflected this mixed experience. The land lease operation under which we either acquired or leased needed lands for distribution to small farmers seemed to cause little or no trouble. This was understandable since it was based on voluntary arrangements for the take-over of lands not actually in use. On the other hand there was obvious concern about the establishment of sugar co-operatives. When the foreign sugar estates were acquired it was assumed that the lands would be divided up into reasonably big parcels to be owned and farmed by medium-sized cane farmers. For the sugar worker who had cut and watered the canes, who had ploughed, weeded and fertilised the land over the years, this would have meant exchanging the former employer whom he never saw for the kind he would see occasionally. Nothing else would change. Another course would be to organise the workers themselves into co-operatives. We decided to go ahead with the more radical idea.

We started to plan with worker organisations and in time established co-operatives in which the former sugar workers would own and control areas of up to a thousand acres under each co-operative. This seemed to flash a signal to the private sector. The word was out that the government wanted to create a different economic structure. The fact that we clearly did not wish to destroy the elements of the former structure, but merely make them a part of a different balance of forces, did not matter. Here was sufficient cause for hysteria.

Every level of government activity generated either voiceless acceptance or overt hostility. The nation's literacy programme and other efforts to improve schooling, provide community centres and daycare centres were accepted. By contrast the establishment of a National Housing Corporation by the Ministry of Housing as an instrument for developing lower-cost housing was treated as an invasion of the private sector's province. Acquisition of unused and up to then unwanted land was not a problem. But the passage of the law providing for land to be leased by the government at a rate as low as that upon which it was taxed was seen as the greatest invasion of property rights.

In retrospect it does not seem that our programme was all that radical. Many of the schemes we tried to introduce already exist in most of Europe. But they were enough to play a part in a process that brought Jamaica to the verge of civil war. This war was to be fought between tribalised poor people in the name of the two parties. Ironically, while it was members of the masses who were to die, the real fight was about class interests. As it is, many died. But they did not know why.

7
THE PERIPHERY FIGHTS BACK

I first met Henry Kissinger in 1974. We talked for about an hour in his office in the State Department in Washington. I had arranged the interview with the US Secretary of State as part of our bauxite strategy.

It was a tense time in North-South relationships. The Organisation of Petroleum Exporting Countries had stunned the world shortly before when they raised the price of crude oil from $3.00 to $11.00 a barrel at a single shot. Of greater relevance to my meeting with Kissinger, however, was the attempt by the Arab members of OPEC to use oil as a weapon in their struggle with Israel. At that time the US had two concerns: the economic consequences for the oil-thirsty industrialised economies; and more seriously for Kissinger, the political implications of a group of Third World countries using a strategic material to exert pressure in an international dispute.

Kissinger was the master of *real politik*, the latterday Metternich and heir to the Machiavellian tradition in the use of power. He was known to be particularly sensitive to the thought that the smaller countries might further complicate the balance of forces in the world, which he sought constantly to manipulate to US advantage.

As it happened, Kissinger's anxiety eventually abated with regard to OPEC because he discovered in time that Saudi Arabia and the Shah's Iran could be manipulated into becoming valuable allies of the US. Saudi Arabia became the instrument of US economic interest while Iran looked after the political interest. Both recycled petrodollars back into the US and European financial systems at a rate sufficient to neutralise OPEC as the economic force it might have been. The political threat receded as the economic force declined.

When I met Kissinger, however, this had not yet happened. In Jamaica, we had spent more than a year and a half working on our bauxite strategy. We had assembled a superb team of financiers, business lawyers, managers and technical experts who had studied the industry from every conceivable point of view. We learned how the industry was organised, financed and planned. We found out where the proven and suspected reserves existed. We learned about mining, alumina production, aluminium smelting, about extrusion and fabrication, about marketing and distribution. We studied the taxation systems of the producing countries and the multi-national corporate structures which created the world-wide network of control.

After eighteen months, the outlines of the strategy had been settled. A quarter of a million acres of land which the first Bustamante government had sold outright to the bauxite companies was to be repatriated.

Fifty-one per cent of the bauxite mining operation was to be nationalised. A Bauxite Institute to supervise the industry was to be established. A national marketing company was to undertake the search for new markets on behalf of the state and to begin the diversification of our outlets. An International Bauxite Association of producing countries was being organised. Talks with President Luis Echeverria of Mexico and President Carlos Andres Perez of Venezuela had led to a decision, in principle, to develop a Jamaica-Venezuela-Mexico bauxite mining, alumina processing and aluminium smelting complex, based on Jamaican bauxite and Venezuelan and Mexican energy. Although we intended to pay compensation after negotiation, there was plenty in this package that the US establishment in general and the multinational corporations, in particular, would not like. They would be specially uneasy about the plan to build an international aluminium producing complex outside the multinational corporation system. But the most important feature of the plan was our intention to replace the existing system of bauxite royalties with a bauxite levy.

The royalties of the past represented a fixed money charge for each ton of bauxite dug out of the ground. There was no way in which Jamaica could be protected as international inflation increased the money value of the aluminium which was made from the bauxite.

As aluminium prices climbed, multinational corporate profits rose with them. The general climate of inflation, in the
meantime, was making all of Jamaica's imports more and more
expensive. Jamaica lost out on both scores. We had decided to
make two changes. Firstly, we would raise the present level of
return to Jamaica for the bauxite mined to a level that would
compensate for the increases in the value of bauxite, since
Norman Manley had last adjusted it some sixteen years before.
This would mean a hefty jump to begin with. Secondly, we
intended to fix Jamaica's take on each ton of bauxite mined as
a percentage of the price of aluminium ingot on the world
market from time to time. At a stroke, we would take what was
then seen as a revolutionary step and lock in Jamaica perma-
nently as a beneficiary of international inflation. For us, this
was a critical move. For generations, Third World countries
have sat helplessly by as international inflation has benefited
the industrialised North and eroded the economic base and
hopes of progress of those who live by selling basic commodities. It had taken the other members of OPEC more than
thirty years to heed the advice of their Venezuelan brothers on
this point; but they had learned at last. We intended to secure
justice for our country through the bauxite levy which would
permit us to share in the benefits of inflation while offering a
measure of protection against its consequences.

We knew that negotiations with the bauxite corporations
were going to be the most difficult our country had ever
undertaken. We anticipated that they would try to persuade
the US administration to support them against us and might
even suggest some form of reprisal if we stuck by our guns. We
knew that we intended to stick by our guns because we were
right both as of today and in terms of every lesson we had
learned from history. We hoped to persuade other bauxite
producers to come along with us and intended to use the
International Bauxite Association for this purpose when it was
formally established. It was important, therefore, to talk to
the political leadership in the USA and Canada to make them
understand exactly what we were about to do and why.

The day before my meeting with Kissinger, I had had a long
talk with Pierre Trudeau, the Prime Minister of Canada. I did
not expect difficulty, because Trudeau and I had met and
established a warm relationship during the Commonwealth
Heads of Government Conference which had been held in

Ottawa in 1973. Trudeau put one firm question to me. Did we intend to negotiate fair compensation for any assets which we might intend to acquire? I assured him that this was so and that was clearly the end of the matter as far as he was concerned. He listened with interest to the strategy which I outlined and seemed particularly struck by the merits of our case for the bauxite levy.

As always with Trudeau, it was a comfortable conversation. He has a fine mind and is quickly at home in the world of ideas and concepts even when a particular formulation is new to him. By training and instinct, he believes that mankind's best hopes lie in reason, persuasion, accommodation, seeing the other fellow's point of view. To these qualities he adds the breadth of vision and sense of history that make the true internationalist. He wished me luck with Kissinger the next day. I did not detect a note of irony in this; or perhaps, I chose not to.

Apart from a careful attempt to communicate a broad understanding of our position to Kissinger, I hammered home two points with particular emphasis. I told him that the action we were about to take was purely economic in its implication. It was not intended as any form of political hostility towards the US, and represented our view of our duty to our country's national, economic interests. Secondly, I told him that we fully recognised the strategic importance of aluminium to US industrial and military interests. I assured him that we would never seek to affect US access to our bauxite through the legitimate channels of its multinational corporation and wished him to pass these assurances on to the President of the United States and the members of the National Security Council.

I found him every bit as quick as his reputation suggested. He was courteous, affable and seemed to be interested. He spoke warmly of a recent meeting he had had with the first Foreign Minister of our administration, Dudley Thompson.

These two conversations represented important insurance against risk. It may not even have been needed in the case of Canada but was, I believe, appreciated. It was very much needed in the US. Careful evaluation of subsequent evidence suggests that it had some effect in Washington. Perhaps it was nothing more than achieving a wait and see attitude; but even that would have been a gain. Later, when the confrontation

over the bauxite levy came with the multinationals, it is believed that at least two of them approached the State Department and asked that Jamaica be black-listed, that aid be cut
off, as a punishment for imposing the levy by law and without
their agreement. Washington did not respond then.

As it turned out, the negotiations with the companies began
as an exercise in pure farce. We had made a formal claim for
Jamaica to be paid a levy of US $11 a ton for bauxite and $14 a
ton for alumina. This compared with the US $1.50 a ton
currently in force. Later we proposed the levy based upon a
percentage of the realised price of aluminium ingot. The first
figure was $8\frac{1}{2}\%$ of the aluminium price per ton allowing for
the tons of bauxite taken to make a ton of aluminium. In the
end our final position was $7\frac{1}{2}\%$.

Throughout all the early talks the companies made no offer
at all. Even at the end they indicated that a figure equivalent to
3% would be the absolute limit they might consider in full and
final settlement. Seven and one-half per cent was a figure which
we demonstrated to be reasonable on any analysis, whether
based on their figures or ours. It was a straight case of intransi-
gence. They resented the basic idea of the percentage; they
resented the level of our expectations; and they were clearly
taken aback by the tough and able manner in which we had
prepared and argued our case. Doubtless assuming that all host
countries approached the bar of multinational corporate
power as supplicants, they were clearly not prepared to deal
with a small island that saw itself as clothed in the rights and
dignity of sovereignty.

The truth is that multinational corporations have grown
used to two types. One is the mendicant of the neo-colonial
syndrome. The other is the revolutionary who simply sends in
the army to take over the operation. Here they were dealing
with neither. This was part of our search for the third path. My
impression at the time was that they did not believe we were
serious and kept assuming that we would suddenly have one of
those midnight meetings when everything would be settled,
more or less on their terms. As it turned out, we never met at
midnight but we did have a final meeting one evening at
around 9.00 p.m. I attended this myself and they discovered
that we were serious after all. They clearly were not and
refused to budge. By then it was too late. We imposed the levy
by law in parliament on May 15, 1974.

In due course, our relations with the bauxite companies returned to normal, particularly after that remarkable and imaginative man, Edgar Kaiser, flew to Jamaica at the suggestion of another remarkable American, former United Steel Workers Counsel and Supreme Court Judge Arthur Goldberg. That visit broke the ice and led to an agreement between the Kaiser Aluminium & Chemical Corporation and ourselves covering all the questions of land, 51% ownership and the rest. This became a model for the industry as a whole. However, they were never comfortable with the levy and have never ceased to argue for its reduction. Equally, they were always unhappy about the prospect of a new aluminium complex involving Jamaica and Mexico with other Third World countries outside the private multinational system.

The fight with the bauxite companies commanded wide support from a majority of the Jamaican people, a support that seemed to stretch across most if not all classes. Only the hardliners of the old oligarchy were outraged by our actions in imposing a levy by law and warned of dire consequences.

At the very time of the imposition of the levy, the world alumina market was entering a slump along with tourism and the rest of the world economy. Production was down everywhere including Jamaica. It was in this highly hostile market that we sought to persuade other bauxite producers such as Surinam, Sierra Leone and Guinea to renegotiate their tax systems. Without exception, they increased their take and adopted our principle of a percentage of the aluminium ingot prices. Equally without exception, they all contrived to fix their level of tax somewhat below Jamaica's thereby securing a competitive advantage for their bauxite by comparison with ours. Whether this happened because the market was contracting at the time and they felt themselves to be under pressure; whether they were simply outbargained; whether they made deals to increase their share of the market at Jamaica's expense; or whether it was a combination of all of these things, we do not know. What we do know is that taking everything into account, Jamaica's bauxite production in the next six years was to slump from 15 million tons in 1974 to 10 million in 1976 rising again to 12 million in 1980.

With all the claims that our levy was unjust, the following figures make a significant comment. Jamaica supplies about one-third of the bauxite used by the four aluminium giants of

North America: Alcoa, Alcan, Reynolds and Kaiser. The immediate effect of the levy was to increase Jamaica's take about sevenfold. 1973 was the last complete year before the levy. The combined net income of the four companies in that year was US$249.1 million. 1974 was the first year of the levy which applied to the whole year. The net income of the four companies after paying the new levy was US$581.7 million. Equally interesting, however, was the fact that Jamaica received US$24.5 million for 12.5 million tons in 1973. We received US$210 million for 12 million tons in 1980.

Although it would seem from these figures that both the companies and Jamaica were doing well after the levy, bauxite production was systematically reduced as an act of retaliation by the companies.

There is a sense in which the bauxite story was the story of our foreign policy. The determination to negotiate an equitable share for a Third World country was an element. So too were the attempts to organise internationally so that other Third World countries could benefit equally and protect each other through united action; to create a new productive capability by co-operation among Third World countries, to make Third World countries direct participants in the benefits of world inflation instead of being its helpless victims. The recognition that the Third World must co-operate in spite of ideological differences between its members and without regard to Cold War issues and East/West tensions, was a fuller element. It was all there. Even the attempt to proceed in a nonconfrontationist way — to work to explain what was intended so as to minimise the risk of irrational hostility due to misunderstanding — was an important part of the exercise.

Whatever may have been the temporary effects on the level of multinational production in Jamaica, the entire exercise was worthwhile. It left in its wake a team of Jamaicans with genuine expertise and, more importantly, self-confidence. Although the International Bauxite Association is still in its infancy, and although we were to be disappointed in the initial actions of some of our international colleagues, potential gains of immense significance for the future abound.

The fact that missions came to us from Haiti and Surinam, that we sent experts to Sierra Leone and Guinea, represents an irreversible gain: to us, to them and to the Third World. Here was the act of sharing Third World technology and expertise.

Another generation will benefit immeasurably from all of this because there will be other times when world markets are not so hostile; times when political leadership will be stronger because it is more experienced and has a clearer grasp of the possibilities of strength that lie in unity. Certainly, the great increases in revenue and the new principles upon which that revenue rests, benefiting so many parts of Africa and the Caribbean where bauxite is produced, are important advances. Nyerere's 'trade union of the poor' was taking its first steps, however faltering.

Bauxite policy was to prove a unifying experience in the main. So, too, were those aspects of our foreign policy in which we acted firmly, offered leadership, developed considerable expertise but where the activity itself was non-controversial. Although the Federation of the West Indies had been repudiated by the Jamaican people, there seemed to be general approval for our membership in the Caribbean Community which evolved from the Caribbean Free Trade Area. In due course, we became leading bargainers for the African, Caribbean and Pacific countries (ACP) who negotiate commodity prices and other arrangements under the Lome Convention with the European Economic Community.[1] There was general pride when our government's second foreign minister, P.J. Patterson, was elected Chairman of the ACP group of countries by acclaim.

In due course, Jamaica became Chairman of the Group of 77 in the UN system and even a member of the Security Council. Both of these reflected our growing status in the Third World: a result in no small measure due to the abilities of both our foreign ministers and our deeply respected permanent representative to the United Nations, Don Mills. A foreign service team which possessed some extraordinarily skilled and dedicated people played an important part at home and abroad.

It may even be true that we carried the majority of the country with us in our aggressive policy of support for the liberation struggles in Southern Africa. We contributed money to this cause and gave it relentless support in every forum in the world in which we had a voice. I used the leverage of my position as Chairman of the Commonwealth Heads of Government Conference in Kingston in 1975 to secure a commitment by the Commonwealth of material support for

Mozambique. This arose from the heroic decision of Samora Machel to close the border between Mozambique and Rhodesia shortly after his shattered country had won its long war of independence with the Portuguese. Machel closed the border to increase the pressure on the renegade white supremacist regime of Ian Smith. But the act cost Mozambique dearly in lost revenue. I persuaded the Commonwealth leaders to accept a moral duty to support Mozambique even though it is not itself in the Commonwealth. Nevertheless they accepted the view that we were all in the struggle against the Rhodesian minority government. Later, I was able to extend the principle during the 1977 London Conference by successfully arguing that all the front-line States — Mozambique, Botswana, Tanzania, Zambia and Angola — deserved special economic support because of the tremendous economic price they paid as a consequence of their help to the freedom fighters of Zimbabwe and Namibia.

In the end, I had the personal satisfaction of being a part of the negotiating process by which the Zimbabwean people secured their rights and won their freedom. The United Nations awarded me its gold medal for the part I had tried to play in the struggle against apartheid in South Africa. It may even be that the majority of the Jamaican people approved of all of this and certainly it would have been difficult for either the local oligarchy or the US establishment to attack it.

But there were problems. To begin with, foreign policy was unfamiliar territory. There was a tendency to feel that the whole thing must involve some kind of personal 'ego-tripping' since many people clearly doubted that small countries could exercise any influence over affairs. Up to then, the word 'foreign' had denoted those places which spoke different languages. England, Canada and America were not 'foreign', but probably represented places where a relative lived, from which investments came from time to time and to which applications for aid were directed. The concept of an international environment of which Jamaica was a part and which contained complex economic relationships, more or less beneficial to Jamaica and more or less subject to change, was new to most people. Our task was to create an understanding that foreign policy had to deal with this world community and had to be directed towards those complex economic arrangements, to try to make them more beneficial and less harmful.

At all times, we worked ceaselessly on behalf of the specific proposals for change in the world economic system which we describe, somewhat rhetorically, as the New International Economic Order (NIEO). This was a global version of the objectives which we pursued in a far narrower sense with our bauxite strategy. A vital part of the effort had to be directed towards the international politics of the situation. How to focus the attention and the political will of more than 120 separate nations with different ideologies, at different levels of development, often with conflicting interests — some Marxist-Leninist, some Arab revolutionary, some African socialist, some vaguely humanist, some revolutionary democrat, some democratic socialist, some social democrat, some Christian democratic, some liberal, some explicitly capitalist, some authoritarian, some one-party state, some plural democracy, some military dictatorship, most in various stages of neo-colonial dependence, some at war with their neighbours —upon a set of agreed international economic objectives is no mean task. But it is the task we all face, because it is only through united action that the Third World can hope to reduce its dependence, create economic viability and give meaning to its independence.

If the commitment to independence is serious, there can be no compromise in the struggle for a new international economic order and the task of building Third World unity. To us this meant that the East-West struggle was secondary, that it was our duty to avoid its entanglements and our duty to resist hegemonic pressure wherever and by whomever it was exerted. The guidelines for policy were set and they were clear. They led us to interesting places but they were never seriously compromised.

The Non-Aligned Movement had tremendous significance for us. Its underlying philosophy was exactly compatible with the position to which we were led by our own experience. Its anti-imperialist ethos was consistent with our interpretation of the past and our perspective for the future. Originally political in its impulses, it was becoming more and more concerned with economics as the new flags of freedom discovered that the winds which drive history are mainly economic. They shape the fortunes of the newly free just as surely as they oppressed the circumstances of those who suffered under the colonial yoke.

In 1973, the Non-Aligned Movement was due to hold its three-yearly summit in Algeria. Algeria was a good choice for the conference and for the chairmanship of the movement in the coming three years. President Houari Boumedienne was a great revolutionary leader and Algeria was emerging as a significant advocate of the NIEO. The Algerian process was already reflecting high degrees of maturity and a grasp of world economics. We intended to participate fully and had various task forces looking at different aspects of the agenda and, in particular, questions dealing with economics and finance. We were already pressing for the creation of a Third World Institution which would provide development finance. Although we could not then guess at the money which could have been available from oil surpluses in the future if the will had been present, we were clear about the need. We discovered that Kuwait had the same idea and later agreed to second a Kuwaiti proposal.

Earlier that year, the four independent nations of the CARICOM group — Barbados, Guyana, Trinidad and Tobago and ourselves — had announced our recognition of Cuba in a move that had startled and displeased the US authorities. Errol Barrow, Barbados's Prime Minister, Forbes Burnham of Guyana, Eric Williams of Trindad and Tobago and I had had no difficulty in agreeing upon Cuba's right to be accepted as a normal member of the hemispheric family and of our right to treat her as such. Now, as the Algiers conference approached and with full diplomatic relations in place between Cuba and the four of us, news came of an invitation from Fidel Castro to fly to the Algiers summit meeting with him in a Cuban government Ilyushin jet. The invitation was to Burnham, Williams and myself, since Barbados was not a member of the Non-Aligned Movement.

It turned out that Williams was not going to the meeting in any case. So, in the end, Burnham and I accepted the invitation. I joined the plane at Piarco Airport in Port of Spain, Trinidad, where we all had supper with Eric Williams. Fidel Castro and Forbes Burnham arrived together from Georgetown. In due course, we set off for Conakry, Guinea, where we were to make a brief stop with President Sekou Toure before the final hop to Algiers.

The news that I would fly with Fidel Castro caused conster-

nation in the Jamaican establishment. The then President of
the Jamaica Manufacturers' Association led a campaign about
it and seemed convinced that I would be cast under a spell.
Others took it as a sign that their worst fears about me and
communism had been true all along. People who had watched
De Gaulle put France on a course which set the example of
detente to the world; who had lived through the Ostpolitik of
West Germany under Willy Brandt; who had seen peaceful
co-existence unfold into detente and were to watch Kissinger
and Nixon set up their marriage of convenience with Red
China — went into virtual hysteria at the thought of Jamaica's
Prime Minister crossing the Atlantic in the same plane as
Cuba's Premier.

Knowing the years of experience which had fashioned my
view of the world and the political policies to which I was
committed, one part of me was insulted to think that they
thought so little of my independence of mind. Of course, I
realised that a part at least of this behaviour was explained by
the very psychology of dependence which we were determined
to struggle against in Jamaica. A tragic lack of national self-
confidence lay at its root. The rest was probably explained in
terms of a general apprehensiveness about Jamaica as they
knew it, as they wished to keep it; a Jamaica they now felt to be
under threat.

As it turned out, Fidel Castro and I talked until five the next
morning, virtually across the Atlantic. We exchanged boy-
hood experiences, stories about our families, and much else
that was simple and human. I was fascinated by stories of the
Sierra Maestra. He seemed genuinely interested to learn about
my father, whom he respected as a great West Indian patriot,
and about the early struggles of the PNP.

Mostly, however, we spoke of international affairs, the
Non-Aligned Movement, the economic struggle and the need
to develop the broadest Third World unity around practical
and attainable economic objectives. Incidentally we were to
discover that we shared a passion for the liberation struggles in
Southern Africa. This arose partly from an intellectual response to the principles involved and partly from the more
visceral reaction that comes from a sense of ethnic connection
between Caribbean and African society. This discovery was to
have a special significance later on.

As happened with Pierre Trudeau, Julius Nyerere and

others over the years, that long, unstructured conversation was to lay the foundations of a genuine and enduring friendship. Forbes Burnham and Errol Barrow had been friends from the days when we were all at London University. These new friendships were unusual experiences because they arose somewhat improbably in that heat and pressure of international events.

The Algiers summit was significant because it witnessed a serious focus of attention by the 75 members of the Non-Aligned Movement on world economic issues. There were fascinating sidelights such as the clear differences of perception about the proper definition of imperialism in world affairs. Gadaffi, looking messianic and sounding like a mystic, spoke of Arab socialism and implied the existence of two imperialisms. Fidel Castro's rejoinder was earnest and passionate. He reeled off the countless occasions on which the Soviet Union had come to the help of the liberation movements in Africa and Asia, pointing out that it was the forces of western imperialism led by the United States which had defended the oppressors over and over throughout history. Both received standing ovations. Jamaica's contribution focused on economic analysis and the liberation struggles in Southern Africa.

After Algiers we were to play an increasing role in the Non-Aligned Movement, the Group of 77 and the Southern Africa struggles. There were state visits to Zambia and Tanzania right after the summit. Simultaneously, we were developing growing relations with Venezuela and Mexico, working on the aluminium complex, establishing a regional shipping line and landing the first major alumina sale to be negotiated by a Jamaican Government. This was with the Venezuelans. We were active in support of Panama in her demand for a new Panama Canal Treaty and constant advocates of Belize's right to independence, free of threat from Guatemala. In 1975, there was an official visit to Cuba. Like many visitors, we were tremendously impressed with what they had achieved in health, education and mobilisation, particularly of the young.

In due course, Richard Nixon was undone by Watergate and succeeded by Ford. The US Government had steadily chilled in its attitude towards us. They seemed particularly upset by our insistence on our right to maintain friendly relations with Cuba.

In the meantime, events were developing rapidly in Southern Africa. Angola had, along with Mozambique, won its independence from the Portuguese, ending the longest continuous colonial rule in history. The Portuguese had packed up and left *en bloc* taking with them virtually the entire infrastructure of skills upon which a modern state depends. Angola now faced two crises. On the one hand, there was the crisis of survival: how to run a modern society when virtually everyone from machinists to stenographers, computer technicians to managers, doctors, scientists and teachers had departed. The second crisis arose from two challenges to the authority of the new Angolan Government. Agostinho Neto and his MPLA (Popular Movement for the Liberation of Angola) had led the fight for independence and managed the transition from colonial to independent rule. He alone commanded broad national support and was capable of providing the organisation and discipline upon which a new administration could be based. Two adventurers, Holden Roberto and Jonas Savimbi, had other ideas. Roberto led a tribally based group to the north called the FNLA, and Savimbi a similar but larger tribal group in the south called UNITA.[3]

No sooner had the new government begun to grapple with the vast administrative problems which confronted it than Roberto and Savimbi moved. Both attacked MPLA forces. Roberto drew his support from two sources: the corrupt and tyrannical regime of President Mobutu of Zaire, Angola's northern neighbour, and the CIA. Savimbi likewise got his money and arms from two sources: the CIA, naturally, and, incredibly, South Africa.

At the outset, Neto had appealed to the Cubans for technical assistance. In response, large numbers of doctors, nurses and teachers along with a few experts in government administration had been quickly organised and dispatched. Interestingly enough, in the days of the liberation struggle, Neto's first appeal for assistance was directed to Washington where they sent him packing. Now that he needed doctors, teachers and administrators to keep his newly independent society afloat, it is understandable that he would direct his first appeal to those who had a track record of supporting liberation struggles.

Even as the Cubans were helping the Angolan Government to build schools, the CIA, Mobutu and the racist rulers of South Africa were funnelling money and arms to Roberto and

Savimbi in the hope that they would crush the new government and set up a docile puppet regime. With Neto's forces increasingly under pressure, he asked the Cubans for arms and military experts who could help him train a more effective army more quickly than he could hope to do alone. The evidence is clear that this request came in response to mounting pressure from north and south. Once again, the Cubans responded, although it is absolutely clear that no Cuban combat troops were sent to Angola at this point, and that no Cuban citizen took any part in the fighting.

It was at this moment, in the middle of 1975, that Savimbi made his pact with the devil. Namibia is Angola's neighbour to the south. It was held, and is still held, illegally by South Africa. In August 1975, regular units of the South African Army crossed the border and began their now infamous dash for Luanda, the capital of Angola. Early on they overran a school being built by Cuban and Angolan workers in the deep south of the country. Neto well knew that no force in Africa can match the South African Army. His guerilla fighters, fresh from a liberation war, just at the beginning of their conversion into a modern army and already extended by the forces of Roberto and Savimbi, would have no chance whatsoever. Neto appealed for direct military assistance urging the Cubans to dispatch combat forces to deal with the South African invaders.[4]

Fidel Castro and the Cuban leadership faced their most difficult single decision since the success of the revolution in 1959. It was by no means their first crisis but involved a decision of epic proportions. They had to consider the enormous logistical problems, since no Cuban plane could fly direct from Cuba to Angola. They had to face a military judgement of profound difficulty. Could they get combat troops to Angola quickly enough and in sufficient numbers to avoid a disastrous defeat for those who would arrive first? This would have tremendous political implications for them at home and internationally. Would South Africa escalate the conflict if the Cubans engaged them in combat? How would the expenses of a protracted war be met?

Then there was the most difficult question of all. There were signs that at long last a thaw in the relations between Cuba and the United States might be coming. They had felt the pressure of economic blockade for fifteen years. They had paid a high price for it. What would the US do if they moved?

In the end, the leadership met for an entire night and took their decision as the first light of dawn appeared to the east of Havana. They decided they must respond to Neto's cry for help. It was a decision that has altered the course of history. Contrary to popular views assiduously promoted by propaganda, it was a Cuban decision. There are indications that Moscow was taken by surprise. Indeed, there is reason to believe that, left to itself, Moscow might not have favoured such a decision at that moment. The Kremlin was preoccupied with detente and the Strategic Arms Limitation Talks (SALT) then in progress. In any event, Fidel Castro's brother Raul was hastily dispatched to Moscow to explain the Cuban decision, and presumably enlist Moscow's support.

Meantime, Cuban transport planes took to the skies within hours. Many had their last refuelling stop in Bridgetown, Barbados, on their way across the Atlantic. Others refuelled in Guyana. They got there in time.

When the first Cuban combat units assembled in Luanda and began moving south, the South African Army was already 500 miles into Angola. They were not quick enough. They were engaged by Cuban forces at Benguella and Malange on November 14, 1975. Their bluff called, the leaders in Pretoria thought again. They ordered the units back inside Namibia once the first defeat had established the quality of the Cuban force which they faced. The fledgling State was saved. In due course, the MPLA government was able to stabilise the situation and Angola thus took its place as an honourable member of that heroic fraternity, the Front Line States. It is this group which has borne the brunt of the struggle for freedom in Zimbabwe, the struggle that continues in Namibia and must one day be resolved in South Africa itself.

It is impossible to overestimate the significance of this Cuban action. You have to go back to the days of Alexander the Great to find a parallel where so small a country by feat of arms has affected so profoundly the balance of forces on a continent. If South Africa had installed Savimbi as its puppet ruler, it is safe to say that Rhodesia's Ian Smith would be firmly in control to this day. By now Zambia might have fallen, Namibia would be a lost cause, Botswana throttled, Tanzania and Mozambique impossibly isolated. Certainly Tanzania could not have lifted the yoke of Amin from the necks of the

Ugandan people. The whole of Southern Africa might now be firmly in the grip of the racists operating through puppet regimes which they could manipulate while isolating the others. This may seem like an exaggeration. But the progressive group of regimes involved face enormous problems.

Multinational corporations and the European political system exert enormous influence in Zaire and Malawi, providing the upper half of a pincer. South Africa is the southern half. The Mozambique economy would collapse without the income remitted by its workers who mine South Africa's gold each year.

Zimbabwe's economy is so locked into South Africa's that she cannot afford to break off economic relations; not yet at any rate. Zambia is one of the biggest producers of copper in the world. Multinational corporation management, technology and marketing are still critical. Tanzania faces acute foreign exchange difficulties. Botswana is half surrounded by South Africa.

Danger lurks everywhere for the regimes which stand firmly against imperialism, and for a different configuration of power in the world. They are threatened by internal sabotage and external pressure. They cannot count on the solidarity of some of their neighbours. The survival of each is affected by the solidarity of the group. The margins are as fine as the dangers are real. It is in this context that we must understand the survival of a progressive Angola in 1975. The Western economic system would have faced an uninterrupted vista of exploitation of those untapped resources which abound from Zaire due east and all the way south.

None of this was lost on the multinational corporations; none of this escaped the attention of the political leaders of the northern industrial countries. Certainly none of the implications was missed by Henry J. Kissinger. Moreover, apart from reading the deeper, strategic implications, Kissinger was personally appalled by the whole turn of events. At home in a world dominated by US and Soviet power, a master of the game plan in which the big pieces dominate the chess board of human history, Kissinger's sense of order was outraged at the thought of a mere pawn behaving as if it were a queen or at least a rook or a knight. How dare a little foot soldier on the world's military stage transport troops thousand of miles as if it were a major power! The normal world of power politics cannot accommodate variables of this kind. If small nations can determine the fate of the weaker brethren, what world order is possible in this view? It is now history that Kissinger reacted with almost ungovernable rage to what had taken place. He was already discomfited by the exposure of the hand that the CIA had played in the entire matter. Now he was to take out his anger by mobilising anybody in Latin America who would listen.

Early in 1976, I had a long conversation with the Venezuelan President, Carlos Andres Perez. It arose in part from an earlier discussion in which Kissinger had asserted to Perez that Cuba's presence in Angola proved the danger which she represented to all of Latin America. Employing the old trick of advocacy which logicians describe as *post hoc ergo propter*, Kissinger scurried around Latin America, whipping its leadership into a frenzy of concern, lest Cuban battalions were about to descend suddenly from Cuban planes in Latin American skies. The militarists were to leap with glee upon the argument, all pressing their claims for increased military subventions. The arms manufacturers of the United States did not fail to benefit from the feverish activity.

Perez wanted my assessment of the situation, which I gave him. I was able to share with him the long talk which I had had with the Cuban President in Santiago while the fighting was at its height in Angola. I had asked to see Fidel Castro because I wanted to get as clear a picture as possible from him of his motivation and intentions in what I recognised to be a critical event in history. He had explained with painstaking care the principles upon which the Cuban action was based and the limits which the government was placing on what their troops would be allowed to do. He stressed that the Organisation of African Unity had unanimously decided to treat all African borders as sacrosanct because of their general fear that any variation of these borders could lead to a catastrophic domino effect in the continent. At the time of the imperialist conquest, Africa was in a state of flux. Certain tribes were expanding, others were in retreat. The situation was strikingly similar to that which had obtained in Europe throughout history and even now sees Bismarck's united Germany once again in two pieces.

The African leaders have always felt that their only realistic hope lies in treating the boundaries left behind by imperialism as fixed and immutable. If they admit change on the basis of old claims there will be chaos. So runs the argument. Secondly, Castro pointed to the fact that a legitimate government had invited the Cuban army to come to its rescue in the face of an invading army from the south. He made it clear that no provocation would ever be allowed to tempt the Cuban army to cross any border of Angola into Namibia or Zaire or anywhere else, even if the conditions of hot pursuit applied. Finally, he said that his troops would be recalled the minute the Angolan government said they were not needed or wanted. He had subsequently made it clear that the troops remained in Angola only because the South African army was still massed on the southern border of Angola and still presented a threat to Angolan independence.

Confirmation of Cuba's sincerity in all of this was to come later when, in similar circumstances, they responded to the appeal of Ethiopia's Mengistu with combat troops. Early in the Ethiopian Revolution, the Government of Somalia, in support of an old claim to the Ogaden province, and believing Ethiopia too weak to resist had invaded the country with the regular Somalian army. The Cubans defeated this army and drove it back across the border. It is known that Mengistu urged the Cubans, then in hot pursuit, to cross the border and complete the rout of the Somalian army. This the Cubans refused to do, halting at the border and refusing to go further.

All this I was able to explain to Carlos Andres Perez, upon whom Kissinger had obviously had less effect than he would have hoped. My own experience with Kissinger in the matter was instructive.

As all this was unfolding in Africa, during 1975, Jamaica was feeling the economic pinch. Foreign exchange was scarce. One of my economic advisers had come up with a plan to ask the US Government to make available trade credits worth $100 million in 1976 to help keep our vital industries going. These were not to be gifts but actual commercial credits to be paid for with interest over reasonable periods of time. At the very moment when this idea was being broached in Washington, the CIA was busy working for the downfall of Neto and the MPLA.

Then, as luck would have it, Henry Kissinger was to spend a short vacation on Jamaica's North Coast with his new bride,

Nancy. The visit was in response to an invitation by our Foreign Minister and took place shortly after the South Africans returned to Namibia. I had invited him to lunch during his stay and he had accepted. During lunch he sat on my right and although probably fuming at this interruption of his holiday was very much his witty and urbane self.

He assured us that the CIA was not interfering in Jamaica's affairs. The question arose because there was considerable speculation at the time that this was indeed the case. As he said it, similar assurances given concerning Chile flashed a little ominously across my mind.

Suddenly he raised the question of Angola and said he would appreciate it if Jamaica would at least remain neutral on the subject of the Cuban army presence in Angola. I told him that I could make no promises but would pay the utmost attention to his request. I pointed out that we were at that very moment dispatching Dudley Thompson to Africa to find out at first hand how the Africans viewed the situation in Angola. I said further that the South African invasion was a terrible thing as far as we were concerned, and that we would be paying close attention to the actual sequence of events as between the entry of South African and Cuban troops. In any event, I told him that before taking any official position on it internationally, I would communicate with him in Washington.

Afterwards Kissinger and I retired to my office for a short tête-à-tête. Again, as if from nowhere, he brought up a subject. This time it was the Jamaican proposal for the hundred million dollar trade credit. He said they were looking at it, and let the comment hang in the room for a moment. I had the feeling he was sending me a message.

We took the Angolan situation so seriously that I spoke to Nyerere and Kaunda on the phone personally, canvassing their views on what had actually happened. Dudley Thompson attended the OAU meeting which was called to discuss the Cuban presence and role. The OAU voted to support Cuba's action although many of its members were bitterly opposed to Cuba's revolutionary government and Marxist-Leninist process. All the evidence confirmed what Fidel Castro had told me. We knew what Jamaica's duty must be.

Within five days of his leaving for home, I let Kissinger know that Jamaica had decided to support the Cuban army presence in Angola because we were satisfied that they were there because of the South African invasion. The Jamaican government then publicly announced its support for Cuba in Angola. I never heard another word about the hundred million dollar trade credit. Of course, I could never say positively that this was an example of the famous Kissinger theory of linkage. But the question has been left hanging in my mind!

Soon after the news that Jamaica was supporting Cuba, a Kissinger confidante, James Reston of the *New York Times,* wrote a vicious and utterly inaccurate article about Jamaica. The article marked a turning point in Jamaica's image in the United States. Reston's wild charges about violence in Jamaica, the alleged presence of Cuban troops and Cuban secret agents, all added up to an impression of a Cuban take-over. This started off a chain reaction in the US press which never ceased until we were finally defeated in the elections of October 1980.[5]

The lunch was in December. Before the end of January, the US Embassy staff in Kingston was increased. Seven new staffers were flown in. Yet all aid to Jamaica suddenly slowed to a virtual halt. The pipelines suddenly became clogged. Economic co-operation contracted as the embassy expanded.

8
GRAPPLING WITH IDEOLOGY

In plural democracies political parties are reflections of the sections of the society from which their members are drawn. The People's National Party, itself typical of this rule, had started out in 1938 with two motives which were by no means complementary. It was an independence movement, which meant it attracted various elements of the society for different reasons. The unemployed, the hillside peasant struggling to survive, the agricultural worker would support such a movement if they made a connection between their personal distress and the dependent colonial status of their country. The middle classes, with a somewhat better education, would be attracted because they would see independence as holding the answer to their own need for national pride. Some would doubtless assume that they would replace the colonial administration and generally be needed to run the new show. In the main, the old plantocracy and the major merchant families would be strongly opposed, although even these groups turned up the occasional patriot who supported the independence movement.

As with other countries, the independence movement is a unifying force in the long run. Not so with the second original motive of our party: the commitment to a democratic system based on universal adult suffrage was originally divisive. Many middle class and most upper class people were strongly opposed to the notion of everyone having the vote, contending characteristically that 'the masses' were not ready for it. Finally, the commitment to Socialism made in 1940 was to set the PNP clearly and irrevocably apart from the oligarchy.

Throughout its history, the party has represented a broad class alliance. With the exception of the oligarchy, which has supported Bustamante's Labour Party solidly and consistently since 1949, the PNP has drawn its support from every group in varying degrees at all times. It is traditionally strongest amongst industrial workers, artisan groups, the white collar middle class, the professionals and the intelligentsia. Starting with almost nothing by comparison with Bustamante, it has steadily grown in strength among small farmers and agricultural labour. It has had a fluctuating relationship with the new entrepreneurial class which built the locally owned manufacturing sector and managed the new enterprises of the Puerto Rican model. Never enjoying majority support amongst this group, it has tended to be much stronger in the ranks of the genuine small business class. Because of socialism and ceaseless propaganda of the 'red smear' type, it has tended to have an uneasy relationship with the Church. In the early days the Evangelical and Catholic Churches were openly antagonistic. Later, the opposition was mostly to be found amongst the more fundamentalist of the Evangelical group. These days the new generation of churchmen who are influenced by liberation theology support the international objectives which we have pursued.

In 1972, the PNP had added the small farmers and the agricultural workers to the columns of its majority strength, but was still itself very much a class alliance and with a leadership somewhat dominated by the more articulate members of the middle class. Immediately after the elections, I addressed the National Executive Council of the PNP, a two-hundred person body which meets every other month and is the governing authority between party annual conferences. Among other things, I reminded them of our socialist history. I urged the view that we could not discharge our historic duty effectively in the absence of a clear ideological position which would serve as inspiration to thought, a guidepost to action and measure of achievement. I drew their attention to the enormous changes which had taken place in the world since the days of the cold war, of Stalinism, of John Foster Dulles and the McCarthy era in the United States. I contended that it would be a dereliction of duty to leave the business of socialism in a half-forgotten corner of the mind, available as a beating stick to our opponents, but of no use as either shield or sword to us, since it was certain that no two of us would any longer share exactly the same idea of what it meant. Equally, then, I argued that it would be irresponsible to take it off the shelf and not discuss and decide upon its meaning. Reminding them of the substantial differences in interpretation which have been applied to socialism, I called upon the party to begin an intensive and continuous dialogue on the subject. The intention was to evolve an interpretation of the ideology which would reflect our experience as a party, our understanding of our country and its needs, our analysis of the world, and provide a framework for the determination of policy. I was convinced that this exercise could lead to a consensus provided the dialogue itself was conducted in a completely democratic manner.

This provoked immediate controversy within our ranks. Many felt that this would, as they put it, stir up trouble. They reminded those who would listen that the party had a history of difficulty with ideology. A left and a right wing had emerged in the 1940s. Eventually tensions grew to the point where there had been an official, in-house enquiry into allegations that the left-wing leadership had been teaching Marxism in secret cells within the party. The charges had been upheld and the top four leaders of the left were expelled in 1952.

This had been followed by the disaffiliation of the Trades Union Congress from the party and the formation of a new body, the National Workers Union. A fratricidal struggle followed which was decisively won by the centre and right wing elements under Manley's leadership. The party went on to win the general elections of 1955. Both quarrel and victory were employed as arguments against reopening an ideological debate.

On the other hand, the party had never disavowed its socialist commitment entered into in 1940. Nor had the ideological argument ever really ceased. It merely went underground to resurface at critical moments. There had been a tense struggle about policy in 1966 This was occasioned by the approaching 1967 elections and the search for a clear policy with which to approach the electorate. Manley had begun to grow disenchanted with the Puerto Rican Model in 1961, and he spoke forcefully on the subject at the party's annual conference that year. He now threw his weight behind a set of radical proposals presented by an emerging left wing. Socialist ideas permeated the proposals. The right wing opposed most of them on pragmatic grounds. For example, it was contended that land reform proposals would upset big landowners who would influence small farmers and lose us votes, therefore 'least said, soonest mended'.

There were no clear, ideological guidelines within which the arguments could be contained. In the end Manley's influence settled matters largely in favour of the radical view. The right were disgruntled and many did not really fight for the programme. The party lost narrowly in the popular vote (JLP 50.7%, PNP 49.3%). To many of us the situation seemed unhealthy, lacking clarity and direction. PNP socialism was a reality yet not quite a reality, like a shadow waiting to take on substance.

The NEC decided at the least to take the shadow off the wall. At first we carried out a general appraisal of the party and in due course looked at ideology. A committee was set up to examine the formulations of the past and to provide us with a basic working document. The groups which formed the democratic base of the party and which are organised in urban neighbourhoods, rural villages and districts were all supplied with copies of the first draft and urged to begin their own discussion of the matter.

In the months that followed, there was intensive discussion at all party levels. The Youth Organisation and recently revived Women's Movement were particularly active in the debate. The National Workers Union, the union affiliate, took much less notice. By early in 1974, a much revised document was ready for consideration by the National Executive Council. The NEC then debated the matter over several weekends and finally passed a rough and much amended document charging the top leadership with the duty of producing a polished version that would reflect all the decisions that had finally been taken. We were also to consider the public relations of the matter: what short name was to be used, how it was to be presented to the general public, and the like.

We then embarked on an exercise which went on for several weeks, exclusively at night, since the days were devoted to the running of the country. The chairman of the party, David Coore, who was also Minister of Finance, the General Secretary, D.K. Duncan, and Vice Presidents P.J. Patterson, Anthony Spaulding, Howard Cooke and William Isaacs all helped. Also active were people like Arnold Bertram, a young member of the party with a strong ideological bent, Professor M.G. Smith, the anthropologist and one of my special advisers, together with a number of others.

As to the name, we considered three possibilities. Christian socialist was rejected on the grounds that it might sound like a political ploy. We decided not to use the word socialist alone because it seemed to invite too much speculation. Quite apart from communism, there were a number of African socialist states organised on a one-party basis. Then again, the local communists were at that time in semi-hiding under the term 'scientific socialist'. Since we were neither communist nor seeking to establish a one-party state, it seemed to invite unnecessary risk to use the term socialist without qualification. In the end, we settled on democratic socialist. The democratic was to be given equal emphasis with the socialist, because we were committed to the maintenance of Jamaica's traditional and constitutional plural democracy; and more importantly, because we intended to do everything in our power to deepen and broaden the democratic process of our party and in the society at large. We reaffirmed the earlier socialist commitment because of our determination to reorganise the Jamaican economy on the basis of a system of social control and popular participation. Both these involved radical alternatives to the free enterprise model of the capitalist system. In addition, we intended to pursue what is now termed a non-capitalist path of development to distinguish experiments like ours from the neo-colonial capitalist model of the Puerto Rican type and the Marxist-Leninist model of the Cuban type.

It was decided that the final draft would be presented to the NEC for clearance and put into booklet form. As soon as the booklet was ready, I would make a speech to parliament summarising the policy, setting it in context and explaining its implications to the nation. This was to be followed that same night by a mass meeting which we would hold at the statue of Norman Manley in downtown Kingston.

All of this was done. The crowd that night was estimated at 75,000 — an incredible turn-out for ideological debate. We can only guess at the size of the radio and television audience which followed the speech in parliament. I will always remember the mood of expectancy in the crowd at that meeting. There was a collective sense of history in the making.

I was worried about the danger of euphoria and made a very sober speech emphasising the great responsibility on all of us, the sacrifices that we must expect to make, and charging our supporters not to treat the decision as an invitation to hostility or bitterness. I tried to place great emphasis on the responsibility to work hard while stressing our determination to make work an ingredient in general progress rather than the basis of exploitative wealth.

To guard against the danger of hostility and divisiveness, we used the slogan 'Socialism is Love'. At the same time, we wished to make a connection between the secular philosophy which we were developing and the natural experience of co-operation and good deeds which the people derive from their Christian faith and church experience. Hence we used the phrase 'Socialism is Christianity in Action'. All of this was in keeping with the level of development within the party at that time and the objective conditions existing in the country. But those simple and quite sincere expressions of faith and intention did not save the country from what was to come. The reaction to them was eventually manipulated to such heights of ferocity that our final defeat was accomplished in a hail of bullets and a river of blood.

The attempts to argue that the reaffirmation of the PNP's socialism caused all that followed is a simplistic exaggeration. Long before October, 1974, important factors were at work. Wealth taxes, national youth service, free education and the land policy were causing strong reactions. Nineteen seventy-four had been a terrible year from the economic point of view as the first winds of the international inflationary hurricane knocked the Jamaican economy sideways. There was panic in the private sector as the prices of raw materials soared. Businessmen were discovering that long-standing overseas suppliers of raw materials and other inputs were suddenly sending cables cancelling supply agreements and demanding up to 100% increases in prices that had been part of firm contracts. At the same time, local crime, which had become a major source of tension in the 1960s was increasing at a frightening pace. Gunmen were terrorising Kingston at night and rape was striking fear into the hearts of the urban house-wives. The police and the government were fighting back with every instrument at their command, but the situation was grim.

Nobody may ever be able to prove a case about Jamaican migration at this period of time. I believe, however, that you would find that many decisions to migrate had been taken long before, even though the actual departure may have occurred after the announcement concerning democratic socialism. What is sure, however, is that the announcement would have provided a readymade excuse for those who had decided to go in any case. And certainly, no one disputes that some were going because they did not like the shift in the centre of gravity of power that was taking place in the society.

The original document spoke of 'equality of opportunity', a range of basic people's rights, and a socially controlled economy with an enlarged public and co-operative sector. It spoke of a dynamic and honoured role for the private sector in a mixed economy. It was strong on the deepening of the democratic process and clear in its commitment to non-alignment and the New International Economic Order.

We had intended to embark upon an immediate programme of political education throughout the party's groups and thereafter, in the society as a whole. As it turned out, this was not to happen for another five years on any consistent and sustained basis.

As soon as the first political education classes got underway, it turned out that a major dispute was developing in the party over the interpretation of everything that had just been agreed. One of the first people to come to me in a state of concern was my brother, Dr. Douglas Manley — the then Minister of Youth and Community Development. A very conscientious member of parliament with a constituency in rural Jamaica, he had acquired his quota of booklets promptly and set his groups to work studying them. From the very first night, a quarrel developed between members of the youth organisation and the older members of the regular party drawn mainly from farming communities. A number of questions were causing difficulty. For example: What was the position in relation to classes? Was there a class alliance? If there was a class alliance — whose class interest should be first served if there was a conflict? In a mixed economy, should the public or the private sector play the leading role? Some were arguing that a class alliance is a contradiction in terms since Jamaica is part of the capitalist system and a capitalist class exists to exploit the working class. There were other minor points but these were the main areas of difficulty.

By the end of the year, the party was in such a state of internal tension and division over the policy that we were forced to call off the political education programme. In some cases, the internal quarrel in a particular group was so serious that no coherent course of study was possible. In other cases, two neighbouring groups would find the courses dominated by opposite interpretations. This led to inconsistencies between the different levels of understanding and perception. Clearly, even the two years devoted to the first exercise had not been enough. The result was superficial and glossed over too many fundamental questions.

Even as some were muttering 'I told you so' in the corridors of the party, we went back to the drawing board. In 1975, a new committee was set up to analyse the serious differences that had surfaced. It was a time of great difficulty for the movement. Younger members of the left, in particular, made a series of pronouncements that lent colour to the propaganda which the opposition was working assiduously to establish in the country. Equally, some members of the right were making statements that seemed to imply that any socialism we might adopt would virtually be meaningless.

Since the days of Bustamante a main element in Labour Party propaganda had been the communist smear. After the declaration of democratic socialism they had, naturally, returned to the attack with vigour under a new leader, Edward Seaga, Minister of Finance in the last JLP government. Every time ultra-leftist statements were made, it was like giving hostages to fortune. This was grist to the mill in the propaganda battle and caused genuine tremors of uncertainty in the society, to say nothing of alarm amongst the old-timers in the party itself. Those who spoke would contend that they were speaking as sincere socialists and that their role was to press for the radicalisation of the party. They would quote statements of the right as evidence of a complete lack of seriousness or commitment. I do not doubt that this was sincere but could not fail to notice that both sides caused damage and created openings which others were quick to exploit. One side helped the anti-red propaganda. The other side made us look inconsistent, if not insincere.

The new committee on policy was slow to start. The difficult, often dramatic and sometimes terrible events of 1976 and 1977 intervened. The party united to fight the 1976 election only to divide again over the handling of the economic crisis in 1977. It was not until 1978 that anyone could find the time and energy to take a new look at the policy.

Throughout 1978 and 1979, the exercise of 1973 and 1974 was repeated. This time, nothing was being glossed over. The ideological claws were out on both sides. Every clause, phrase and word was scrutinised, often to become a battleground between left and right forces which had emerged in full battle array.

On the left of the right wing was a group not unfamiliar with political ideals and with a high degree of flexible political intelligence. They called themselves the moderates. On the right of the left wing was a group who were not strangers to pragmatism, who also possessed flexible political intelligence. They did not call themselves anything in particular, seemingly content to be identified as part of the left. It is these two groups, sharing the quality of flexibility, who established the dialogue that eventually led to the resolution of the difficulties and the development of a far more advanced, sophisticated and detailed statement. This is now the official policy of the party and is published as *The Principles and Objectives of the People's National Party.*[1]

It took all the time up to the annual conference in September 1979, to resolve the difficulties. In the end, in a remarkable example of democracy in action, two thousand delegates spent three days of a five-day annual conference going through the document clause by clause. Hour by hour, compromise language was being sought and agreed in the corridors, often finally decided by the officers on the platform. It was as dramatic as it was exhausting. Once again, the top leadership was charged to take the mutilated mass of papers which resulted and reduce them to a reasonably smooth and coherent body of language. This time we were even to attach a glossary of political terms offering agreed definition of words like imperialism, capitalism and mixed economy.

A basis for political education existed at last. The Secretariat of the party went into action. Special cadres were trained as instructors and a well co-ordinated, island-wide programme of political education commenced. Sophisticated teaching methods were employed involving the most up to date techniques of group involvement and feedback. As it turned out, the time was too short. The election of October 1980 intervened before the programme could begin fully to achieve its objectives. At the least, however, the party had demonstrated its commitment to and capacity for democratic process; its concern for ideas and principles; its dedication to the view that democratic politics presuppose a politically educated people.

The new document sought to clarify the two major questions involving classes and the economy. Both nettles were grasped. Emphasising the role of the class alliance, it stated unequivocally that it is the interest of the working class which must predominate. With respect to the mixed economy, it asserted with equal clarity that the public sector must play the leading role in a mixed economy of which the private sector is to be a vibrant part. This was clearly in keeping with the programme on which Norman Manley fought his last election in 1967. In all of this the party had come a long way from the night in December 1975 when I had heard a leading member, a long standing Mayor of one of Jamaica's principal towns declare to a public meeting in my presence: 'You don't have to be afraid of socialism. All it means is that you will pay a little more to the maid in your home.' Needless to say, that particular comrade did not remain with us for much longer. When he discovered that even our mild form of socialism meant considerably more than that, he grumbled, at first privately. Later he made his disaffection public. Later he was expelled, whereupon he joined and found his place in the more comfortable surroundings of the Jamaica Labour Party, where he is now a bastion of conservative values. That he had remained so long in the PNP is an interesting comment upon the tribal attachments which keep people fixed in traditional allegiances to parties long after a rational basis for loyalty has disappeared.

By the time the more developed version of the policy was available to the public, Jamaica was so deep in the political crisis which the opposition was committed to provoke, that it is difficult to estimate whether there was any strong public reaction. Sides had been taken. The battle lines were drawn. By now propaganda was perceived as truth and truth as propaganda, depending on who was listening. To the extent that the document represented an advance in seriousness and no retreat from commitment, it would have been noted by the oligarchy and filed as further evidence of the importance of removing us at any cost. The CIA would doubtless have fed similar advice to the US establishment.

9
TACKLING DESTABILISATION

By the end of 1975 Jamaica had become like a time bomb. The atmosphere was charged. A programme of change had begun and some of its effects were being felt. Crime was the cause of mounting fear. Inflation, running at 20.6% in 1974 and 15.6% in 1975 was eroding not only hard won living standards but confidence in the future as well. No one could fail to notice that something was seriously amiss in the world and some might be tempted to feel that the old order of things was under serious assault, if not on the verge of collapse. Who and what was to blame? Obviously, we were responsible for the programme of change and could not escape some responsibility for the crime situation since that is something governments are supposed to be able to deal with. Inflation was certainly not our fault and we could hardly claim credit or accept blame for the state of the world. The degree to which we were responsible for the decline in the economy was the major point of controversy. These were times ripe for propaganda and agitation, particularly from the right.

When Kissinger lunched with me at the height of the Angola crisis, the JLP was well into its programme of opposition. Under its new leader, red-baiting was the order of the day. Top priority was given to ceaseless anti-communist propaganda at every level and on every conceivable occasion. Nothing was spared. Facts and truth were simply disregarded. Initially I was to wonder why this savage and, at first, seemingly unproductive emphasis! Later, the meaning was to become quite clear.

The second aspect of the JLP campaign was, more logically it seemed, the economy. Oil prices had hit us hard as had world inflation and the recession affecting aluminium and tourism. A lot of money had been spirited out of the country by the defecting members of the upper classes. Nobody had ever felt inflation at the levels that were smiting the people during those years. All this, plus the attempt to run a wide range of new institutions, placed enormous strain on the government management sector which was inevitably not altogether prepared to cope with problems of such magnitude.

The opposition clearly had a pipeline right into the system and penetrating close to the top. It became commonplace for them to make dramatic revelations about the state of the economy and, in particular, of national finances. Almost invariably these statements would be based on the information contained in documents prepared under oath of secrecy for the government at its request.

Interesting ethical questions will always arise about secret government documents. In the end, there can be no hard and fast rules. Official secrecy cannot become a blanket under which malpractices are hidden. Equally, effective government can be severely hampered if there is no level at which sensitive material can be assessed and made the basis of decisions before the rest of the world is made aware of what is going on. For example, if a body of economic information, when analysed, brings a government to the conclusion that it must devalue its currency, advance information opens the door to speculative action in which private citizens can make a killing at the expense of their own country. Clearly, circumstances alter cases, but in the end commonsense tells us that there is a proper role for official secrecy in any intelligent view of government. Equally, commonsense tells us that an opposition has the responsibility to accept this principle, unless it is of the view that wrong-doing is afoot and must be exposed. Such a view cannot be held lightly since it could easily become the excuse for a general disregard of the principle.

There was no wrong-doing in the Jamaican government but rather an anxious search for answers to a deepening economic crisis. On the other hand, the opposition had clearly established an effective espionage network so that it could appear to the public in the role of economic wizard and prophet of doom. If the figures with which you play this game are the very figures prepared for the government by its own experts, you are at least certain that your reputation as prophet cannot be shaken because of the inaccuracy of your information! This reached such a pass that late in 1975 an

actual cabinet submission was published in the local
opposition daily newspaper, having found its way there
through the parliamentary opposition. The whole sordid
episode eventually led to a court trial. A cabinet member was
acquitted and, appropriately enough, found his way into the
ranks of the opposition party. Interestingly, his permanent
secretary was convicted at first instance. The decision was later
reversed by the Court of Appeal.

While all this was happening, the local conservative
newspaper, the *Daily Gleaner*, was emerging as a major focus of
opposition. Founded in 1834, the *Gleaner* had been for more
than a century the bastion of conservatism, defender of the
status quo and the leader of reaction to any attempts at change.
Originally the voice of the plantocracy and their merchant
allies, it had been, in turn, the staunchest champion of the
empire, the monarchy, and now of western capitalism and the
NATO alliance. In the days of empire and particularly after
1865, its views were those of the mother country. Subsequent
to World War II, its views were those of the Washington
establishment with an occasional nostalgic nod in the direction
of Whitehall. It had rejoiced in the hanging of Bogle and
Gordon and hounded Marcus Garvey in these words in April
1924:

> It is with profound regret that we view the arrival of Marcus
> Garvey back in Jamaica, and it is with more than profound regret
> that we picture any leader of thought and culture in this island
> associating himself with a welcome given to him.

It had regarded even Bustamante with concern until he
emerged as a champion of the anti-socialist cause. When
Bustamante was arrested on May 24, 1938, as riots and strikes
rocked Kingston, the *Gleaner* wrote with genteel concern on
May 25: 'No doubt, many good people will breathe easier at the
thought of Bustamante in gaol.' Even then there was none of
the contempt with which it battered Garvey, the revolutionary, fourteen years earlier. It must have sensed early on
that Bustamante's declaration for higher wages was familiar
ground. In other respects the paper ran true to form. On May
23, 1938, it had commented upon the disturbances at a sugar
estate named Frome. There had been riots and workers had
been shot and killed. Men and women were letting it be known
that they could not continue as underpaid wage slaves free in
name only. The *Gleaner* commented editorially: 'It was noted

that persons from Cuba or certain persons here receiving emoluments from the Communist Party in Cuba were responsible for the recent Frome riots and the present strikes in the island.' With the *Gleaner*, protest and progress always cast their shadow. The shadow always led to communism and to Cuba.

The paper could not but respect Norman Manley's unrivalled gifts of intellect, advocacy and disciplined application, but it opposed him throughout his career. Whereas it was constantly fulsome in its praise of the conservative Bustamante during his lifetime, it reserved its warmer thoughts on Norman Manley till he was safely in his grave. With every breath he drew, Manley challenged the structures and assumptions of colonialism. The system was unsafe in his presence.

It must be next to impossible for outsiders to understand a newspaper coming to occupy so dominant a position in the life of a country as the *Gleaner* does in Jamaica. The paper has been the only source of popular reading in the country for so long that it has become a part of the country's unconscious system of habits. One often notices the fact that Jamaicans in a foreign country do not ask for a newspaper but enquire whether they can see the *Gleaner*.

For the establishment and most of the middle class, the *Gleaner* sets the daily agenda in Jamaica. It has the power to invest particular events with a moral or immoral character. For example, I once reported in a speech that a certain company had increased its exports by 115%. The figure had been double-checked by the statistical source, but was still wrong. The *Gleaner* battered me for deliberate dishonesty. On another occasion when a conservative prime minister made a similar error, the paper politely pointed out that ministers are bound to make mistakes occasionally. But this was only a minor incident when compared with so many others.

By 1975 the *Gleaner* was on the warpath. It had not yet attained the levels of orchestrated venom which were to mark its performance later, but it was already sounding a strident cacophony of abuse and sowing the seeds of discord and suspicion wherever it could. From that time on, the *Gleaner* was in fact indistinguishable from the opposition, its tactics similar to that of the notorious *El Mercurio* in Chile.

In the midst of all this, the oligarchy was beginning to

mobilise the major elements in the private sector against the government. It was not a difficult task. Businessmen in both the manufacturing and commercial sector were a part of a pattern of middle class anxiety. Many were under great pressure at home from wives who resented developments in education and feared for their own safety at night. The opposition propaganda was ceaseless and directed at business fears that we really had something bad up our sleeves, perhaps even the expropriation of their businesses. The two main business organisations at the time, the Jamaica Manufacturers' Association (JMA) and the Jamaica Chamber of Commerce were against us. We held many meetings with this private sector leadership explaining, answering questions and doing what we could to maintain an atmosphere of bare sanity if not reason. Each time we calmed things down, something or somebody would manage to start them up again.

What is sad about all this, in retrospect, is that we did far more than talk. We knew that the private sector was taking an economic buffeting. Throughout this period and later, we did much to help them remain viable. A series of ministers were appointed with good credentials among the business community. Special loan funds were earmarked; an export credit facility was introduced in April 1974; Bank of Jamaica loans were available at special interest rates for exporters; the Jamaica Export Credit Insurance Corporation was created to provide guarantees for exporters on as much as 80% of the value of their exports; accelerated depreciation rates were arranged for private enterprises operating two or more shifts; tax rebates were provided for training workers required for expansion of production; the consolidation of group profits and losses was permitted where companies were 100% owned by the same group; credit facilities through the Jamaica Development Bank were expanded.

Who says that 'deeds speak louder than words'? Our 'deeds' to the private sector were the most eloquent testimony to our sincerity with respect to the mixed economy. To these 'deeds' were added countless words of categoric, official reassurance.[1] Against this were ranged some cases of irresponsible comment from our side and a ceaseless stream of provocative, manipulative and patently dishonest propaganda from the opposition. It was obvious that the private sector chose to assume the worst, presumably because we were challenging the system in the pure form which they prefer. They were not prepared to accept the entirely honourable place which they were being offered in a modified system.

In the meantime, the foreign press began to campaign against us as well. The first clear sign emerged when a writer from the *Wall Street Journal* wrote a piece which was strikingly similar to the James Reston article following Kissinger's return from Jamaica. The peg upon which he hung the story was a demonstration staged outside a Kingston hotel where the International Monetary Fund was holding its annual gathering of Finance Ministers. News had got out that a South African would attend the conference. This struck deep chords in our movement and junior government ministers advised me that their consciences demanded they take part in an anti-apartheid demonstration outside the hotel. Permission to take part was granted.

In due course the South African arrived at the insistence of the IMF authorities, and the demonstration was held. It was peaceful, although it did become somewhat noisy on the first day. When asked by our Minister of Finance to quieten down, the demonstrators did so.

The *Wall Street* writer used this simple episode to write a scurrilous piece about Jamaica. Every sort of claptrap and lie about Cuba's presence in Jamaica was trotted out. I was subsequently to learn that the particular writer is believed to be one of the hacks the CIA keep to do their dirty work when they want to start 'hatcheting' a country or foreign political figure.

During 1976, there was a mounting flood of American articles against Jamaica. Some would make honest and even telling comments about our economic difficulties; some frankly disagreed with our policies or took exception to our democratic socialism. Still others expressed resentment of our non-aligned position and our relations with Cuba. All this was fair enough, though it was tedious to have to explain over and over that the relationship with Cuba was no closer than that with Mexico and Venezuela; that I did not have a deeper friendship with Fidel Castro than I enjoyed with Pierre Trudeau and Julius Nyerere.

Quite different were the increasing articles which represented us as a communist surrogate, a cat's-paw of Soviet and Cuban adventurism. These sought to prove their charges by describing Cuban troops stationed in Jamaica and making similar lying references. To conceal Cuban troops in an island as small as Jamaica would be impossible. Clearly this kind of coverage was part of a plan and not an element in the spontaneous reaction of a free press.

But these media efforts of the opposition were like the nuisance factor that irritates but does not altogether destroy. The key to those times was to be found in a particular kind of organised violence which passed itself off as crime, but was really something quite different.[2]

In 1974 we had introduced controversial legislation in which we made the illegal possession of a firearm a crime punishable by mandatory life sentence. We had even stopped bird shooting and asked the sportsmen to hand in their guns for safe-keeping in the military armoury. Under the Gun Court Law, as it was called, we had made special arrangements to provide for the quick trial of those charged with offences involving guns. Acting upon the advice of a team which included a sociologist and a psychiatrist, we had tried shock therapy in the hope that this would buy time for the society and give us an opportunity to gain control over the situation through improved methods of detection and police activity generally. We had also hoped that the home guard would be an important element in changing the situation for the better. For a time, things did improve and the Gun Court enjoyed widespread support. But as 1975 proceeded on its anxious and tense way, crime was on the rise again and public concern increasing with it.

Meanwhile political violence was becoming serious. There was a period during 1975 when the leaders of our party in the ghetto areas of the western section of the capital were on the verge of panic. Gunmen owing their allegiance to the opposition had mounted a reign of terror. The doors of well known PNP supporters would be kicked down at night and the one-room shacks in which they lived shot up. Sometimes the occupants were killed. In an attempt to combat a mood of despair in the party I paid several visits to the worst areas to try to bolster morale. Of course some elements hit back, some giving as good as they got. But it was very clear that we were not the aggressors.

At the beginning of 1976, we held a series of discussions with the heads of the security forces. Among the things which we discussed was the question of the declaration of a State of Emergency. If we took this course, the government would be able to empower the security forces to detain people without trial on the basis of intelligence concerning their activities.

We were reluctant. A State of Emergency signals to the outside world that you are in crisis. It is damaging to tourist industry and investment prospects and generally involves the tacit admission that the normal democratic process has failed. In any event, we were warned that we were in no condition to impose a State of Emergency. Although large criminal gangs were operating all over Kingston, criminal intelligence was such that a State of Emergency would scarcely have helped. When asked the question: 'Do you know whom to detain and where to find them, were you to possess these powers?', the answer of the security chiefs was an emphatic if regretful 'no'! It was thereupon suggested that there should be a complete overhaul of our methods in the field of criminal intelligence as part of a precautionary preparation.

As things went from bad to worse, it became clear that we were dealing with something far more sinister than ordinary crime. The word that has emerged in the modern lexicon to describe what we were experiencing is destabilisation.

Destabilisation describes a situation where some source either inside or outside a country — or perhaps two sources working in concert, one outside and one inside — set out to create a situation of instability and panic *by design*. John Foster Dulles' brother, Allen, has boasted of how little it cost to use *agents provocateurs* to create chaos in Teheran, to bring down Iran's radical prime minister, Mossadegh, and set the Shah on the Peacock Throne. By the time the CIA was finished with Chile, many citizens and particularly members of the middle class were hysterically convinced that Allende intended to destroy everything of value in Chile.[3]

Jamaica in 1976 took on these characteristics. For instance, there was a terrible night when two gangs operating in neighbouring areas in Kingston became locked in a vendetta. A member of one gang was killed and reprisals began. In due course, the leader of the other gang was shot dead on a main highway early one evening. Before we knew it, members of his gang had surrounded a huge tenement yard in which over 500 people were crammed into some 200 small rooms including areas to wash, cook and do all other domestic activities. Fires were set at several points on the outer perimeter of the old buildings and shacks that comprised the yard. The whole place went up in flames. Eleven people died. The victims included five small children, and two babies, who were trapped in the flames and died as their parents listened helplessly to their pitiful screams.

The Orange Lane fire, as it became known, shocked the society to its core. It seemed an ultimate example of man's inhumanity to man, a new dimension in senseless brutality. It was clear that the fire was a part of the gang war intended as an act of reprisal because it was believed that the gang leader's assailants had taken refuge in the yard. Is it, however, credible to believe that a group of tough, battle-hardened street fighters would really have thought that a fire set in that way could catch equally battle-hardened and street-wise gunmen alert to a danger they knew to be imminent?

We know that the incident did more than shock the national sensibility. It was quickly taken up as an example of a crime situation out of the government's control. I do not believe that the Orange Lane fire was simply a case of the members of a gang getting angry one night. The whole history of the escalating difficulty between the two gangs reeks of provocation. The final setting of the fire suggests not anger but the coldest calculation. Needless to say, the official enquiry had no evidence upon which to come to such a conclusion. There had been trouble between the gangs. Gang members had been killed. A fire had been set. The question is whether this was spontaneous or skilfully stage-managed.

Then the problem with the police began. A number of men in uniform were gunned down. The force was tense. One night two policemen were doing fixed guard duty at a housing project. At around midnight gunmen surprised them and shot them dead. Before day could break, the section of the police force known as the Mobile Reserve, a tough group, trained to deal with anything from riots to gunmen, was on strike. There was no industrial dispute with the government at the time. Nor was there any evidence of a quarrel between men and a commanding officer, as can sometimes occur in a security force. Like a bolt from the blue they stopped working because gunmen had clearly beaten two of their own to the draw. One would expect a logical response. When this happens to police in another country and at other times in Jamaica, the normal reaction is for every man to reach for his gun and go hunting. The blood boils as the adrenalin pumps in response to the sense of comradely outrage. Not so with our Mobile Reserve on that February morning 1976. Instead, as if on cue, certain police voices were ready to take charge of the police network jamming the line with the most filthy abuse of the government, the Security Minister and of me personally.

At the headquarters of the Mobile Reserve, an activist leadership had suddenly emerged, as if from nowhere, calling upon the men to refuse to work. What is particularly instructive about the strike call was the fact that it was made in support of no claim.

We never did discover what it was the men struck in support of on that macabre morning. I drove straight to the scene of the strike. I still imagined that there may have been some festering grievance of which I had not been informed and which had caused this completely irrational and unprecedented behaviour. I was anxious to discover what moved a group of men, trained to deal with the very problem that had overcome their comrades the night before, to react in this way.

I arrived at headquarters to find several hundred policemen milling around in various states ranging from surliness to confusion. Shortly after, they all went back to work, having made no claim and consequently secured no concession. By then, however, much damage had been done. The government's credibility took a blow. The press was filled with dark forebodings as an explanation was sought for these grim events. When even the police stop working 'things have come to a pretty pass' was the battle cry of the establishment and its spokespersons.

Looking back at the events of 1976, and I have not gone into detail here, I have no doubt that the CIA was active in Jamaica that year and was working through its own agents to destabilise us. They deny it to this day, but I prefer the judgements of the heads of the Jamaica security forces at the time. Police, army and special branch concurred that the CIA was actively behind the events. My commonsense left me with no option but to agree.

By the middle of 1976 things had indeed come to a 'pretty pass'. By constitution, the election could be held no later than June of 1977 and would normally be expected by February at the latest. The police were battling manfully with their problems and there had been no hint of a recurrence of the weird aberration in February amongst members of the Mobile Reserve. Our criminal intelligence had been brushed up and I was now assured that, should a State of Emergency be called, the security forces would have a thorough grasp of the situation. They would know who to detain and where to find them. Once again, the situation was crying out for the declaration of a State of Emergency. By now our minds were finally made up. Only timing and the method of handling the news overseas were under further and final study. The event which finally precipitated the decision to call the State of Emergency was the killing of the Peruvian Ambassador in his home on June 14. The security heads insisted that the decision could no longer be postponed. A special sub-committee of the cabinet had been set up in May to keep this question of a State of Emergency under constant review. It consisted of Coore, Patterson, Rattray, Munn and myself. By now we were meeting almost daily. After the killing of the Ambassador the committee decided that the actual date should be the following Tuesday, June 22, when it could be announced in parliament. In the event, the date was brought forward by three days because of other developments.

Long after the 1976 election the opposition revived the question of the State of Emergency, alleging it to have been corruptly called and improperly used to secure the defeat of the JLP in the election for which they were already campaigning.

But the facts are clear and incontrovertible. Crime and political violence were virtually paralysing the society. We were satisfied that a considerable proportion of what was taking place was the result of calculated provocation. We concluded, as had a JLP Government in 1966, that the national interest demanded the strongest action that is possible under our constitution. No reasonable observer at that time could doubt that the situation in the country came entirely within the intention of the constitution in providing the emergency powers which were in fact invoked.

At that stage things were so serious that the heads of the security forces were meeting me on a daily basis to review the state of affairs in the struggle with crime and violence. The security chiefs were unanimous and emphatic in the advice to act. There was overwhelming popular support for the move.[4]

In calling the State of Emergency, it was made absolutely

clear to the Minister of National Security, Keble Munn, and to the heads of the security forces themselves that the powers conferred were to be used with the greatest care and discretion and were not to be directed against the opposition in any way. It was pointed out that we were going to hold the elections. I regarded it as critical to the preservation of confidence in the democratic process in Jamaica, that no one should be able to say or feel afterwards that the opposition JLP had been unfairly hampered in the conduct of their campaign. There was to be no banning of public meetings.

The State of Emergency was maintained for approximately one year. Throughout the period, 593 people were actually detained. Three candidates of the opposition and one of the governing party were detained. Two other members of the executive committee of the opposition were detained along with a prominent figure in the constituency organisation of West Kingston, held by the opposition. A prominent member of the constituency of South St. Andrew, held by the government, was also detained. The rest were underworld figures and members of the political gangs which had grown up over the years, attaching themselves to one party or the other.

The JLP hit the road with a vigorous campaign of public meetings preparing for the election as soon as the dust settled. I personally invited the Leader of the Opposition to see me and assured him that we intended to hold the elections and that he and his party would not be harassed, but would have absolute freedom to organise and campaign in the normal way. I regard the subsequent attempt to suggest that the State of Emergency was corruptly used to guarantee our return to power as the most disgraceful single case of political and journalistic dishonesty that I have witnessed in my long years in public life. Anything the opposition could lay their hands on was put to use. We thus decided to have everything out on the table. We set up a Commission of Enquiry into the State of Emergency under the Chief Justice of Jamaica, the Honourable Kenneth Smith, O.J.

Smith's reputation for absolute integrity and moral courage had made him a legend in his lifetime amongst those who practise law in Jamaica. He was made the sole enquirer on a commission with the widest powers to subpoena witnesses and otherwise probe all allegations of corruption against our government. This had been expanded to include all allegations arising out of the declaration of the State of Emergency.

For months on end, the finest lawyers available to the opposition had full power of cross-examination of any and all witnesses who were called or cared to offer themselves to give evidence about the State of Emergency, its calling or its implementation. I, myself, faced days of cross-examination. Chief Justice Smith found that there was absolutely no corruption, illegality or impropriety in connection with the calling of the State of Emergency. He stated in the end that one or two detentions were questionable, although he said that no question of corruption on the part of the political directorate arose in any case. He found one detention corrupt and attached blame to a particular police officer.

Two things have never been properly explained in connection with two of the opposition candidates who were detained during the State of Emergency. One was found with a document in his possession. It was headed 'Operation Werewolf'. It consisted of a carefully elaborated plan for what could only have been a guerilla-type operation. The plan spoke of guns and other types of equipment needed and where they were to be hidden; and of training needs. It was in every sense a most unusual document to be found in the possession of a candidate for a supposedly peaceful democratic election. The candidate had an earlier connection with the military and obviously knew of what he spoke.

In the case of the second candidate, a tape was found in his home. On that tape was an extensive recording of the radio transmissions of police patrol cars. The cars were speeding along various roads trying to head off gunmen to whom they were giving chase. It was obvious on the tape that the gunmen were also in cars and trying to escape. One of the things which intelligence had been reporting for some time was that shortwave radios were being used to monitor the police so as to tip off the get-away cars which were used by gunmen in the political attacks which were common in lower Kingston. Neither the document nor the tape was by itself enough to make a successful case in court. Equally, neither document nor tape has ever been explained.

Perhaps the final comment to be made about the State of Emergency concerns the crime figures. During the Emergency all crime decreased by 17.9%; during the first six months there was a 33.2% drop in gun crimes even though an election was fought in this period. Forty-two people were killed in the month before the Emergency, 11 were killed during the first month of the Emergency.[5]

10
VICTORY IN 1976

Nothing like it had ever been seen in Jamaican history. Normally cautious estimates put the crowd at 120,000. A team who were over the scene in a helicopter said it could have been as high as 150,000. All day the cars, the buses, the trucks, the mini-vans, the motor bicycles had been streaming along the highways from the east, the west and the south. Now they were gathered in historic Sam Sharpe Square, Montego Bay at night.

The Square itself has deep significance. It was here that Sam Sharpe was hanged after his abortive but ultimately successful slave rebellion. He had looked across this very space as they erected the gallows from which he would hang and uttered his deathless words of defiance. For generations, it had been known as Charles Square after the King of that name who had kept both head and crown. We had renamed it after Sam Sharpe.

It was from this very spot that we had launched our successful 1972 election campaign. On that occasion, it had been estimated that 90,000 attended. Now, the people stretched as far as one could see, disappearing up the side streets, which empty into the square, in great solid columns.

Everyone knew that they were there to hear the election date and to be a part of the launching of the campaign. I arrived with my family promptly at 9:00pm. I spoke for an hour, starting at 10:00pm, and ended by announcing the election date as December 15. The cheer that greeted the announcement was tinged with relief like an underlining to the excitement. Everyone had endured so much, of violence, of propaganda, of sheer tension. It would probably get worse in the next couple of weeks, but everyone could hope that relief would follow the day itself.

The issues were sharply focused.[1] The opposition JLP

campaigned on communism and the economy. In the light of
the attacks that were to follow, it is particularly interesting to
note that they did not make either the State of Emergency or
the electoral system a campaign issue.

We campaigned on our record of performance and called for
a mandate for democratic socialism as we had proclaimed it in
our policy. We laid great stress on the fact that all our best
programmes of the last four years had been part of a general,
socialist design to make Jamaica a place in which the majority
of its people, its workers, farmers, professionals and middle
class would have a better life, better opportunities and, above
all, a bigger share in their country. This share was to involve its
wealth. It was also to involve power in the country at large and
in its institutions.

I was particularly careful to stress the role of our foreign
policy and the fact that we were not communist, in fact or
intent. I reminded everyone that our relationships with
communist countries were part of a principled international
policy. In speech after speech, I hammered at the themes of
hard work, sacrifice and co-operation. I was at pains to explain
that we had serious economic difficulties and called upon the
people to prepare to co-operate so that we could work our way
out of our difficulties in the years to come. I always ended with
a strong appeal for a mandate for democratic socialism and the
continuation of our policies.

I stress this because it became clear subsequently that not all
members of the party campaigned in this carefully modulated
way. In the last days of the campaign, a slogan emerged which
was another example of differences in perception within the
movement: 'Forward to Full Socialism'. This was not part of
the official campaign. It was important because the use of the
word 'full' was to take on a special significance after the
election. The official slogan was the basis of a campaign song:
'Forward to socialism, no turning back, no turning back'.

It was a vigorous campaign with both sides slugging it out at
full blast. In spite of the State of Emergency, there was far too
much violence. When the gunmen were detained earlier, few of
their guns had been found. Obviously, other hands were ready
to come forward and put new trigger-fingers in place. Two
days before the election itself, one of our candidates, Ferdie
Neita was gunned down in broad daylight. It took three hours
on the operating table to save his life. I was shot at in my own

constituency. So, too, were several others among our candidates. In the last week, my schedule was altered more than once to visit areas in which it was felt that morale was collapsing because opposition gunmen had been on the rampage. Perhaps the other side can tell similar stories.

Throughout the year, a social scientist, Dr. Carl Stone, had been conducting opinion surveys. We had been in the lead throughout the year, although the opposition had closed the gap somewhat in a poll about two months after the State of Emergency. They had been campaigning very hard and we had not hit the road as yet. From October onwards, his poll showed us pulling steadily away.

My own programme put me at about 150 public meetings in the last six weeks. The entire party was galvanised and on the move. Internal differences had been firmly shelved for the moment and everyone concentrated on the task at hand. In the end, Stone was within 1% in his final election prediction. In the last days of the campaign, I had no doubt that we were heading for a landslide. It could be felt in the size of the meetings, their quality of enthusiasm and attention.

On the eve of the election, something was to happen which was to cast a shadow nearly four years forward. There had been a meeting in a town called Old Harbour, which in typical Jamaican style is about six miles from the sea at the nearest point. (It is not unusual to find oneself in a Mount 'Something' and search in vain for a slight rise in the terrain, much less a hill.) After the meeting, there had been a row between Duncan and an officer of the Reserve Battalion of the Army. The officer had struck Duncan while the latter was requesting protection for a group of PNP supporters returning from a meeting. They had to pass through a hostile group of JLP trouble-makers. Things were tense and I was urged to come to Old Harbour before they got out of hand. I duly arrived and began questioning the officer, a captain, about the incident. Suddenly he turned his back and strutted away. In a flash, his men surrounded me. There must have been ten or twelve of them. There was the rattle of rifles readied to fire. I hesitated for a moment and then decided this was a situation which could not accommodate two bosses. I walked straight at one of the men, doubtless looking as angry as I felt. It was his turn to hesitate. The moment before he lowered his rifle and stepped aside seemed interminable. The others followed suit.

That moment of melodrama was significant for what it anticipated, though we could not know it at the time. It was a reserve group, the members of which spend eleven months of the year in civilian life and a month in army training. They were correspondingly less disciplined and more involved in ordinary politics than their colleagues of the regular force. Nonetheless, the incident then was still a straw in the wind.

We won 47 of the 60 seats in parliament, polling 56.8% of the popular vote to 43.2% for the opposition JLP. Once again, we had set a record in our majority. 85.2% of a voters' roll of 870,972 voted, which was itself a record. Afterwards, the opposition leader commented that he had never seen the Jamaican people vote for a government in the way that they had in that election.[2]

I mention this because it makes for an interesting memory in the light of subsequent attempts to pretend that we had somehow stolen the elections.

On election night, I had a good sleep until they woke me to say, in effect, that we had won. The same thing had happened in 1972. It was an emotional moment because we had been through a great deal. The migration of many Jamaicans had been a blow and the constant problem of violence a terrible source of strain. The incessant propaganda about communism lent an air of unreality to the political climate, which in itself was a source of tension. Now that the people had spoken decisively, perhaps there could be some respite from the irrelevance and the ugly 'red herrings' which were constantly introduced into a political dialogue that already had so much to cause serious debate.

I was deeply conscious of the tremendous economic problems which the country faced and determined to try to hold the party on a steady and sober course. If I could, I wanted the party to see the election result not as an occasion for either rejoicing or recrimination, but as a challenge to work and effort. It was a mandate for us to continue on the course which we had set and for the democratic socialism which we had carefully proclaimed.

Manley with constituency supporter.
Announcing democratic socialism, 1974.

Addressing Parliament.
Edward Heath on holiday in Jamaica in 1974.
A day-care centre in Manley's constituency.

...anley with Judith Hart at Jamaica House, 1980.
...m Sharpe Square, 1976. A crowd of some 150,000 gathered to hear Manley speak.

Manley meets Fidel Castro on his arrival in Jamaica in 1977.

Manley training for the Home Guard.

A school lunch programme.

Runaway Bay Summit. December 1978. (l. to r.) Trudeau, Manley, Perez, Nordli, Obasanju, Schmidt, and Frazer

chael Manley with his wife Beverly at a Labour Day celebration.
th Nyerere in Tanzania, 1973.

A self-help extension to a primary school in Manley's constituency, 1975.

na Manley, Manley's mother, next to Edward Heath.
th Mohammed Ali.
eracy Campaign graduation ceremony.

Runaway Bay planning meeting in Hamburg, 1978, with Schmidt and Brandt.
Michael Manley arriving in Cuba, 1976.

11
CRISIS AND THE IMF

Our second term problems were upon us immediately. The economy was in deep trouble. The balance of payments crisis had us by the throat and production was down everywhere. A number of factors had combined to create the crisis.

First in the sequence and most significant in effect was the combination of oil prices and world inflation. Jamaica is 97% dependent on oil for energy. In addition, it is a surprisingly big user of energy per capita for a Third World country. This is so because of the substantial growth in manufacturing which had taken place during the previous thirty years. Ironically, the situation had been exacerbated by a decision of purest folly taken by the sugar industry a few years before. Most of Jamaica's sugar factories used to burn the sugar cane waste, bagasse, to supply the energy for the sugar factories. This involved quite a labour force since the bagasse had to be stored and shovelled into furnaces. Needless to say, bagasse workers were a fractious, not to say militant group. Bagasse dust is a miserable business particularly when facing the heat of a furnace into which it is being shovelled. Many are the days I had spent as a trade unionist arguing for respiratory masks and premium pay for these groups.[1] In due course, the sugar manufacturers were to be seduced by the low price of oil and the prospect of no more bagasse workers. At a stroke, and at the cost of an investment which is best forgotten, they converted the entire industry to oil-burning furnaces. At the time, the foreign exchange needed to pay for all the new equipment was bad enough. So was the loss of more than 1,000 jobs. However, all that was to pale into insignificance beside the implications of $11.00 a barrel oil which was soon to become $14.00, $21.00, $28.00 and now $36.00 a barrel. By such means does the Puerto Rican model flatter to deceive. How proud the manufacturers were when they laid off their people and admired the shiny new equipment that could not talk back!

Oil was not the only factor putting pressure on Jamaica's foreign exchange. We were heavy importers of food and between 1973 and 1974 average food import prices soared. Our manufacturing sector was and still is heavily dependent on imported raw materials, equipment and spare parts. Prices were soaring here as well. Bauxite and alumina exports were falling rapidly, originally as part of the world recession and later as the multinationals hit back over the levy.

Tourism was in sharp decline. Again, the recession provided the general framework. We were particularly hard hit, however, because years of neglect of our tourist product was catching up with us. The industry had never been planned but had mushroomed, helter-skelter, in the fifties and sixties. As the demand for hotel workers grew, the quality of training fell. Luxury hotels had sprouted cheek-by-jowl with the worst slums. It was common for taxi drivers to rook the visitor and for pimps and prostitutes to provide daily harassment. In twenty years, Jamaica's image had slipped disastrously in the marketplace. In times of recession the places with the good reputations stand up remarkably well. The ones with the bad reputations go to the wall. We went to the wall.

Then there were sugar and bananas. From a peak of 500,000 tons of sugar in 1965, production had declined to 350,000 tons a year by the middle seventies. Burning of canefields was reducing yields. More importantly, the big overseas operations, Britain's Tate & Lyle and the US United Fruit Company had taken strategic decisions to pull out. During the sixties they began to run their plants down, extracting the last cent of return from their investments before the inevitable rescue operations would predictably commence, as circumstances forced countries like Trinidad and Jamaica to buy them out.

It would be a long time before the capital could be mobilised to refurbish near-derelict factories and replace creaking rolling stock as part of the effort to arrest the decline. Even as I write in 1981, the turnaround has not started yet. Production is only 210,000 tons.

The banana industry almost defies analysis. Inefficiently organised, its top-heavy control body and transport costs to the docks of London leech its potential profits. In the most quality-sensitive market in the world, Jamaican bananas were consistently failing the highest quality tests and missing out on the best prices. Yields per acre run anywhere from ten to fifteen tons in Central America. Jamaica's growers were averaging between two and three. To non-existent product-ivity was being added, each year, the further problem of diminishing acreage. From a high of 200,000 tons in 1965, national production had slipped to 70,000 tons by the middle seventies. Every Jamaican government since universal adult suffrage had tried its hand at the re-organisation of the banana industry. We were no exception. Our failure stood upon a consistent precedent.

To oil, inflation, and declining export production, one had to add the flight of capital. By 1977 it was conservatively estimated that some US $300 million had left the country illegally. Often the skill had followed the capital. Finally we had been obliged to borrow in a tightening money market to keep the economy afloat during 1974, 1975 and 1976. Suddenly, eight and ten year money had disappeared and reasonable interest rates with it. Three year money at 12% had become the order of the day as the world system reeled under successive blows. Now the question was: what to do?

The quartet who were responsible for the management of the economy were David Coore, the Minister of Finance, Horace Barber, the Financial Secretary, G. Arthur Brown, the Governor of the Bank of Jamaica, and Gladstone Bonnick, the Director of the National Planning Agency. This group had been in touch with the International Monetary Fund about our situation as was their duty and Jamaica's right. Jamaica had become a first class member of the IMF in 1963 under Article VIII, thus signifying our intention to pay our contributions as if we were a developed country and entitled to support on the same basis.

During the latter part of 1976, there had been talks with the IMF in which representatives of the Fund had stated the view that Jamaica should devalue its currency by 40% and take various other corrective measures including sharp cut-backs in budget expenditure. Obviously, this could not have been done in the middle of an election campaign and it was agreed that the matter would be discussed immediately after the election if we were still the government. All this was of critical importance because the foreign exchange situation was acute and the country was beginning to suffer as a consequence.

As soon as the new cabinet was in place, it turned to the economic situation as the first order of business. Even while it was being formed, the crisis was being discussed among the leadership. The nature and extent of the foreign exchange crisis was outlined and the need for a new programme providing sustained inflows of foreign exchange was indicated. All this was for the benefit of the new members of the team. It was a familiar litany to the veterans of the first term. The proposal called for an application to the IMF for a stand-by facility under which specific sums of foreign exchange would become available on a regular basis as part of a financing plan. This would include further loans from the commercial banking sector. With IMF support, these loans would be for more reasonable periods and on more manageable terms.

Having set the stage, it was then announced that the IMF would expect, as an integral part of these arrangements, a 40% devaluation and severe cuts in budget expenditure. To say that the news exploded like a bombshell would do considerably less than justice to what occurred. The reaction came in waves. First, there was the political realisation of what so massive a devaluation would do to the cost of living and, in particular, to the poor. To this was added the further insight that heavy cutbacks in the budget could only come from the programmes which helped the poor. The major part of the budget was already committed to the fixed operating overheads of the government itself.

The second wave of reaction came shortly afterwards as many members of the cabinet began to question the net impact of a devaluation upon the economy as a whole. If devaluation is ultimately justified by the expectation that exports will increase, how do you justify it if there is reason to doubt that your particular export industries are in a position to respond to the opportunity which a devaluation is supposed to provide? For example, our sugar exports could not increase because of a devaluation, since falling exports were not caused by the over-pricing of our sugar but by problems in sugar production itself.

The third and most serious reaction to the proposal surfaced within days. To the left wing of the party, dealing with the IMF at all gave rise to profound difficulties. They were aware of the history of the IMF, particularly in its dealings in Latin America. It was, indeed, a sorry story. Time and again IMF programmes which were supposed to cure ailing economies had resulted in massive pressure on the poor, rioting, often the collapse of civilian government and a general history of mayhem. The monetarist demand management approach of the IMF was designed by the representatives and planners of developed capitalist economies for the typical ailments of those economies.[2] The left pointed out that there was not a single case where these prescriptions cured a Third World economy. On the contrary, there were a number of cases where economies had remained sick, but democratic government had died. To them, reliance upon an IMF programme for adjustment and recovery meant delivering Jamaica into a trap. Once in the trap, they argued, the Jamaican economy would not recover but merely stagger deeper and deeper into the very position of dependence from which we were pledged to extricate it. In the meantime, the democratic socialist process would be the most probable casualty of the exercise.

The left of the party argued a different course of action. They believed that we could survive the foreign exchange crisis in the short run by careful rationing of our earnings, supplemented by loans and other kinds of material support from socialist bloc and progressive OPEC countries. In the meantime, they called for the mobilisation of the people in a national productive effort that would place great reliance on community involvement in planning, greatly increased mobilisation of domestic agricultural production and a rapid expansion in community-based small business enterprises. They argued, accurately, that the manufacturing sector used up large sums of foreign exchange to maintain production and that this group should be asked to bear their proportionate share of a general national sacrifice under a tight programme of foreign exchange budgeting.

In the end, these arguments carried the day. This was so to the extent that it was decided to make every effort to see whether the means could be found to mobilise the programme that they advocated and to secure the survival of the society and its economy at the same time. The IMF was advised that we did not agree with the devaluation proposal, whereupon those talks became deadlocked. In the meantime, the cabinet unanimously decided to try to see whether we could get the economy moving and out of the crisis without the devaluation. We never actually broke with the IMF at that time. We wanted the programme to succeed without them because they were demanding such a high price in terms of the effect on the people. I summed it up in these words in a speech to parliament on January 19, 1977. Having described the issues involved in the devaluation proposal, I said: '. . . And this is not a condition which we are prepared to meet *as long as there is a viable alternative*'. I went on to say: 'We did these things fully conscious that they might mean — and I stress might mean — that we might not now be able to obtain the IMF seal of approval . . . ' We were going to try with everything we possessed, but we were keeping the lifeline open, should we fail.

The best of the left wing and progressive economists at the University of the West Indies were mobilised for the planning effort under the leadership of the distinguished economist and an expert on the aluminium industry, Norman Girvan. A newly formed Ministry of Mobilisation under Duncan stumped the countryside, mobilising communities and villages to identify land which could be brought under production, or simple productive projects which could be undertaken. After weeks of feverish activity, a people-based 'Production Plan' was ready.

The Plan identified specific production possibilities sector by sector. It had involved hundreds of Jamaicans in the business of planning for the first time. Whole communities, villages and sectors now had leaders who could speak of a production plan as their own. It represented the first attempt at economic mobilisation in Jamaican history. Hitherto planners had been drawn from the elite of the bureaucracy, the political directorate and, perhaps, the captains of industry. Disciplined obedience supported by rhetorical injunctions to hard work had been expected to guarantee that the 'people' played their part.

Now the leadership of the same 'people' at basic levels had helped to prepare the plan. Authorship should provide a better foundation for commitment than the platitudinous exhortations in which governors general and other ceremonial heads of state specialise.

The plan had weaknesses without a doubt. Some of the production targets were unrealistic. Foreign exchange requirements were underestimated in a number of cases. There was also a general miscalculation about the amount of foreign exchange that would be needed and could be forthcoming.

At that time the party was divided into three groups. The left was on fire with enthusiasm, confident that the plan could work. A goodly part of the rest were co-operating fully and hoping that it would work since the alternative posed by the IMF seemed to call for unprecedented levels of suffering by the Jamaican people, to say nothing of the political catastrophe that it clearly invited. There was a minority who were quiet but sure it could not work. For some of these, it was a matter of scale. They simply did not believe that the Jamaican economy could survive at a level that would maintain social viability without the infusion of foreign exchange which they were sure the IMF alone could provide. I do not doubt that there was also an element who would have looked askance at all these young Turks of the left, often sporting beards, tams and jeans, playing so prominent a part in affairs.

As the work on the production plan proceeded, the foreign exchange situation rapidly approached crisis point. Coore advised that our reserves were exhausted and that we would shortly face a dreaded import choice. We would have to decide whether to maintain minimum imports of basic foods and drugs or the raw materials for the factories with their tens of thousands of workers. In an agonising session, Cabinet debated the matter and decided that there was nothing for it but to resume the negotiations with the IMF. In due course, the executive of the party was advised.

Beginning with the cabinet decision itself, there was great bitterness and disillusionment on the left. Looking back, I believe it to be clear that we had no choice at that time. We did not have the developed relationships with the countries that we approached which would normally precede help on the scale that was needed. Nor did we occupy any position of military and political significance of the sort which attracts help like a magnet, even where there is no distress. On the other hand, the decision itself could have been much better handled. If we had developed by early 1977 the party's Economic Commission, which we created by 1979, it would have ensured the full involvement of the party in government planning and decision-making. Consequently, the brutal realities which compelled the decision would have been generally understood and appreciated so that the action would have reflected a consensus

of commonsense, however sad. As it was, the decision was
divisive in the extreme within the party.

The decision made, we went into action. Two sub-
committees of the cabinet began working. The first examined
all options which could be followed to minimise the effects on
the people of the IMF budget demands. The second
concentrated on the economic issues in the negotiations. We
were not about to lie down and accept the IMF programme
without a fight. This was not because there was a compulsion
to fight, but because we genuinely believed that the
programme itself was inhuman and counter-productive. A
major quarrel developed around the question of the
devaluation. We counter-proposed a dual exchange rate in
which our traditional exports along with non-essential
consumer goods would be subject to a 37.5% devaluation.
Imports of essential foods and drugs along with the bauxite
alumina industry would remain on the old rate. This was
important because we would have lost considerable foreign
exchange if devaluation applied to the bauxite industry.
Bauxite and alumina sales do not come to account in our
banking system. Our benefit derives from the dollars which are
sent to Jamaica from the US to pay for wages and other local
inputs into the industry.

The negotiations which commenced in April 1977 were soon
deadlocked. We then played our trump card. We raised the
matter with Prime Minister Jim Callaghan of Britain and Pierre
Trudeau. Both countries had directors on the Board of the
IMF. Callaghan had been through his own torment with the
IMF. I outlined the situation to them and enlisted their
support. Both promised to help and did. In fact, it was during
the week-end of the 1977 London Commonwealth Heads of
Government Conference. I was working on the Gleneagles
Agreement under which Commonwealth governments
promise to fight against apartheid in sport when Callaghan got
the news from the British director on the IMF Board that our
proposal had been accepted.

As a result of all this, the new agreement was far more
satisfactory than the formula originally proposed by the IMF.
The dual exchange rate had reduced the average value of the
Jamaican dollar by about 15% in comparison with the 40%
which was the original IMF position. Most importantly, the
goods on which the poor depended had been spared the huge

increases in price which the original plan entailed. There was to be a lot of controversy because of my attempts to explain the difference between a general devaluation of the normal kind and the rather complicated operation which had just been concluded. Because I used the phrase 'depreciation in the average value of our currency' as part of a general explanation, I was roundly attacked. That apart, however, we had an agreement. Additional foreign exchange would now become available and the country had a chance to settle down and try to work and produce its way out of its difficulties.

At around this time an economic mission visited Moscow. It was not immediately successful but laid foundations that were to lead to alumina marketing and other useful areas of co-operation later on.

IMF agreements of this kind include quarterly performance tests in which targets are set for a number of areas of activity. For example, at the end of each quarter the level of foreign reserves should be at a particular level; the amount of credit extended to the public and private sectors should be within certain totals and consistent with agreed proportions as between the two sectors; the net domestic assets ratio should stand at a certain level, and so on. These indicators are important guides to general performance and have to be monitored extremely carefully. Where the IMF is well disposed towards a particular client, they will actually help with the monitoring and point out ways in which last minute adjustments can be made which enable the client to pass the test. Depending upon the level of cordiality between IMF and client, tests can even be failed without precipitating a crisis because in certain circumstances a plea of 'guilty with explanations' will be accepted. Where the relationship is negative, however, no allowances are made.

Towards the end of the year, Coore became ill and had to have an operation. While he was recuperating and only partly back at work, the time for the December test was approaching. A number of meetings were held at his official residence, to deal with present and future questions affecting foreign exchange and the management of the economy. Among other things, we were trying to deal with an unexpected turn of events.

During 1976 I had visited Trinidad and Tobago, Barbados and Guyana to discuss the foreign exchange crisis. Dr. Eric

Williams, Errol Barrow and Forbes Burnham, the respective prime ministers, had all been extremely helpful within their means. Of course, only oil-rich Trinidad and Tobago was really in a position to offer substantial relief. Williams, a great figure in Caribbean history, was a man of moods. On this occasion he was at the top of his form. We worked out a broad trade agreement in which priority status would be afforded to certain types of goods being produced between us. Meantime, they would lend us US$50 million on normal commercial terms. This was a real help and we both felt that the trade agreement was a genuine step forward in the Caribbean integration process.

The loan was promptly forthcoming and equally promptly serviced as the months passed.

At the time when the IMF agreement of 1977 was made, Dr. Williams had agreed to a further loan of US$50 million as part of the foreign exchange package. This was no burden for Trinidad and Tobago whose reserves were then well over a billion TT dollars and rising with the world-wide tide of oil prices. We were a reliable customer with a good repayment record.

The problem was internal politics. A wave of criticism was sweeping Trinidad concerning loans to her Caribbean neighbours while roads needed fixing at home, to say nothing of the telephones which wouldn't work. A calypso summed up the mood with the words: 'Charity begins at home!' In fact it was a silly argument because the problem was not the loans, a drop in the financial bucket, but the capacity to spend money effectively. Trinidad had oil wealth, but was still a typical developing country. Like the rest of us, she lacked the administrative and technical capacity to spend money effectively. The sudden extra income from the new oil prices could not solve that problem.

But politics is not always about rational things. When the second US$50 million was well overdue and a new foreign exchange crisis upon us with some of the commercial sources lagging as well, a letter arrived. It was handwritten and from Dr. Williams. It spoke of political difficulties. The bottom line, literally and figuratively, was: no second loan! Coore, Barber, the bauxite team and myself were wrestling with all of this in our meetings. They thought they could find other ways out of the difficulties.

In the meantime, I had no indication of what was shortly to follow.

Early in December, I was due to pay my first official visit to Washington for talks with President Jimmy Carter. The day of the meeting came and, ironically, President Carter duly congratulated me on the success which he had been advised we were having with the economy. He was obviously under the impression that we had passed the December test. But it was upon my return to the hotel that evening that I received a call on the telephone from Jamaica. We had not passed, but failed.[3]

This news was nothing short of a disaster. It was taken as confirmation of the view being advanced by our critics at home that we were incapable of managing the economy. Far worse was the use to which it was put by the IMF. They obviously decided that their chance had now come to punish us and put us in our place for challenging their judgement in the first place. Then there was the matter of bringing political pressure to bear from Britain and Canada. This could not have endeared us to them.

The negotiations which were to follow would be one of the most ghastly experiences of my life. So great had been the blow to our credibility that I felt it absolutely necessary to make a change in the leadership of the financial team. The IMF programme called for rigorous monitoring on a day by day basis. I no longer had confidence that the team would be driven hard enough in this respect. The fact that the failure of the test took us by surprise was decisive in my mind.

Accordingly, I asked Coore, who was also the Deputy Prime Minister, to discuss an alternative senior post in the government so that I could name some new person as Minister of Finance. He was unwilling to move and so I had no alternative but to accept his resignation. This had a deep personal sadness for me because he had been my closest friend for all of 42 years, since the day, in fact, that we met as ten-year-olds at the school which we had both attended for nearly eight years.

Coore, a fine lawyer and a man of great charm, urbanity and high intelligence, left the government and public life and is now an official at the Inter-American Development Bank. I missed him and particularly his wit when things were darkest.

I named as new Minister of Finance Eric Bell, a man who had shown the qualities of a tough administrator. He had been first

Minister of Public Utilities, and for the last year was in charge of education. To him fell the unenviable task of negotiating the completely new agreement upon which the IMF insisted.

As it happened, it took us five months to complete this agreement which was finally concluded in May 1978. It must represent one of the most savage packages ever imposed on any client government by the IMF. They insisted upon the reunification of the exchange rate along with a further immediate general devaluation of 15%. Of course the unification was set at the lower level. This was to be followed by a crawling peg arrangement under which there would be a further mini-devaluation every two months. The cumulative effect of the crawling peg was to be 15%. The upshot of all this would result in a movement of the Jamaican dollar from a position slightly at better than parity to the US dollar to an exchange rate of J$1.76 for US$1.00. This was to be absorbed in a period of just over one year. There were to be further severe reductions in budget expenditure on social programmes together with the most massive tax package in the history of the country. Finally they demanded a mandatory limit on wage settlements of 15% per year in comparison with the predicted increase in the cost of living of at least 40%.

In the final days of the negotiation, the most conservative and pragmatic members of the Cabinet were in revolt, appalled at the wholesale slaughter that was being insisted upon. In the end, however, we could neither prevail upon the IMF to modify its position nor convince ourselves that any alternative source of foreign exchange could be found. We signed the agreement and announced it in parliament immediately.

The effect was devastating. Not only were there immediate increases in prices but the prospect that these would continue month after month for at least another year. These increases were, of course, to be in addition to those caused by the general international inflation which was continuing to rage and such local inflation as would have occurred in any event. The tax package would put further pressure on the people along with compression of demand. The budget cuts and the wage increase limits would complete the sad picture.

Even the private sector was shocked and contended immediately that the compression in demand was so great as to diminish the prospects of recovery severely. The IMF reply was bland. They were not expected to make a recovery in the local market but through the development of new export markets.

The union movement was in shock. They naturally rejected any notion of wage limits, but seemed more in a state of disbelief than anything else. Our excellent relations with the movement as a whole probably saved Jamaica from a terrible confrontation at that time. We did our best to rally the country. In the end, all one could feel was the disillusionment and bitterness on all sides.

All this dealt, as might be imagined, a severe blow to the party itself. Already divided on the question of dealing with the IMF, this latest agreement seemed to confirm the worst fears of the left wing. It must be said, however, that by now there was a general, if reluctant, agreement in the party that for the time being we did not have any choice.

The effect on the opposition was something else again. This was the break they had been waiting for. The government had gone to the people in the election on a particular basis. That campaign had been a consistent extension of more than four years of work in office. Now, everything was in contradiction and confusion. The 1978 IMF agreement was like the moment when a jet, having just landed, puts those mighty engines in reverse to achieve the quickest possible stop on the runway. By the second half of 1978, the jet was in reverse with a vengeance.

Throughout the rest of 1978 and into 1979, the experience with the IMF was harrowing. Naturally, a critical part of this kind of recovery programme is the foreign exchange which it is supposed to provide. The IMF itself does not provide all or even the bulk of the money which a country will need. In those days its own contributions were still relatively minor. What was important was to secure the IMF 'seal of approval'. Once the 'seal' was affixed, the private commercial banking system was supposed to come up with the rest of the money. In fact the IMF would work on these supplementary packages of commercial finance even as they were negotiating with a client government. The final agreement would indicate with absolute precision the amounts of additional foreign exchange which would be needed, the times at which the blocks of finance would become available, and the rough terms on which these would be provided.

In our experience it never worked out this way. There was never an occasion when the commercial banking system either came up with all that the plan called for or even produced lesser sums on time. In spite of Herculean efforts by Bell, Barber and Herbert Walker who had replaced Arthur Brown as Governor of the Bank of Jamaica, there were always shortfalls. The result was that our cash flow situation with respect to foreign exchange was never satisfactory. The shortgages would occur at the most awkward moments. Planning of the foreign exchange budget became almost impossible. Those manufacturers who had geared themselves for great efforts in patriotic and practical response to the needs of the situation would be frustrated because at critical moments they could not clear the licences that they needed. We could not clear the licences because the foreign exchange would not actually be there, although it was planned for in the agreement.

We attempted major improvements in the situation. The whole management of foreign exchange flows was put on a highly sophisticated basis. Careful budgets were worked out and efforts were made to improve and streamline the procedures for the granting of licences. Elaborate attention was paid to the balance between raw materials, spare parts, fertilisers, agricultural chemicals, drugs, essential foods.

The State Trading Corporation was established. It was an outstanding success enabling the government to buy food, drugs and building materials in bulk, and at the lowest prices from whoever made the best bids after international competitive tender. It also provided flexibility, permitting internal cross-subsidies for price sensitive items from the point of view of the poor.

We set up comprehensive systems of consultation with the major institutions. A National Planning Commission was established on which were represented the major bodies in the trade union movement, the Private Sector Organisation of Jamaica, which had recently been formed, the older bodies like the Jamaica Manufacturers' Association and the Chamber of Commerce and representatives of agriculture and the commodity associations. These would sit with the major technical officers of the government. There were weekly meetings under the chairmanship of the Minister of Finance, along with the key economic ministers in industry, agriculture, utilities, mining and labour.

There is a sense in which all of this was like providing a basket to carry water. As long as the foreign exchange was not forthcoming at the outset, the effort was doomed. By 1979 a number of fundamental things had become clear to me about the technical fallacy that underlies the IMF approach to Third World economies.

IMF demand management is predicated on two basic factors which are supposed to provide a particular result. The two factors are devaluation which reduces the demand for imports by making them expensive, while stimulating exports by making them comparatively competitive. The second factor is a compression of local demand by reducing government expenditure or increasing taxation or both so as to leave less spending money in the economy. Tight wage controls are imposed to ensure that both factors are effective. With less spending money in the economy the producer finds he can sell less on the local market and so is driven to make up his lost markets through exports. This is the 'stick' of the process. The 'carrot' of the process is that the devaluation has made his product more competitive overseas and so helps provide the opportunity for the market which he is driven to seek.

This is all well and good where you have a developed economy with substantial industrial, manufacturing and agricultural productive capacity in place. The medicine is then applied where this productive machine is not being fully utilised because the basic economic equations have gone out of kilter. If local costs, for example, have made exports uncompetitive, the system earns less. Where there has been a lot of surplus demand in the economy bringing in imports for its satisfaction, the system spends more. There would be a cumulative effect upon the country's reserves of foreign exchange because of increased expenditure upon imports. In due course, this would lead to a balance of payments crisis which would then be solved by the IMF demand management prescription.

For this prescription to work, two conditions should be present. Firstly, there must exist a productive capacity which can respond to the challenge and the opportunity which the medicine provides. Secondly, it is important for the society to have in place a system of social welfare which can shield the population from the worst effects of the medicine when it is first applied and before its benefits can begin to be felt. IMF medicine may produce temporary unemployment in the distributive trades that are accustomed to handling large imports. It will certainly provide sharp increases in prices which may bear down with intolerable effect upon the poor. All of this will be mitigated if there are the social welfare provisions that are now a standard part of the workings of the welfare state.

Now, let us consider the situation of the average Third World country. To begin with, one can assume that this type of economy is not blessed with a sophisticated productive apparatus in manufacturing and agriculture already in place and merely awaiting the right stimuli to produce. On the contrary, it is of the very nature of the Third World condition that development is what is needed and, by the same token, what is lacking. In the absence of developed factors of production, the stimulus of IMF medicine cannot apply by definition because there is little for it to work on. In the average Third World country, the problem is not the search for markets for, say, a sophisticated wheat farmer already capable of high levels of productivity. The problem is how to get a simple peasant hillside farmer to become an efficient producer in the first place; how to find the capital with which to help him terrace his hillside; how to find the money for the extension services to ensure that he is trained in the use of fertilisers and followed up, at first, to ensure that he applies the right ones at the right times in the right amounts; how to find the capital to provide him with some modicum of the modern machinery which is a key to agricultural productivity. The problems, therefore, are structural and fundamental. The right demand climate can provide the framework within which production increases but it cannot, as it is assumed to do in a developed country, create the increased productive capacity.

The basic premise of an IMF formula, therefore, is misconceived in the Third World situation. Given the need for the development of productive capability, typical two or three year IMF agreements simply miss the point of the Third World dilemma. One sees, therefore, a situation in which the population is subjected to severe pressure in pursuit of benefits that are unattainable. To compound the crisis, however, this social pressure is applied in a society which probably does not have the kind of social welfare system which can protect its people from the worst initial consequences of the medicine. Therefore, people are hurt in a situation where they enjoy no safety net and for gains which cannot materialise.

The IMF was created by the capitalist countries after World War II. It is designed to apply capitalist techniques and to serve the ends of those who created it originally. For developing economies this kind of short-term, sharp, demand management approach is inappropriate. What is needed is that the whole analysis should begin at a different point. The fact of the foreign exchange shortage is not the correct point of departure. That is to be found much earlier in the process by an examination of the structural deficiences of the particular economy. The approach should therefore begin with a plan for the development of the necessary productive capability. There should be no attempt to impose upon the client economy a particular type of economic model. If the country wishes to pursue a capitalist path — well and good. If they wish to pursue a socialist path — well and good. If theirs is a mixed economy option, so be it. Whichever the model, the search must be for the development of a productive capability that exploits the natural advantages of the society and aims for the most rapid development of its production for home needs and for trade. Clearly this contemplates development planning of seven to ten years' duration at least.

The second essential involves the provision of foreign exchange on a consistent and reliable basis over the period. Particular attention must be given to the foreign exchange that is needed early, up front: an economy cannot recover under a plan which begins to stumble and gasp for air at the very first hurdle because there is not enough oxygen for the system at the start. Thirdly, great care has to be taken with demand management itself lest the social shocks to which the population in the ailing economy is subject are greater than it can bear. In short, we need a genuine international institution, controlled internationally and flexible enough to assist different types of economies.

There has been an attempt to spread a *canard* to the effect that Third World countries do not want to manage their economies. Excepting corrupt regimes or the governments of deranged despots, this is just stupid. We never questioned IMF insistence on strict financial controls. We tried to apply these ourselves and were glad of their assistance in devising better methods. The quarrels were about strategies, time-spans, capacity to endure, levels of shock, maintenance of foreign exchange flows, relative roles for private and public sectors, and the like.

We have been constant critics of the IMF, not in pique but in the conviction that the body needs radical overhaul as part of sweeping changes in the world's economic system and the operation of the multilateral institutions which have emerged since World War II. There are signs recently that some of our criticisms have not gone unheeded. Certainly, we played a significant part in mobilising world opinion in favour of change; but nothing has happened to date to suggest that changes on the scale that are needed are likely to occur in the near future.

As I look back, I doubt if we ever really recovered from the 1978 package. In many respects worse was to follow. Indeed, could we but have seen into the minds of the people we might have discovered that 1978 was irreversible. The jet engines, once in reverse, did not again seem to develop forward thrust.

I certainly spent many hours at the time considering resigning either on behalf of the government or personally. In the end I rejected both and stayed on. It may have been my biggest personal mistake.

REACTION

12
OPPOSITIONS AND ENEMIES

Norman Manley was once bitterly criticised in a *Gleaner* editorial because he referred to the JLP opposition as 'the enemy'. It was nearing the end of the 1967 election and although the *Gleaner* put forward a rational argument, my sympathies were with him not only out of normal loyalty but because of the nature of the issue. He had just been the target for a sustained burst of gunshot while standing at the front of an open truck touring lower Kingston. It was only months before that we had been burying several supporters a week, casualties of what had been called 'The West Kingston War'. This had been serious enough to lead to the declaration of a State of Emergency by the JLP Government, and had ended with the complete destruction of any pretence at a PNP political machine in the constituency of that name.

In the months and years that were to follow the 1976 election, I came to develop a deep understanding of what must have prompted Norman Manley's choice of that word in preference to the term 'opposition'. A consummate lawyer and supremely rational man with a finely honed sense of the meaning and use of words, he never used terms lightly.

If plural democracy is to work it must rest upon two acts of self-restraint, firstly on the part of those who hold power, and secondly on the part of those who seek it. No constitution can provide for this. Rather, it must flow from an understanding of the delicate human balances that must be preserved. Power needs to be used; but a judgement has always to be exercised concerning the limits which must be imposed upon its use. Oppositions must oppose, but must likewise exercise judgement about the degree and the manner of that opposition. The Reichstag fire was a brilliant political tactic which wreaked havoc with the fortunes of the left within the democratic process of the German Weimar Republic in the 1930s. Hitler was the beneficiary and the world paid a high price for a classic case of political success achieved through methods which the democratic process simply cannot handle.

The West Kingston War is another, albeit smaller case in point. It was contested by supporters of the two political parties in the constituency of that name. Guns were brought into play in a consistent and systematic way. In the end one side achieved, through fear, a complete political dominance throughout the constituency.[1] It had been pretended, with utter cynicism, that the war was merely an attempt by the forces of the JLP to protect themselves against attack by the 'wicked' leftists of the PNP. Norman Manley, however, knew the truth and always felt that something evil and dangerous had been unleashed in the Jamaican political system. He felt that it was a clear example of Fascist methodology and was convinced that Jamaica would pay an increasing price in terms of our capacity to develop a viable plural democracy.

In spite of the events of 1966 and up to 1974. Jamaica had been essentially the scene of a politics of dialogue. Of course there was propaganda, some of it mindless, some nasty, some calculated, like the communist smear. There was often shocking favouritism in the distribution of scarce benefits, like work and housing for the poor. There was a certain amount of street fighting with stones and knives and even the West Kingston War itself, which was fought out with sidearms. But these had all been sporadic and restricted to the worst ghettoes in Kingston where they often owed as much to inter-gang hostility as to political calculation.

In 1974, the principal beneficiary of the West Kingston War took over the leadership of the JLP. Changes were soon apparent. In addition to the leakages out of the Ministry of Finance which soon attained haemorrhagic proportions, there was a rapid build-up in political violence and propaganda. Throughout 1975, there was a single-minded concentration along these lines. By-elections would be held and contested in the face of uniformly hysterical doses of the 'red' smear. In every by-election, the JLP would be routed in results that indicated that our mass support was firm and not responding to the propaganda. Still it was maintained.

It was only in 1976 that I began to understand the reasoning behind a tactic which was not working by any visible, objective measure on the surface of the democratic process. Then the coin dropped. The tone of a document like 'Operation Werewolf' which had been discovered in 1976 suggested the mood of a religious crusade. By then, other bits of information were coming to hand. The pattern was clear.

The new point of the communist smear was that it created a condition in which people could be brought to a frenzy of alarm. In turn, the alarm triggered would create an atmosphere in which violence would be seen not as aimed at the destruction of the democratic process but at its preservation! In a stroke, the image of political violence, so normally abhorrent to the great majority of Jamaican people, could be transformed into the virtuous struggle to 'save democracy' itself. Here was a pretty variant on the Reichstag fire theme. Only this time, a fictional enemy was first created and then the 'fire' openly set. Thereafter, the act would be clothed in virtue in the eyes of those who could see only the enemy that had been created.

The attack upon the legitimacy of the government began with allegations that the election had been stolen. There was, in fact, a weakness in our electoral system to which no one has yet found an answer.[2] The weakness is revealed wherever three conditions are present. One party must be overwhelmingly strong in a particular community; the community itself must be prone to violence; and the political machine in the particular area must either intend to exploit this combination of factors or fail to control them. Where all this happens, the party with the controlling strength is able to take charge of the particular polling station, refusing to allow the few, terrified supporters of the other side anywhere near the polling booth. Thereupon the controlling side can proceed to stuff the ballot box until the name of every voter has been used in support of the candidate of their choice. This is shocking and completely undemocratic. It had its counterparts in certain wards of the Chicago system, particularly in the days of Mayor Daley. But the effect of all this upon the outcome of a national election in Jamaica is about as great as the effect the Chicago wards used to have on the presidential elections of the United States.[3]

However a programme was orchestrated by the opposition which had as its premise, sometimes spoken, sometimes not, that the electoral system was a veritable quagmire of corruption — somehow more so in 1976 than in previous elections. This despite the fact that in 1977 we had entered into bi-partisan discussion with the JLP to see what could be done to improve the system.

The second leg of the attack on the government was directed at me personally. There is no need here to go into the details of the vilification to which I was subject. In the picture that emerged I was a strange hybrid, suspended somewhere between tyrant, liar, mismanager and weakling. But I leave the portraits to future historians.

Throughout these years, incidents of every kind, large or small, grave or trivial, were seized upon to create an impression of corruption. Lies and misrepresentation were plentiful. I began to understand how in the hallowed name of press freedom, newspapers like *El Mercurio* in Chile and our own *Gleaner* used existing freedoms to pursue tactics clearly aimed not only at character assassination, but more significantly at spreading panic: at destabilisation.

Shades of Chile, too, when in 1979, the government was subject to an employers' strike 'to protest against the crippling economic conditions and official brutalities'. Then there was the propaganda capital to be made out of a strike against petrol prices throughout the inland but particularly in tourist areas where it was sure to hurt the most; our foreign policy; our friendly relations with Cuba.[4] According to the local and foreign press, there were thousands of Cuban troops in Jamaica, presumably hidden somewhere in the country along with mysterious radio transmitting masts. The US government, of course, was equally worried about these 'friendly relations', but more about that in due course.

By the middle of 1979, it was beginning to be clear that the economy was not turning around. The substantial negative growth which had occurred earlier in the first shock of external crisis and local reaction to change had abated. It was as if the decline was bottoming out but with no real sign that we would start climbing. There was never enough foreign exchange. This put a premium on accurate planning. But the planning work carried out by the various sectors was often shoddy and some elements in the private sector were clearly more interested in political propaganda than hard work. Some sections of the economy, it is true, performed magnificently in spite of the difficulties. There was hardly a year that the small farmers did not record an increase in production which would be reflected in the domestic agriculture sector of the gross domestic product. The Jamaica Exporters Association, comprised mainly of younger businessmen in the export field, was patriotic and energetic. Under the leadership of successive, dynamic presidents, they set an unfailing example to the rest of the country which might have fared differently had others followed. The small business sector was bursting with energy and ideas at the time. It is the spectacular growth of this sector together with the tens of thousands of small farming opportunities created by the Land Reform programme which account for an interesting fact about unemployment.

During the great period of massive investments and steady growth in GDP from 1962 to 1972, unemployment moved from 12% to 24%. From 1972 to the last quarter of 1980 unemployment moved less than 3% more, from 24% to 26.8%. Both figures reflect social disaster, but the comparison is still profoundly significant. In nine years from 1972 to 1981, GDP had declined a cumulative total of 25%, an average of nearly 3% per annum. In the period 1962 to 1972, GDP had virtually doubled in real terms and yet unemployment had increased by 12% as against the 3% in our time.

This second term in office witnessed two milestones, one political and the other social. The parties reached an agreement that led to the establishment of an Electoral Advisory Committee which was charged with the implementation of a number of agreed reforms in the electoral system. The constitution was to be amended to entrench a permanent Independent Electoral Commission. As part of these understandings, the opposition accepted our insistence that Jamaica make the final break with the British monarchy and become a republic with appropriate constitutional amendments at the same time as those entrenching the electoral body.

In the social field, we introduced legislation requiring the registration of fathers, a companion to the Status of Children Act and the establishment of the Family Courts. The new piece of major social legislation was the new Maternity Leave (With Pay) Act. This completed the quiet revolution in the legal status of the Jamaican working classes and, particularly, women. As important as the legal specifics of these various acts may have been, the change in the workers' perception of their status in society and the society's perception of the workers' place was even more critical. This had undergone a radical transformation.

The Maternity Leave Act was our last specific confrontation with the business classes. As usual, there was everything from supplication to threat. Dark mutterings about another employers' strike could be heard. The case for protection was unanswerable. The average poor mother faced childbirth in a state of unrelieved anxiety. At the very moment when her financial needs were greatest, to say nothing of her need for a sense of security, she faced the loss of everything. In the face of widespread employer resistance, we passed the Act providing for job security and a minimum of three months leave (two with full pay). It was modest but a beginning.

As the year drew to a close we once again headed for trouble with the IMF tests. The IMF were to claim that they had warned Minister of Finance Bell and that important areas of financial control over the Budget were slipping. Between the accounts given by the IMF's representative on the Jamaica case, Omar Albertelli, Financial Secretary Barber and Bell himself, it was never possible to decide finally who or what was to blame. Meantime the economy was not responding, and by December we had failed more than one test.[5]

This failure occurred in spite of continuing efforts. In the attempt to improve efficiency and restrain costs, we had carried out a major reorganisation of the government reducing the number of ministries from 20 to 13, along with a number of realignments in the administrative apparatus. Feeling that agriculture was going to prove critical, I decided, after long thought and careful consultation with my colleagues, to take over the agriculture portfolio myself. I started a series of sectoral analyses to try to locate the blocks standing in the way of revival in crops like sugar and bananas. At the same time, I held staff meetings all over the island, trying to infuse a new sense of dedication and purpose.

The failure of the tests in December 1979 precipitated another of those interminable pauses in economic planning while a new IMF agrement was being worked out. In the interim a meeting with the United States administration was to give me cause for reflection.

13
NON-ALIGNMENT AND US PRESSURE

The smiles were polite, but there was an underlying tension. Former US Ambassador to the United Nations, Andrew Young, was to my immediate right; across from me on a couch was State Department veteran, Phillip Habib, at that time President Carter's Special Representative for Latin American Affairs. Away to my left was Bob Pastor, one of Carter's bright young men and a member of the National Security Council. With me were Dudley Thompson, now Minister of National Security, and Danny Williams, our Minister of Industry and Commerce. It was December 1979, and I had just finished addressing a large group of American and Caribbean businessmen who were holding a conference on Caribbean economic affairs and investment possibilities in a Miami hotel.

It was about midnight, and after pleasantries which were more perfunctory than usual, we were settling down to a serious discussion in my suite high above the Convention Hall where I had spoken. This meeting had been arranged at the President's request and it was soon clear that Habib was to play the leading role on their side. Andy Young had been removed as UN Ambassador in response to Zionist pressure some time before, but was still personally close to the Carters. He alone seemed perfectly relaxed and at ease as always.

I knew that the US administration had been very upset by the speech which I had made barely three months before at the Non-Aligned Summit Meeting in Havana, Cuba. They had affected to be hurt and angry because I had said that I would be happier if the Puerto Rican people were to choose independent status. They chose to ignore the care with which I had insisted that, whatever other people's preferences might be, the choice was theirs alone to make and could only be made by democratic means. I had already been over this ground with the greatest of care with the US Ambassador in Kingston and suspected that the objection to the speech rested upon deeper foundations than any question involving Puerto Rico's political status.

All this was very much in my mind as I looked across at Habib indicating that it was time to get down to business.

I gave Habib, a veteran if ever there was one, full marks for the element of surprise. Before uttering a word, he reached into the inside pocket of his jacket and produced a document. Fixing me with an accusing look, doubtless practised in long years of international bargaining, he charged me with allowing the People's National Party to accuse the United States of destabilising Jamaica. I reacted with genuine astonishment since, whatever suspicions might have been harboured by many and convictions held by some, the PNP had not been making that charge during the Carter Administration. I wondered, as I was supposed to, what document was being held with such confidence in his hand.

Habib went on to say that the document had been circulated at a meeting of the National Executive Council of the Party, held recently in Montego Bay, and accused the United States of interfering in Jamaica's internal affairs. My astonishment deepened because, for the life of me, I could remember no such document and could only assume that Habib was describing the contents of the paper accurately.

Suppressing an urge to ask him how he came by the document, as if I couldn't have guessed, I asked to see it. Literally wondering what I would find in it, I settled back to read. At this stage my astonishment was complete, but for a different reason. It was a short pamphlet, most of which consisted of direct quotes from a US Army Manual on Psychological Warfare. The Manual, which was properly identified in the pamphlet, set out a number of recommended steps for creating alarm and despondency among the enemy, and a state of confusion and panic in the ranks of the civilian population. No particular country is identified, but it sets out various elements of a methodology which it claims can be depended upon to work in any situation where the need arises. The Manual reflects the US passion for reducing everything to a simple, explanatory guide. It is written with that absence of passion which characterises the instruction sheet which you might get with anything from a US-made vacuum cleaner to an infant's feeding chair.

The PNP pamphlet not by so much as a word suggested that the US was doing any of these things in Jamaica at the time. It was obviously intended to warn that these techniques could be used in Jamaica and recommended that the techniques themselves be studied carefully so that the people could be warned of dangers that might lie ahead. I had never seen the document myself but was immediately struck by the similarity between some of the methods suggested in the manual, as quoted in the document, and things actually happening in Jamaica at that very time. I pointed out that the paper did not support his complaint and that we were not, in fact, accusing the US of destabilising Jamaica at that time.

To the extent that Habib had clearly failed to read the document carefully, and based his surprise attack on a false premise, the ploy backfired. However, that was really beside the point. He and Pastor had come to go over the whole question of US-Jamaica relations, Cuba's role in the Caribbean, and a number of issues that flowed from all of that. Young had clearly come to listen.

As I had originally expected, we then dealt with the Havana speech. We covered the Puerto Rican ground again. We dealt with my reference in the speech to Fidel Castro as one of those figures who come to symbolise a turning point in history. Apart from the courtesy which one owes to the host and chairman at a major international gathering, I would have thought the matter self-evident if not platitudinous. Apparently, the obvious rankled.

I think it was Pastor who then came to the real point, which was the general tone of the speech. He reminded me that Carter had offered the hand of friendship at the start of his term of office and I reminded him that I had accepted it gladly. He retorted with a reference to the general anti-imperialist tone of the speech asserting that this had to be equated with an anti-US position. I suppressed a rejoinder about 'caps fitting' and instead went into yet another careful exposition of our foreign policy.

I reminded them of the complexity and heterogeneous nature of the US political and economic system. I traced the history of the present world economic system, the extent to which it is dominated by multinational corporations and financial institutions, the effect which the system has upon Third World countries and our determination to work to change it. I pointed out that I had always spoken of our friendship with and affection for the US people as people. I ended by saying that just as I would never abandon the struggle to which I was committed, equally would I never tire of trying to explain to the American people that the problem is not with them, but with the multinational corporations which act in their name, over which they have no control and which earn for the American people such a bad reputation abroad.

Pastor then turned to Cuba and I wondered that it had taken so long. At this point, I was not so much speaking as hearing myself say for the umpteenth time what I believed to be true. I drew a careful distinction between the days of Che Guevara, of which I confessed I knew little and had no direct experience, and the present. I spoke of the Cubans in the Caribbean as we had known and dealt with them for nearly eight years. I said that Cuba had long since come to terms with detente, peaceful co-existence and the acceptance of a pluralist world in which different societies with different histories and at different levels of development pursued different economic and political paths.

I urged a very important point. As Marxist-Leninists, the Cubans do not believe that revolutions are created by a subjective desire to have one. Objective conditions must exist before they are possible. Our experience of the Cubans indicated that they were too sophisticated to go running around encouraging childish enthusiasts to confuse their subjective desires with objective realities. In addition, as a small country, they were deeply committed to the principle of respect for sovereignty and the non-interference in the affairs of others which is the critical reverse side of that coin. Hence their care in staying out of other countries' normal political problems and disputes. Obviously if a genuine liberation process were struggling against an obvious tyranny, they would help. But then, I pointed out, so would I and many others. Perez of Venezuela, Torrijos of Panama, Portillos of Mexico had all given strong support to the Sandinistas against Somoza in Nicaragua. Who, I asked, had ever accused them of plotting revolution or even of interference on that account?

I ended by urging them to stress to the President what a service he would render to us all in the Western hemisphere if he were to act boldly and establish a mini-detente in the Caribbean. The normalisation of relations between the US and

Cuba would remove an unending source of tension throughout the region.

I could never say that they specifically asked me to downgrade our relations with Cuba or anything as crude as that. They spoke of the role that I could play in the Caribbean and I pointed out that I had always been totally committed to CARIFTA and CARICOM and the Caribbean integration process generally.

Granada and its revolutionary government came up for inevitable mention. I said that I thought it was a serious mistake for the US to behave with hostility to Maurice Bishop's government, which could only drive him to react correspondingly. I reminded them that external pressure upon any revolutionary government forces the radicalisation of the internal process. Surely the wiser course was to hold out the hand of friendship. I suggested that a friend can advise moderation with some hope of response. An enemy can demand what he likes with no hope of attention.

The talk went on for three hours with Habib saying less and Pastor more as time wore on. Andy said little throughout but was clearly listening with the closest attention. He hardly needed to speak because my views were strikingly like those he expressed from time to time. In fact, he had been constantly in trouble with the US Establishment because of his refusal to be a part of the simplistic claptrap which passes for analysis in the establishment view of Cuba and the Third World. As old friends, Andy and I knew where we agreed and where we agreed to differ. Much of what I was saying was similar to the view that he had urged with less and less success as the Carter administration began to flounder towards the end.

It was after 3:00am when we saw our guests to the hotel elevator. I sent my regards to the President. As they left, I was sure that the discussion had accomplished nothing. There was nothing that I could concede, no ground that I could offer to yield because the positions we held flowed from a set of principles and a body of experience.

This meeting took place soon after the Havana Summit of the Non-Aligned Movement. This had opened to a blatantly unfair piece of US interference. President Carter accused Cuba of breaking the Krushchev-Kennedy understandings reached after the missile crisis of 1962. It was claimed that the Soviets had suddenly increased their military presence in the island and a build-up of US forces in Florida was announced. It is difficult to describe how deeply this angered the great majority of the delegations in Havana. It was so obviously untrue, so clearly a case of CIA disinformation that a child would have seen through it. Carter himself was a victim of a move by Senator Frank Church who had sought to forestall a right-wing attack in his state of Idaho by himself pre-empting the story of the alleged Soviet build-up in Cuba. Carter, then under increasing pressure, had done his own pre-empting.

This problem aside, the conference reflected an increasing concern with economic issues. OPEC members began, at last, to enter into serious dialogue about energy and the role of oil surpluses in Third World development. Both Venezuela and Mexico attended as observers and we had valuable talks about a Venezuela-Mexico oil rebate scheme for their Caribbean Basin customers. This was eventually to provide 30% relief on the price with the difference turned into a balance of payments loan convertible to development purposes. The details took a long time to iron out and it actually went into effect the month after we left office!

Meantime my speech enraged the establishment at home and was to cause concern in Washington. I realised that we represented an enigma to many US policy-makers. The 'hawks' could simply dismiss us as crypto-communist surrogates of Moscow via Havana and conclude that we must be removed forthwith. To the more sophisticated exponents of US foreign policy, the 'doves' of the liberal establishment, it could not have been that simple. We were obviously democratic. One could pick any day at random and know that there was the fullest freedom of speech and press. Our human rights record was untarnished. We had never so much as threatened much less expropriated a dollar's worth of US property, or anyone else's for that matter. We had a vigorous opposition which had operated without let or hindrance even during the State of Emergency. From the point of view of the classic liberal, the credentials were impeccable. Yet the position was frankly anti-imperialist, aggressively non-aligned, openly trying to maintain good relations with Latin America, with Western Europe, and with Washington and Ottawa; but equally with Moscow and Havana.

We had made peace with our bauxite companies but were working assiduously to establish an internationally owned bauxite-alumina-aluminium company which would mine bauxite and process alumina in Jamaica for state-owned smelters in Mexico, Algeria and Iraq with the balance of the production going to the Soviet Union. The technology for this alumina plant was to be Hungarian. Algeria and Iran had agreed to provide finance for the equity. An English finance house was mobilising the loan finance. Much of the equipment was to come from West Germany; and an American firm, Kaiser Engineers, had been approached to be the principal construction contractors.

At the same time, we were working with the government of Norway and the American multinational corporation Alcoa on an expansion of Alcoa's alumina plant in Jamaica in a Norway-Alcoa-Jamaica partnership. Simultaneously, our advocacy of the New International Economic Order had made us, with Algeria, the foremost exponents of that cause in the world even as we continued to give open and vigorous support to the liberation struggles in Nicaragua and Southern Africa. Clearly we did not fit into any familiar pattern and were, therefore, a source of puzzlement if not irritation. I kept explaining that we were neither Puerto Rico nor Cuba but were just another country searching for that 'third way'.

Earlier that year Carter had casually asked me about Castro and Cuba over lunch. The discussion was courteous and frank. He obviously wanted to hear my views. One bit of the conversation will always stand out in my mind. We were discussing Angola and the typical US reaction to it. I had stated the position as our research had revealed it; as my trusted African friends had confirmed it; and as Fidel Castro had always stated it. The President disagreed on one critical point of fact. He said that evidence had been shown to him which indicated that Cuban combat troops had been crossing the Atlantic by ship prior to the South African invasion from their Namibian bases. He did not claim that Cuban troops were in Angola but that they were on the high seas. I replied that this was absolutely contrary to our information which indicated that construction workers, teachers, doctors, administrators, nurses and even military advisers could have been involved either in Angola or on the high seas up to that point, but not combat troops. He stuck to his guns and I to mine. Since then I have probed the matter again and remain convinced that we are not only right but that our version is consistent with the logical unfolding of events. No one has ever offered to show me this evidence which so conveniently contradicts the commonsense of the matter.

We had nearly caught Carter's sympathetic interest once before at the end of 1978 when we held a meeting at Runaway Bay involving Chancellor Helmut Schmidt of the Federal Republic of Germany, General Ulusegun Ubasanju, Head of the Military Government of Nigeria, Prime Minister Udvar Nordli of Norway, Perez of Venezuela, Trudeau of Canada and myself as host and chairman. I had discussed the idea of the conference with Andy Young by telephone after the basic idea emerged between Schmidt and myself in Hamburg. Both members of the Socialist International, we had met there to talk about the whole state of the North-South dialogue. We had decided to try a small, informal gathering of carefully chosen heads of state who could spend a couple of days looking at the problems and possibilities in a confidential and unstructured way. I offered to host and Schmidt liked the idea. Young liked it too and promised to discuss it with the President, due to meet with the North's Big Seven shortly after the Jamaica meeting. But Carter was persuaded to decline the Jamaican invitation on grounds of pressure. As it happened, the Runaway Bay meeting went very well. In fact, the Common Fund negotiations which were then hopelessly stalled in Geneva soon recorded a breakthrough which led to an agreement in principle about the Fund itself.

Although Carter himself had a sympathetic ear for the New International Economic Order, political developments intervened before he could devote serious attention to it and to the North-South dialogue as a whole. Cuban troops went to the support of Mengitsu, whose Ethiopian revolution was under attack, and predictably outraged the Carter Administration. In due course this was to be followed by the Iranian revolution, the Iranian hostage crisis and Afghanistan. The days of Carter's attention to any question of reform in the world economic system were numbered.

14
THE BREAK WITH THE IMF

Throughout 1979 there was a growing sense in the ranks of the PNP that the IMF programme was getting nowhere in terms of economic recovery. The party was deeply conscious of the complete loss of momentum, the drastic curtailment of expenditure on the social front. In a more profound sense, it resented the intrusion of a foreign authority which seemed to the average PNP supporter to hold almost sovereign sway over Jamaica's internal affairs. To him, the situation was fraught with contradiction. Group leaders claimed to find it almost impossible to deal with the membership and it did not take a political genius to detect that the party was losing ground steadily at its critical grass roots.

All of this was uppermost in the mind of every delegate at the Annual Conference of 1979. In 1978, three complete days had been devoted to the party's policy and had made history when the final plank of the policy was hammered into place as midnight approached on the third day. Now, three days had to be set aside for the discussion of the economy and future economic strategy.

Once again, some 2,000 delegates participated in nearly thirty hours of non-stop discussion. PNP democracy is no ordinary phenomenon. Hour after hour, the delegates from town and country, from bauxite plant and sugar mill, from tiny hillside holding to Kingston's waterfront, from trained professional to unemployed ghetto youth, said their piece. Well over 100 took part in that epic debate. No one felt that the present strategies could work, although few could voice their concern in terms of standard economic jargon.

The upshot of this marathon effort was a decision to set up an economic commission to carry out an exhaustive review of economic strategy and performance since the first IMF agreement in 1977. It would have full access to ministers, who were to be given every opportunity to explain policies and defend strategies.

Having reviewed the past in the light of the party's principles and objectives — a job made difficult because of the traditional resistance of civil servants to outside meddling — the commission was to turn its attention to the future. In four month's time, it was to make preliminary recommendations concerning future economic strategy and policy with particular reference to the IMF.

Accordingly, in January 1980 two critical exercises were converging: the negotiations between government and the IMF for a new agreement to replace the one which was abrogated with the failure of the December tests; the examination of basic economic strategy by the party commission. Once again, the first exercise proceeded against a background of trouble. Foreign exchange drawings were suspended as before and the economy suffered further damage. The IMF was insisting upon more massive cuts in expenditure and seemed, as usual, to be offering too little foreign exchange too late. Not even they had the nerve to propose a further devaluation but were insisting on lowering the wage increase guidelines from 15% to 10%. Unless we were to do something insane, like shutting down a number of schools or hospitals, we could only hope to close the gap by firing about 15,000 workers.

Meanwhile the commission, having analysed recent developments and canvassed views of party members throughout the island, advanced a preliminary conclusion at the delegates' meeting. They were of the view that it would be impossible to develop the Jamaican economy in a manner consistent with our principles and objectives within the framework of agreements made with the IMF. They saw an absolute and disabling contradiction between the philosophy of the IMF and the model of economic development on which its programmes were predicated, on the one hand, and the goal of a socially controlled, egalitarian society seeking to maximise its independence of economic action, on the other. They recommended unanimously that the government should, at some appropriate time, disengage from the IMF. The mood of the conference was overwhelmingly in favour of this basic recommendation.

I made a careful speech reminding delegates of the complex and delicate nature of a country's economy. I concurred in the view that Jamaica should not remain dependent on IMF-type programmes for its salvation. However, I stressed the importance of timing and planning; and proposed that the commission be charged to come back to a special NEC meeting with the most precise answers possible about the timing and implementation of an alternative plan.

By March 8, when the NEC met, the political equation had changed radically. I had announced five weeks before, on February 3, that there would be a new election as soon as the Independent Electoral Advisory Committee could advise me that the new machinery for elections was ready and in place. The news took the country completely by surprise and involved one of the most difficult decisions I ever took in my public life.

I had two major concerns, neither of which had to do with electioneering tactics. Firstly, it seemed to me that the Jamaican system was coming apart under the pressure of events. Such was the state of hysteria, tension, fear and bitterness in the society that I feared for our ability to continue to function effectively as a national community. It seemed pointless to me to continue to preside over a society increasingly succumbing to paralysis merely because I had the constitutional right to another two years in office. I reasoned that it must be better to create a situation in which the issues could be put to the vote and determined.

The new electoral system would hopefully ensure that the legitimacy of the government that emerged would be beyond question. It would be important that the resulting election be contested in a manner that put the issue of basic economic strategy squarely to the people so that the vote could be treated as a mandate by the winning side. I was encouraged to hope that this last might be made possible by the fact that there were such clear differences between the two sides and their view of national and international policy.

The second consideration involved the IMF itself. Like the overwhelming majority of my party colleagues, I could see no long-term future with that body under its present policies, management and control. It seemed to me that the sooner Jamaicans were forced to make a choice between the IMF path, with its clear implications for deeper and deeper dependence on the Puerto Rican model, and a more self- reliant alternative, the better. But I had no illusions. I knew fully well that the self-reliant path which we might plan to take in the future would require levels of dedication and sacrifice beyond anything in the past experience of the present generation of Jamaican people.

It was still the 'third path' of our original intentions. But now we knew far more about the demands that such a course makes upon the people. Furthermore, we now had the fullest grasp of the extent to which the international economic environment had changed since those simpler times in 1972! Although the 1976 election should have set the stage for such an enterprise, the fact is that it did not. The issues of that election had become unfocused. They were lost somewhere between a mass euphoria induced by the unprecedented range of social and legislative changes, non-specific proclamations of socialist intent and anger over violence and 'red smear' propaganda. Too little attention had been given to the development of an understanding of the demands which could be made on the people and their institutions. We paid a high price for our failure to implement and maintain an effective programme of political education during the two years following the announcement of democratic socialism in September 1974.

Now it seemed to me that only an election announced with a lead time of approximately eight months could create the conditions in which one could hope to confront the people with a choice which they might understand. Such a decision would have to include a choice between a future with the IMF and all which that implied, this being the JLP alternative; and a future without the IMF and all which that implied, the PNP alternative. Whatever the outcome, I was convinced that the whole country had to make the choice.

I put my thoughts to my closest colleagues who agreed after exhaustive discussion of the pros and cons. It is noteworthy that the decision was taken by all these political leaders in the face of the knowledge that our own polls showed us far behind the JLP at the time.

Hence, when the NEC met on March 8, 1980, to hear the further report of the Economic Commission and the latest report on the IMF negotiations, it did so in a new political situation. Elections would be at most seven or eight months away. It turned out that neither team, commission nor Cabinet, could make a full report. The commission's calculations with respect to foreign exchange contained obvious gaps. On the IMF side, the negotiations simply were not concluded. It was clear that the NEC was more firm than ever in its determination to break with the IMF, but I was equally determined to have no decision until both exercises were sufficiently advanced to provide the kind of information on which serious decisions of the gravest national importance could be based.

It was beginning to be clear that the early election was facilitating one point of consensus. I sensed a virtual unanimity around the idea that we should fight the election campaign on a clear and unequivocal assurance that we would discontinue our relationship with the IMF and seek a mandate for the kind of economic strategy and national effort which such a course of action would demand. In the meantime, the party seemed to be dividing around the question of whether there should be an immediate break with the IMF, contesting the election from that position; or whether there should be a final IMF agreement to cover the next year as far as the economy was concerned and provide the time to put in place an alternative foreign exchange strategy. In the end, we adjourned for a final two weeks to give the commission time to address the gaps in its presentation and the Cabinet time to complete its research of the exact and final shape which an IMF agreement could take, down to the last comma.

The final meeting of the NEC was held on March 22, 1980, in the Hotel Intercontinental in Ocho Rios on the North Coast. It was to last into the night. By now the commission had done more work and its final document had gone a long way to cover the deficiencies that were so glaring two weeks before. It was still, however, stronger in what it could promise in the long run, than if there were to be an immediate break. It had clear soft spots. For example, it assumed that multilateral institutions such as the World Bank could be persuaded to forego repayment of principal on their various loans and programmes in Jamaica for periods of time to be negotiated. There was no concrete basis for this other than the assumption that it should be possible. This proved to be wrong. It correctly predicted that a number of progressive European countries would continue to support us even in the new context of a break with the IMF. It wrongly assumed that Britain would keep in place funds that were already in the pipeline. It correctly predicted a willingness on the part of the commercial banks who had lent us money to negotiate roll-over provisions with respect to payments of principal. It correctly indicated a number of areas in which the cash flow situation could be adjusted. It assessed accurately the benefits to flow from the Venezuela-Mexico oil facility although it was a little optimistic, as were the rest of us, as to how soon the facility would actually be put in place.

It was clearly over-optimistic about the loans which Jamaica could raise from other sources and, in particular, OPEC countries. On the other hand, it correctly assessed the range of suppliers' credits that could be put in place in Socialist bloc countries and elsewhere among progressive members of the Western European Community and with our Third World friends generally.

The IMF agreement which we could make was similarly flawed. Last minute adjustments in the foreign exchange flows had been secured and made it a more viable package, from that point of view, than anything previously considered. It was still unconscionably harsh in the area of budget cuts and still seemed to imply a considerable lay-off programme, though this would not have to be as heavy as originally thought. On the other hand, the party's economic commission was equally clear about the need for strict control on expenditure and the budget which their plan contemplated involved no 'gravy train'. This was very much to their credit.

The real problem with the IMF programme was, as one might have guessed, with the performance tests. It had emerged in cabinet in the course of the week leading up to the NEC meeting that the way the tests were being proposed by the IMF would inevitably create a crisis point at the time of the September tests. This arose because Jamaica's foreign exchange earnings are seasonal in a number of respects. One test, the Net International Reserves Test, which requires particular levels of reserves in the Central Bank at specific times, did not properly reflect the seasonality of our foreign exchange flows. The test called for higher levels of reserves than could possibly have been achieved. We had all by then become well versed in the problems that follow upon the failure of an IMF test. While the new negotiations are set in train, the economy starts to gasp for the oxygen which it needs.

When we met in Ocho Rios, Bell was obliged to advise me that he could not guarantee to the NEC that we could pass the test. I opened the proceedings with the most careful presentation of which I was capable. Hours of discussion ensued, but in the end the factor that proved to be decisive was the profound and, by now, engrained suspicion of the IMF. The intentions of its officials and decision-makers towards a Government of our type was simply not trusted. Against this background the question of the Net International Reserves Test became critical. Speaker after speaker was to point out that if we failed it, literally weeks before an election, our situation would be irretrievable. Not only would this be the final confirmation of the enemy propaganda about mis-management, but the foreign exchange flows themselves would be abruptly cut off on the eve of an election. Surely, they argued, the position would be untenable. Others pointed out that it might still be possible to persuade the IMF to modify the test. To which the reply came that we had no protection against the possibility that IMF hostility might act against us to such an extent that if this test were not failed, something else would be made to go wrong. Speakers reminded the conference of the consistent failure of the IMF to deliver the concurrent private banking finance on time. They stressed the dislocations that this had caused. What guarantee would we have, they asked, that the same would not happen again? They argued that the danger would be even greater on the eve of an election which so many forces in the US economic, military and political establishment obviously wished us to lose.

The truth of the matter is that the history of the last two and three-quarter years made the outcome a foregone conclusion. Late that night the debate closed and it was time to decide. Two votes were put: the first asked whether there should be a permanent break with the IMF. This was understood to mean immediately after the elections at latest and that the election should be contested on that basis. This vote was unanimously 'yes'. Later, Bell alone was to ask that he be recorded as against that proposition.

The second vote asked whether the break should be immediate or post-election. By a 2-1 majority the NEC voted for the break there and then. The actual score was 103 to 45 with four abstentions.

I immediately offered to resign on the grounds that I had led the movement during the last two and three-quarter years on a path that had included successive agreements with the IMF. I said I felt it to be very important that the movement should consider whether it needed a new leader in the new circumstances.[1] I made this offer with the deepest seriousness and believe it was understood in that light, but it was instantly and overwhelmingly rejected. The alternative path had its ups and downs. The private sector were apoplectic at first. The opposition predicted for the hundredth time or so that the economy was about to collapse. In fact, they had first predicted its early demise as inevitable in the course of 1976. Now it was four years later and, tough as things might be, the economy was still alive and kicking. In fact, we now know that unemployment was actually declining from a high of 31% in late 1979 to 26.8% by late 1980. At the very moment when this was happening, the opposition and much of the foreign press were proclaiming an unemployment rate approaching 40%. Never mentioned was the fact that the 31% was a freak result. Terrible floods in 1979 had put great numbers of small farmers off their holdings and on to the lists of those seeking work. This was duly reflected in the figures for October and used to press the claim that we had collapsed. Such is the regard which propaganda pays to fact.

With hindsight one can measure precisely the successes and the failures of the alternative path in its first, and only, seven months. We were disappointed to the extent that the foreign exchange targets were not met. On the other hand, the predictions stood up or were exceeded in bauxite, tourism, non-traditional exports, domestic food production, and agricultural exports, except bananas and sugar. In the end, we fell 15% short of the foreign exchange target. It will be debated for a long time whether this was an unacceptable margin having regard to the minimal nature of the predicted figures, or whether this represented a reasonable level of performance.

Interestingly enough, the economy did not collapse, proving yet again that economies are more resilient than their principal actors care to admit. I do not doubt that the foreign exchange situation continued to benefit from the 'invisible' results of the ganja trade. I suspect, equally, that the raw materials situation received support from an unexpected but understandable quarter. Some businessmen, calculating on a JLP victory, used the dollars which they had 'salted away' illegally in the US, to finance raw materials and other inputs during the period up to the election. They would have preferred this course to a possible shut-down involving the problems of a future start-up should their party win. This was nothing more than a marginal factor but is associated with an amusing sidelight on the character of this type of operator. As soon as the JLP won, the repatriation of their illegal overseas capital ceased. Once again, the patriotism of this kind of Jamaican was to succumb to the more cynical dictates of self-interest.

In weighing performance at home, one factor must be remembered. We suffered from the fact that many things went into limbo because the election was known to be in the offing. For example, in the international community some feared seeming to favour the government side by offering assistance and made it clear they would act as soon as a result was declared, regardless of the outcome.

The break with the IMF was regarded by the opposing forces at home and abroad as the final confirmation of their view that we must be removed. The argument was couched in terms of foreign exchange statistics and needs. But there was a deeper concern. The IMF was seen as a guarantee of dependence upon an economic strategy in which the free enterprise system would be increasingly entrenched. Foreign banking support would baulk if free enterprise was not promoted visibly in successive programmes. The logic of events would drive us along that path. A break meant freedom to explore the non-capitalist path, the democratic socialism of the third way.

As it happened Jamaica began to mobilise world opinion against the IMF, joining forces in this with Nyerere's Tanzania. Progressive OPEC countries like Algeria and Iraq made foreign exchange loans. Some social democratic governments in Western Europe helped with loans or lines of credit. Norway and Holland were particularly co-operative. Certain members of the Eastern bloc with whom we had developed relations also offered lines of credit. An earlier state visit I had made to the Soviet Union had laid a basis for co-operation: a substantial trade agreement, including a long-term alumina sales contract, was supplemented by lines of credit in several areas.

In the midst of it all and whatever the outcome of the

elections that were to come, it was beyond question that by the act of March 1980 the PNP had recovered its soul — at least as far as the rank and file were concerned.

15
DESTABILISATION TRIUMPHS

Violence was mounting as the weeks left for the election ticked away. By now Jamaica had become like an echo chamber specially designed to make rumour and bad news reverberate. After the election, people were to comment on the comparative silence as if it were some gift from the new government. Not so. It was just that the thunderstorm had passed, leaving behind an exhausted population relieved to discover that the world could be silent. People were to luxuriate in that silence as a countryside basks in the sun when the storm clouds have passed. Since the JLP made most of the noise themselves as an important part of their political tactics, it is hardly surprising that the noise abated when they got what they wanted.

An argument was advanced at the time that the JLP were ahead in the polls and therefore did not need violence. By contrast we were behind and so we must have been responsible. The reasoning was, of course, faulty. Our polls confirmed to us that we were behind. At the same time we were convinced that our only hope lay in being able to get to people to talk to them, to answer their doubts and allay their fears. The more violence spread fear, the harder was it for us to carry our side of the arguments. It was we who had lost ground, we who were the victims of the rumours and the propaganda. We would have had to be insane to want to increase the panic, increase the impression of a society collapsing. On the contrary, it is precisely this impression which had helped put us behind. Violence had been one of the critical tools. Why would the JLP have wanted the society to suddenly heave a sigh of relief and feel that things were coming back under control? We were the ones who needed peace from every point of view and wanted it. Unless there is overwhelming and widely accepted evidence

laying the blame for violence at the door of one party, it tends
to damage the government in power, since it is the government
that people look to for their personal security.

We started to close the gap in the polls the minute the
campaign began in earnest in July. By August all polls showed
the gap closing fast. Clearly we needed to talk to people and
benefited whenever we did. Or could!

Seven hundred and fifty people were to die violently in the
months leading up to the 1980 election. Each side was to
proclaim itself the principal target and main victim.
Unquestionably, there were losses on both sides. There can be
no doubt, however, who was the aggressor and who stood to
gain.

The violence was a primary cause of migration. It killed any
hope of significant foreign investment which we continued to
seek consistently up to the end of 1979. We only stopped
trying in 1980: nobody would be interested in investment while
we were in the throes of an increasingly bloody election.
Violence struck at the foundations of local confidence. For the
first time, even rural areas were beginning to succumb to the
general panic. They were now finding themselves targets.

The JLP obviously had big money to spend. Their
advertising campaign was massive and had gone for years. They
seemed to have more cars and jeeps than they knew what to do
with. For months the opposition had claimed that they were
raising this money from Jamaican migrants in various parts of
North America. There is no doubt that they held fund-raising
meetings. There is also no doubt that they had developed very
close relations with some of the most right-wing elements in
the US political system. Seaga's close relations with
reactionary figures, such as Congressman Larry McDonald of
Georgia, were notorious. Making every allowance for what the
JLP could raise from the local oligarchy and the overseas
migrant population, it is simply not on the cards that they
could have raised money by ordinary means to match the level
of their expenditure. They obviously had a godfather or
godfathers somewhere in the international system.

Up to 1976, the .365 Magnum was the deadliest weapon in
common use in the political battle. It certainly was deadly
enough! The 1980 campaign was to be dominated by the M16
rifle, smuggled into the country in large but unspecified
numbers at that time. Their rapid-fire chatter became like a

theme song of the campaign. The whole period was an
extended nightmare from which, it seemed, we would never
awaken.

Both sides claimed their particular horror stories, though we
were only aware of one major incident affecting the JLP. This
was what came to be known as the Gold Street Massacre, a
terrible shooting which took place at a JLP function just inside
my own constituency in East Central Kingston. Five died, and
I make no comment on this ghastly event as people even now
have been charged and await trial in connection with it. There
was a big funeral and considerable attention was paid to the
event by the churches and private sector bodies, all of whom,
appropriately, denounced what had happened.

The experiences of the PNP could fill a book. One night
during the campaign, I addressed a meeting in one of the rural
areas.

The meeting took place at one end of a long ravine with high
cliffs on either side and the river running alongside the
highway. Most of the buses and vehicles which had brought
people to the meeting had to return along this gorge on their
way home. That night, after the meeting, they were ambushed.
Two traps were set: the first trap allowed a number of our
buses to pass through and then cut the group in half, the latter
part having to withdraw in the face of automatic rifle fire. The
first section which had been allowed to pass, then ran into the
second trap at the outskirts of Spanish Town, the island's
second largest city. No one died that night but about a dozen
people were admitted to hospital with gunshot wounds. The
weapons used had been heavy enough to blast whole chunks of
metal out of the sides of the buses.

A few days later there was the news that five youths had been
machine-gunned to death as they slept in a shack close by the
single-track railway line out of Kingston. I was on the scene as
soon as I could be. A crowd had gathered waiting for me. They
were tense and angry, each trying to tell me the story at the
same time. As we walked along the railroad tracks to the shack
where the young people had died we could feel that special
charge in the atmosphere that is half fear, half anger. There is
an inner sense that detects this like a smell.

In the early hours, a masked group had kicked open the door
of the derelict shack in which seven young people slept, four
boys and three girls. The first four, two boys and two girls

must have been dead before the first burst of gun fire was finished. Even as they died one of those in the next room was shouting: 'A girl is in here, a girl is in here. Don't shoot, don't shoot.' That was dismissed with another burst of automatic fire.

One was to escape, a boy of ten. Sleeping at the end of the one bed in the room, he had been able to hide himself under it even as his sister and her boyfriend died before they could move. Numb with shock, the little fellow was trying to tell us what happened. It took a long time, as his stammer recalled the terror through which he had passed more vividly than any words he could have found. There were no arrests. The five had a funeral but no representatives of the private sector attended; the establishment neither mourned nor denounced the manner of their passing. The *Gleaner* was not moved to give the event a label to fix it in the public mind. All who died were young stalwarts of the PNP.

Within days, five youths would be machine-gunned to death in one terrible minute. In the past year they had formed a party youth group in the same constituency. Inspired by the ideas of self-reliance which we were teaching, they had erected their own club house with discarded pieces of board and sheets of zinc which they had spent months collecting. They had painted their own sign to hang over the doorway. It read simply: 'The Socialist Joint'. They were caught inside the club house which they built with their own hands and at no cost to anyone, save their own time and effort. Five minutes later, all five were dead. So efficient were the methods and so deadly the weapons that not a single one of the five survived long enough to fight for his life on an operating table. Again, there was a funeral. Again, the private sector took no notice; neither did they mourn; neither did they denounce. No labels were attached. Yet these, too, had been 'massacres' in the most terrible sense.

On each occasion, the *Gleaner* set the agenda to which people were expected to react. The major JLP tragedy at that time, the shooting at Gold Street, was built up day after day by the *Gleaner*: the church and the private sector following suit. As killing after killing took place affecting PNP supporters on a scale unheard of in our previous political history, the news stories always managed to bury the political affiliation of the dead and their identity in the fine print.

Until October 1980, no candidate of either party had ever been killed during an election campaign or at any other time. Many of us have been shot at, some more than others. Ferdie Neita, a candidate of the PNP in 1976, was the first to be actually shot, and he had, mercifully, survived. Now on October 13 we were a mere seventeen days from the election. It was the eve of Nomination Day. In the Jamaican system, all candidates are formally nominated on a designated day usually two or three weeks before the actual election day itself. Suddenly the PNP radios which provided our island-wide communication network began to give out frantic appeals for help. Throughout the system our people could hear gunshots in the background and the calls for help being repeated with increasing desperation by Roy McGann, Junior Minister of National Security. McGann was MP for a constituency that stretches from the foothills which rise outside Kingston, through the great coffee country of the Blue Mountain Range up to the island's highest peak, 7,400 feet above sea level. McGann was explaining that he was pinned down by gunfire in Gordon Town, a village that stands astride the only highway leading up into the mountains that formed the eastern half of the constituency.

Suddenly Party radios could hear McGann's voice calling over and over, 'I am Roy McGann, the Minister, don't shoot!' A further burst of gunfire was heard and he was silent. By the time PNP supporters had recovered from the shock and rushed to the scene, McGann was on his way to the big University Hospital on the outskirts of Kingston. He was pronounced dead on arrival.

Later, we were to discover that McGann was driving home some of his supporters from a meeting. On reaching Gordon Town they had run into a mass of JLP supporters who blocked their passage home. A confrontation developed, obviously the responsibility of the JLP. At some point it is clear that a police party arrived, drove through the PNP group to the south, then through the JLP group to the north. Thereupon the police vehicle parked and the men, some with side arms, some with rifles, descended. It appears that the police detachment then took up positions on either side of the road. Some climbed on to the roofs of the buildings above and across from where McGann was standing on a verandah at the front of a shop. Piecing the evidence together it seemed that McGann had been trying to identify himself to the police when his voice was picked up on the PNP radios shouting 'I am Roy McGann'. McGann was shot immediately after, the bullet entering his right side and coming out through his left chest. It was not recovered as it passed clean through.

Trying desperately to save his life, his bodyguard carried him several yards down the road. At a point where there is a small bridge over a narrow gully-course, the bodyguard tried to get McGann to safety over the railing of the bridge into the gully below. He had to do this because the shooting was continuing. Even as he tried to drag McGann to safety he himself was shot, falling to the gully bed below. He dragged himself along a few yards then collapsed and died. McGann was carried from the bottom of the gully into which he also had fallen, but he never had a chance.

The killing of McGann sent a shock through the system. The PNP were numb, emotions hovering between dismay and outrage. The JLP and the *Gleaner* propaganda machine went into action immediately. In no time the little group which McGann had been trying to shepherd home had grown into a hostile PNP force threatening a peaceful merry-making JLP gathering in the Gordon Town Square. As I write, a coroner's inquest is yet to be held and I reserve comment on this aspect of the matter. However, the propaganda was preposterous. The JLP and the *Gleaner* version had McGann shooting at the JLP. So far from regretting the death of a minister, to say nothing of the sense of outrage that the death should have caused, McGann was described as an aggressor. His death was represented as arising from the necessity to defend hundreds of 'helpless' JLP supporters. The fact that several of them were armed, to say nothing of the presence of a police detachment complete with rifles, was conveniently disregarded. So ran the propaganda.

The campaign itself had started two weeks before McGann was murdered. It was by now almost a tradition that we should begin at Sam Sharpe Square in Montego Bay. On the night of October 5, people gathered in response to another of those great feats of mobilisation of which we were the acknowledged masters. The crowd was at least as big as in 1976, in spite of the earlier rains. When I saw the vast assembly stretching as far as the eye could see in the brightly lit square and up the side streets, I thought we might win in spite of everything.

We had held our annual conference immediately before in Montego Bay so as to reduce logistical problems. Our overseas friends had attended in force. Dame Judith Hart from the British Labour Party, Pena Gomez, Secretary General of the ruling party of the Dominican Republic, were present. There were messages from Carlos Andres Perez and our African friends. Bernt Carlsson, Secretary General of the Socialist International, was there, bringing special words of cheer from Willy Brandt, as did Judith Hart from Jim Callaghan. The Soviet Union with whom trade relations were developing satisfactorily and Hungary with whom we had worked for so long on the alumina project were represented by strong delegations. Cuba was present as were Vietnam and representatives from Grenada, Mexico, Iraq, Algeria, Yugoslavia, the Socialist Party of Puerto Rico, the Chilean Radical Party, as well as the US and Canadian Embassies in Jamaica. The Swedish and Norwegian Labour Parties, old friends, were there too. A particularly bright note was provided when the High Commissioner for Trinidad and Tobago advised us privately that Prime Minister Eric Williams had denounced the IMF for having met Seaga before the election.

There was no mistaking the wide interest in the election or the degree and depth of our support in all those parts of the world which could be described as 'progressive'. Small as Jamaica is, it was clear that the world community reflected and duplicated the lines of battle as they were drawn in the island. Clearly, the multinational corporation, the conservative elements of the Western press, the champions of the capitalist system, the US establishment and those who defended the *status quo* generally, were lined up solidly behind the JLP.

I spoke for two hours that night in the Square. By the end of the first hour it was clear to me that we were in trouble. The vast crowd was silent and seemed to hang on every word, as if seeking answers to their own private doubts. They had, every last one of them, been through an extended period of disturbance and pain. Much of this was due to propaganda and finely calculated violence. But the economic problems were grave, the shortages real. The Jamaican establishment had mastered the ways of destabilisation. It knew how to use fact and create fiction for maximum effect. We do not know what was the part played by the CIA in the last year. By then it may not have mattered because the *Gleaner* and the JLP had clearly reached postgraduate level.

The first hour of the speech was directed to history, beginning with our roots and setting the last eight and a half years in that context. The second hour dealt with our accomplishments and the future which we foresaw. No attempt was made to gloss over the hardships which had been endured or the sacrifices which would be expected. At moments during the second half, the crowd clearly came alive as sections of the speech beckoned to memory through the fog of propaganda in which Jamaica was, by then, wrapped. The announcement of the dates, October 14 for nominations and October 30 for the election, set off the usual clamour, and at 4:00 the next morning some forty to fifty thousand were still dancing. So we dispersed for the last twenty-five days.

About a week before the election we were due to hold the final meeting which I would address in Spanish Town. This is an area that tends to swing but had been predominately PNP in recent years. There had been increasing terrorism. We were sufficiently worried that I had twice walked areas of the town to try to boost morale. For days JLP thugs had spread the word that no meeting could be held. In spite of this a big crowd had gathered by eight o'clock when the 'warm-up' speakers were keeping things going. I was due at around nine o'clock.

As I was driving along to the meeting I heard reports on the crowd on our internal radio. The adrenalin was beginning to flow mercifully dispelling all hints of fatigue. Then the second report came. There was trouble at the meeting and Duncan also on his way to Spanish Town was parked just outside the town. I instructed him to meet me and when we did I gathered that the shocks of this election were not yet finished. Incredibly, soldiers had fired in the direction of the crowd and pandemonium had broken out. By all accounts the meeting was a shambles. I decided we must get to the spot as quickly as possible. A couple of hundred yards down the street from the beautiful old square in which the meeting was being held, some local police officers met me and tried to stop me from going any further. They said that the situation was tense and dangerous. I overruled them and led the entire party, which included Duncan, up the street and into the square.

Of the estimated ten thousand who had been there when the soldiers opened fire, perhaps a couple of thousand had stood their ground. The rest had long since fled in the general panic. We gathered on the platform to discuss what to do. The atmosphere was tense; people who had come from afar were stranded; others feared for their safety in getting home; everybody was trying to tell what had really happened.

We were trying to decide whether to try to restart the meeting with those who had remained or whether to fix another date. The discussion suddenly became irrelevant. A new burst of gunfire started. It was coming from every direction. People were diving for safety, running with that sort of abandon which only panic causes. In a flash, the platform was almost empty. There would be no more meeting that night.

Here was a development of staggering seriousness: the military firing on a political gathering. Of course, the Jamaican army had always been a potential problem. Nurtured in the tradition of constitutional neutrality, it was nonetheless made up of individuals affected by social moods and currents. The theory is that training is supposed to insulate them. In fact, however, other factors intervene. To begin with, the officer group of the Jamaican Defence Force is traditionally drawn from upper and middle class families, and class bias persists, despite training. As the establishment increased its campaign amongst the middle class and as the latter, angered by shortages and frightened by anti-communist propaganda, became increasingly hostile to our government, the officer group reflected this mood. Even the lower ranks began to succumb. The opposition's constant assertion that we were about to bring the Cuban army in to take over the country kept the whole defence force in a state of tension. After all, who would of necessity be the first target if a foreign army were to land?

Then too, the entire traditional system of military training is designed around the concept of an enemy. Most of our officers had been through Sandhurst. They had been exposed to a world configuration in which the enemy is seen through the eyes of M15. For people of this kind of class background, early cultural experience and training, it is exremely difficult to accept that a foreign communist — and perhaps even a local socialist — is not an enemy. Their unconscious assumptions lead them into a precarious contradiction. For example, military dictatorships of the most corrupt and repressive kind

abound in Latin America and throughout the world. Were
they to take over in Jamaica, they would represent a complete
reversal of every value which the Jamaican establishment
claims to hold dear. Yet they do not appear as enemies in the
assumptions of that kind of Jamaican.

The break-up of the Spanish town meeting constituted
another shock, another mystery for the average voter to digest,
to try to understand. Neither episode of gunfire could be
rationally explained. In the case of the first it turned out that
there had been an incident between a group of youths and the
soldiers at one corner of the meeting. Stones were thrown. The
incident could have been contained without the slightest
difficulty. Instead, apparently upon a signal from the officer in
charge, there was sustained firing until the meeting was
completely destroyed. They did not fire into the meeting, of
course: if they had, many would have died. All they needed to
do was to fire to ensure that the proceedings would be at an
end. The second instance could not even be blamed upon a
stone. There was no cause for the firing which I witnessed. No
explanation has ever been forthcoming.

Was it panic? Was it the mood of the times? Or, was it
something else?

No words can adequately reflect the strength and loyalty of
thousands of cadres who braved everything, not least the
propaganda of the last three years, to stand firm with their
party. Day after day they braved the gunmen, endured the
privations, went hungry if necessary to carry the campaign
through town and village. But in the last days of the campaign I
could sense that we were losing momentum. Unlike 1972 and
1976, attendances at meetings were beginning to slip. There
was a level of violence sufficient to keep any but the bravest at
home. The majority of both branches of the security forces
were by now openly siding with the JLP and often harassing
and intimidating our supporters. The JLP had only to name
someone to a police officer and an innocent but tactically
important PNP agent would be arrested. Some of these cases
were so bad that an accuser who led to the arrest of one of the
people shortly before the election has now been sent to prison
with one year's hard labour. The sentence was for perjury. In a
tough part of Kingston a JLP and a PNP candidate accused
each other constantly of the resort to violence and the use of

guns. The soldiers and police, by now acting under joint command, raided the PNP campaign headquarters in the area more than thirty times. Party cadres were forced to strip to the waist and lie face down for long periods. The JLP headquarters, against which equal evidence existed, was raided twice. No one was forced to lie down.

In the police, particularly, hostility was increasingly directed against the groups in the force who tried to remain impartial and loyal to their oath. This was to reach extremes in the case, for example, of those whose jobs required them to provide security for the prime minister and other members of the cabinet.

As election day approached the opposition, often enjoying the quiet and not so quiet support of elements of the security forces, gained confidence. Equally, the PNP found itself driven back upon courage alone.

October 30 came and when the polls closed at 5:00 that evening, I had my own private way of knowing the outcome before the first vote was counted much less announced. Going back twenty-seven years, I have been through countless campaigns. In the early days there were union elections between the Bustamante Union and our National Workers Union. At times thousands of workers were involved. Then, as on election night on the last two occasions, I had always been perfectly relaxed once the final occasion for effort was over. Indeed, in 1972 and 1976 I had slept soundly as a rather logical response to the efforts of the days before. That evening, in 1980, sleep would not come. We had lost — and massively.

REASSESSMENT

16
PSYCHOLOGICAL WARFARE AND ITS EFFECTS

The raw statistics were intimidating. 58% had voted for the JLP; 41% voted PNP. Almost a million persons had registered to vote. 86.9% of these had voted. Every figure was a record. Even the 350,000 persons who voted for the PNP represented the greatest number of votes ever cast for a losing party in Jamaican political history! These figures provide an interesting contrast to what was to occur in the United States a few days later. There, the only record that was set arose from the fact that an American President had just been elected by the smallest percentage of the American electorate that had bothered to vote in this century. Whatever else might be said, no one could accuse us of putting the political system to sleep.

A great poet once said that if you want to write poetry, your emotions are best recollected in tranquillity. Equally, if one is to attempt historical analysis, trauma is best recalled from a distance.

The first trauma to consider concerns the movement of percentages. 57% of the people voted *for* something in 1976 and 58% of them voted *against* something in 1980. Of course, neither assertion can be altogether accurate. However most observers agree that the largest factor in the 1976 vote arose from a positive impulse. A majority of people had been touched, moved, benefited, made to feel more important and they wanted this to continue. The 1980 vote sprang from an essentially negative impulse. The majority of people were frightened, insecure, confused, unsure of the future, and reaching for safety. The 1976 vote was not a vote for an opposition, untried and full of promise, but for a government that had been in place for five years. That vote was an act of confirmation, not a gamble with the unknown. What then, happened between January 1977 and October 1980 to cause so large a turnaround?

Looking back just ten months after the debacle, it becomes increasingly clear that a number of factors were working in combination to set the stage for the final outcome. The economic crisis and the IMF programme created the conditions in which the credibility of the government began to erode. The opposition accelerated the process by collaborating in the tactics of destabilisation. In the end the communist bogey wearing Cuban robes became the focus of a hysteria in which the original issue on which the election was based, the IMF itself, was increasingly obscured.

Basic to everything that happened was the question of the economy. There had been negative growth. There were shortages. Unemployment had crept up from 24% to 26.8%. By 1980 the foreign exchange crisis had been at the level where the ordinary man and woman could feel it for nearly four years. From one point of view, we were another in a long line of casualties amongst the democratic governments of the world who have gone down before the economic storms which have shaken the world since 1973.

World economic crisis and its effects placed unprecedented strain on Jamaican management. It took us a long time to respond adequately to this challenge. Unquestionably we overestimated the capacity of the bureaucracy and the management sector to run the wide range of new institutions. In a sense we overloaded the circuit. In future we intend to be better prepared.

Economic hardship, insecurity, poor management un-doubtedly accounted for some part of the larger than usual swing — a staggering 16%. But that is only part of the story. It continues with the factor of violence.

Jamaicans were psychologically exhausted by violence by the time the election came. It was as if the collective, psychological landscape had been laid waste. People were tired, scared, distrustful and uncertain. It was not only the killings and rapes, but the rumours of killings and rapes. It was not only that so many died but that there was so little rational explanation as to why.

I had always felt that violence represented the greatest single threat to our political fortunes. As long as it was there, economic recovery was improbable and confidence that the government was in charge of the situation more and more difficult to maintain. Not for one instant did the JLP and the *Gleaner* ever relax in the charge that our economic difficulties were solely and exclusively the fault of our bad management. The level of crime and violence seemed to suggest that we were unable to manage security either. Hence, the level of violence added credibility to the charge that mismanagement was really behind everything.

The part played by the security forces was a factor within a factor. With violence out of hand, the security forces became a focus of attention. In the end, they were more against than for us. The 'anti's' were openly hostile and many played a partisan hand in the election. It was only a minority but that is enough. Much can be done by a few to swing a marginal area. To this must be added the general impact of the news that the security forces were against the government at a time when violence had most citizens shaking in their shoes.

Then there was the communist bogey. There had always been a steady flow of propaganda acting like an undertow in Jamaican society. Our foreign policy had involved developing relations with everything from communist to liberal democratic, free enterprise processes. We developed fraternal relations from Moscow to Lagos, from Hanoi to Canberra. We had a visible and vocal left wing and, of course, there was Cuba.

In the last couple of years there had been a number of occasions when the local communist movement had supported us in some of the confrontations with the oligarchy. They had often criticised us too, and bitterly, but this was never highlighted. On occasion, affiliated organisations of both the socialist and the communist movements had made common cause and combined to press for a particular change. Such had been the case with maternity leave. There was plenty here that could be misconstrued, exaggerated, misrepresented and even made the subject of downright lies.

As elections approached, there was considerable uneasiness about this whole question of the PNP and communism. During the election itself, the Workers Party of Jamaica took a tactical decision that was to have a distinct bearing on the result. They had every reason to fear a JLP victory. Equally, they could hope to claim some credit for a PNP victory, if they could be seen to have contributed to it. In such an event, they would have legitimised themselves as a significant part of the political system. Whatever the reasons, they decided to campaign openly for the PNP. We made repeated statements to explain that this was not of our seeking and to keep the distinction clear. Nevertheless, this did us real harm because it seemed to confirm the years of propaganda asserting that the PNP had 'gone communist'.

At that very time, the 'boat people' were leaving Cuba for Miami. It had its effect among those who feared that we were heading towards communism. This fear was strengthened by the shortages, the unofficial rationing and queues at the supermarkets which made it seem to some that communism had already arrived.

The communist scare was bolstered by the fact that many PNP leaders had resigned: Coore, Bell, William Isaacs, Dr. Ken McNeill. None had resigned from the party as such and there were different reasons why each had left the government. McNeill, for example, left for reasons of health. Nonetheless, propaganda had it that the real reason was that we had been captured by the communists. Finally, there was the whole question of our credibility. If we were bad managers; if the communists supported us; if we could not stop violence; if the security forces were against us; if many of our own people had resigned: were we a credible choice?

Considerable effort had been devoted by the JLP to undermining any credibility. I make no special point of this on its own, because it is the very stuff of which the cut and thrust of party politics is made. What is significant is the way in which events were manipulated, sometimes even staged, to create particular impressions.

Perhaps the best way to illustrate the point is to quote from the US Army Manual of Psychological Warfare. This was the instruction sheet which we quoted to warn our cadres what to expect and which had upset Phillip Habib. It reads like a description of Jamaica between January 1976 and October 1980. It is headed: *The Field Manual of the Department of the Army, Psychological Operations:* published by the Central Office of the Army in Washington, D.C. USA. It goes on to say:

Psychological operations are actions destined to influence foreign nations. Psychological activities are those carried out in peace time or in places other than war theatres, planned and carried out to influence the feelings, attitudes, behaviour of

foreign groups in a manner favourable to the achievement of the policies of the United States. The climate for psychological warfare can only be developed successfully if the daily life of the nation is kept in a state of commotion . . .
STRATEGY
  i) Create discouragement, demoralisation, apathy;
 ii) Discredit the ideology of the popular movement;
iii) Promote disorganised and confused behaviour;
 iv) Encourage divisive and anti-social actions to undermine the political structure of the country;
  v) Promote and support movements of resistance against the authorities.

The local exponents of these techniques had been good students. It is not altogether surprising that we were no longer a credible choice for so many people.

Régis Debray wrote the following description of Chile on the eve of Allende's overthrow after three years of systematic destabilisation:

Consequently what developed was a rampant crisis, insidious, intangible and invisible, responsibility for which could never be laid at the proper door. The enemy advanced in disguise. From without it took the form of processions of 'housewives', and from within it wore the mask of 'natural catastrophe' — of inflation, poverty, the transport strike, locked petrol pumps, and rationing. Anonymous and faceless, parliamentary obstruction, by preventing tax reform and refusing to finance the social sector of the economy, forced more and more currency to be issued; omnipresent but fleeting; generalised and consequently depersonalised, there was stockpiling by shops, hoarding by customers, smuggling of goods out of the country, and a black market among the well-to-do; ramifying and secret, strike funds were supplied to the owners' associations by the CIA. Nowhere were there any identifiable enemies or targets.

This was Chile at that time as understood by scores of observers, though none expressed it with more telling force. The 'rampant crisis, insidious, intangible and invisible'; 'the enemy advancing in disguise'; the lack of 'identifiable enemies or targets' could all have applied to Jamaica at any time from 1976 to 1980.

We had no parliamentary obstruction but could not finance the social sector of the economy adequately. This was so because the economy was shrinking, caught between world crisis and sabotage. What these two could not do was completed by the IMF. In the end that was the inevitable element of self-inflicted damage, because our capacity for management was unequal to the extra burdens which were placed by crisis upon an already difficult situation.

Unlike Chile we had a visible 'enemy' in the *Gleaner* and the JLP. To some extent, these masked their role in the traditional respectability of the positions they occupied. Behind the facade of constitutional propriety, both 'advanced in disguise' to spread the 'insidious crisis' that eroded public confidence. In the end they did not even bother with the mask. Norman Manley's 'alien force' was here, at the bidding of the guardians of Quincy Adams' 'commercial interests'.

One is thus led to the conclusion that the basic cause of the electoral collapse was economic but that violence, together with confusion about communism, contributed mightily to the outcome. Assisted by the destabilisation programme, all three acted in a mutually reinforcing manner to produce a sudden decline in credibility. Instead of, say, 8% of those persons who voted for the PNP in 1976, deciding that two terms were enough, an astounding 16% made that decision.

An interesting reinforcement for this analysis comes from a poll conducted by Dr. Stone just nine months after our electoral defeat.

During these nine months the new government had secured an agreement with the IMF more favourable than any previously worked out with the organisation anywhere in the world. The Venezuela-Mexico oil facility was now in place. US aid had been pouring into the country for months. President Ronald Reagan had made the new Prime Minister his first official visitor from overseas. David Rockefeller had been named chairman of a special committee to mobilise US investment for Jamaica. It had been announced that over a thousand proposals for new investment in Jamaica had been received. With huge loans from every quarter of the free enterprise economic system in place, the shops were now bursting with goods. The *Gleaner* front page had been like an extended soap opera recording triumph after triumph as the days passed. The editorial page was like an extended panegyric to the new Prime Minister. Not for one moment had the columnists let up on their attack upon me. With everything going the JLP's way, we awaited the result of the poll with interest, some even with anxiety.

The poll, which might have been expected to show an increase in the standing of the JLP, or at the very least, shown them holding firm at 58%, showed an astonishing decline of 6%, the exact level of swing which had put the PNP in power in 1972! Already, a substantial proportion of the 16% had vanished. We were back to more normal magnitudes. It is early to draw conclusions. But it is at least arguable that this supports the view that the election result had a substantial element of panic to it. It tends to confirm my own, admittedly subjective, impression that at the very end, many people voted out of a confused desperation and not because of a settled, rational commitment to another policy. Everything for which they could be supposed to have voted was in fact happening. Why, then, so sudden a switch?

It is also interesting to observe that the same poll showed the leader of the opposition already 4% ahead of the new Prime Minister in personal standing with the voters. For a variety of personal reasons, I have been even more inactive than the PNP in recent months. When asked the question 'Which party is more interested in the poor?', 54% named the PNP, and only 36%, the JLP. This was the same poll-taker who predicted the last two election results to within 1%.

That Jamaica was destabilised, as we have defined the word, is beyond question. Any objective review of the sequence of events from 1976 to 1980 reveals the matter as impatient of debate.

17
POLITICS FOR DEVELOPMENT

As I reflect upon the experience of the last eight years in office, certain strands of thought emerge with growing clarity. The first has to do with our positive accomplishments, irreversible in themselves; the second with the nature of the dilemma which all of us in the Third World face.

The PNP sowed the seeds of a social revolution, hammered out a foreign policy and a bauxite strategy each of which represented a radical departure from the past. Household helpers enter a house by the front door now. Jamaica's position on the right or left of world affairs is noticed now. Multinational corporations have learned that we cannot so readily be treated with contempt or taken for granted as their natural accomplices. But perhaps of greatest importance is the fact that no government will again be able with impunity to run Jamaica as if by *fiat*. Short of out and out repression, the politics of participation is hard to turn off. When over 100,000 people out of a population of 2 million come to political meetings, something irreversible has begun to happen in terms of their self-definition as citizens.

During our two terms in office grass-roots democracy began to form part of the normal expectations of Jamaicans. Suddenly the right to be heard became an extension of the right to vote. Voting may be the skeleton on which the democratic system hangs. But participation in decision-making is the body of democracy itself. And that body must needs grow to maturity. Future Jamaican governments will inevitably discover that the democratic process cannot afford to be static. Democracy will have to enter the workplace, become the avenue for community self-expression as men and women increasingly demand a voice in affairs. If the process is thwarted, sooner or later there will be growing dissension from the electorate.

The dilemma we faced as a party in Jamaica is sharply focused. We were and are trying to build a democratic socialist society by constitutional means within a plural system. In this we are not so different from our European counterparts. The mixed economy is a permanent objective; a class alliance the working method. Social engineering is required on a fundamental scale, since organisational structures as well as personal attitudes and motivations must change if a viable society is to emerge.

But the dilemma in Jamaica is compounded. Not only must change occur within an economy that is capitalist and a political system in which opposition is institutionalised, but in a geo-political environment in which we, as part of the Third World, are on the receiving end of the imperialist whip.

Imperialism itself is not a single-faceted entity. Its definition is often contentious or simply obscured by political rhetoric. For some, imperialism implies any situation in which one set of people acquire dominance over another. For others, imperialism is capitalism in its highest contemporary phase, no more, no less. Both of these definitions leave something to be desired. Without going into the history of domination from Roman times, it is essential to develop a vocabulary which distinguishes between the forms which domination takes in the modern world. Perhaps the best way to begin is with the question: to what purpose is domination put?

Two clear patterns can be distinguished. First we have the case where domination is used to guarantee the transfer of wealth from one set of people to another; second, the case where domination is exercised to protect national borders, to ensure the absence of hostile governments who threaten security. If the second happens without an actual process of economic exploitation, then clearly we have a distinct kind of domination. Both forms may involve political, cultural and psychological consequences that are utterly objectionable, but I believe it dangerous to confuse them. Therefore, I prefer to use the word imperialism to describe the first form of domination and hegemony to describe the second. Imperialism thus describes a situation in which domination and exploitation are both present; hegemony, one in which domination exists for purposes other than economic exploitation.

Obviously domination can be achieved in many ways. It does not have to be the result of explicit political control. If the economy of a small country is totally dependent upon a set of external factors, this is a form of domination as effective as anything that existed in colonial times. The effect of all the economic factors adds up to a sort of cumulative *force majeure* from which there is no escape. That is why the entire group of countries who make up the industrialised North of the enterprise world are at the centre of an imperialist system, even though they have long since divested themselves of their former colonies insofar as political ties are concerned. Similarly, the Soviet Union can exercise considerable or even complete dominance over the countries of the Socialist bloc and still not be imperialist. To be imperialist, there would have to be evidence that the domination was associated with the transfer of wealth. There are no multinational corporations, no monopoly of transport, no unilateral pricing of products under exclusive license in countries dominated by the Soviet Union. The closest study of the economic relations within the COMECON countries provides no evidence of exploitation by the USSR. All economic exchange is negotiated and applies reciprocally by agreement. Impartial analysis, within the facts available to me, suggests that the exchanges are fair and reasonable.

This is not in any way to deny that the Soviet Union's domination of the Socialist bloc can be ruthless. Yet for the purposes of clarity, it is critical to distinguish this hegemonic process of domination from imperialism with its economic motive.

It is, of course, possible for a country to be both imperialist and hegemonic. Generally imperialistic, the USA also acts from other than economic motives. It is sensitive to its defence and ideological interests. After a brief flirtation with pluralism under Carter, it has now in fact reverted to a traditional, aggressive posture towards ideologies of which it disapproves and exerts pressure even where economic interests are not directly at stake.

Yet those commercial interests formulated in the Monroe Doctrine are still at the heart of hemispheric policies. From the start, the Americas were declared 'home base' by the US. Nobody was asked to agree to this, only to listen to it. In simpler times, the marines were enough to deal with any who had a contrary view. When world opinion became more sensitive, the CIA was ready to step into the breach.

As imperialism developed over the course of the century European and US interests often merged in a multinational corporate structure increasingly dominated by the US component. Throughout this process, the people of each Third World country were divided into two kinds: beneficiaries and victims. Hence, when Jamaica became independent, patriotism could not be assumed to run deeper than support for the national cricket team. The economic interests of the people reflected two divisions. One was the internal division common to all forms of capitalism, early or advanced: the division of interests between those who own the means of production and whose who sell their labour power. The second division was between those who owed their economic status to the international system and those whose labour provided its raw materials cheaply.

This leads to a situation replete with internal contradictions. If any policy in Jamaica — or indeed most other countries locked into the imperialist network — appears to challenge the international system in the name of national interest, one part of the population can be relied on to stand firm with the imperialist forces, the guardians at the centre of the system.

It is this which makes a mixed economy, with social and political aims of a socialist nature, so difficult to manage. Central to the mixed economy is the understanding that both private and public sectors will co-operate to promote economic development. When the private sector feels there is no threat to its class interests and that the public sector is merely engaged in productive capitalist activity for the state, all is well. But where the development of a public sector is part of an overall strategy to change the balance of relations between classes in the society, the private sector reacts differently. True, some elements co-operate once they feel assured that this mixed economy really has a place for private business. Indeed, they may feel more secure in a society which they see tackling injustice.

But other parts of the private sector do not co-operate, doubtless feeling that their class interests are threatened. Some mark time, do not reinvest their profits. Others actively seek ways to sabotage the economy, running down their businesses, exporting their capital illegally. Still others simply depart, complete with worldly goods, often to set up points of overseas resistance to the government which tried to disturb their power.

This was the case in Jamaica. And it became increasingly clear to us that we could not hope to change internal conditions without also working to change the wider international environment which created our dilemma in the first place. Both Nicaragua and Grenada in the Caribbean area are now finding how difficult this can be.

What is particularly sad about the Jamaican case is the cynical extent to which a small group in the leadership of the opposition — acting on behalf of the beneficiaries of the imperialist system — were willing to manipulate their own party and the country at large. Unsure of their ability to beat a party which had once again taken on the characteristics of a movement, they decided to take no chances. They acted in alliance with the most reactionary elements in the US power structure. The consequence was to deliver the country once again fully into the hands of imperialist interests.

Yet Jamaica is not Chile. In Chile one had only to create the conditions for Pinochet's army to do the job. In Jamaica the JLP as official opposition had a good chance of winning the election without resorting to tactics which brought the country to the verge of civil war. Inflation was high, the economy was in trouble, crime was a headache: all the ingredients necessary for marking the end of a two-term government were present. The fact that the recourse to destabilisation tactics seemed necessary throws us back again into the nexus of imperialist relations, their intolerance of ideological and economic independence of any kind. It must never be forgotten that the JLP had a choice. They could have acted as a traditional opposition. They chose not to. A lot of people are dead today on that account.

But what of the future? Every aspect of the recent Jamaican and Third World experience reinforces the conviction that the third way must be pursued.

We have learned many things. Political ideas and strategy, ideology, must be more rigorously defined and taught within the movement. On a general level, political awareness needs to be raised throughout society. Otherwise political movements become the mirrors of popular confusion rather than the mobilisers of change. Economic strategy must be more clearly calculated and the requirements of management more precisely anticipated. Without this, progress cannot be financed and the society at large becomes vulnerable and insecure.

Further it is essential that a new focus of international co-operation be defined and co-operation itself brought to new levels. We of the South must begin to make a reality of this. Collective self-reliance among Third World countries must become more than a slogan, because it is an important step on the long, hard road to economic independence for us all.

Progressives of the North need to emerge from their present paralysis and recognise that their own hopes can best be realised in a world economy that functions and expands because it is organised with equitable exchange in mind. They would do well to realise that they cannot create the just society of their ideals by purely national programmes conceived in isolation from the world's economic superstructure and its controls. The entire Third World is part of an economic periphery. But social democracy, even when in power, has become part of a political periphery. Would they but realise it, the progressives of the North need an international economic strategy as badly as does everyone in the South.

Finally, it needs to be stressed that the antipodes of domination and liberation cannot coexist; that the 'pecuniary interests' of the Monroe Doctrine and Norman Manley's charge of economic self-determination cannot live side by side. The Third World and the Non-Aligned Movement are exploring a new view of international relations based upon respect for sovereignty. The cornerstone of this approach is the affirmation that co-operation is more important than differences. A whole new tradition is developing in which countries of the periphery, with different pasts, ideologies, political formations and religions, are attempting to make common cause in the struggle to create a new world economic order. In the pressure of national struggle, a paradox has emerged: self-determination, rather than being the focal point of aggressive self-interest, has become the basis for mutual respect and unity. It is as if in this new situation each nation desires the success of its neighbour's attempt at self-determination, perhaps simply because we have, for so long, been the victims of imperialism. One does not pretend that this is universally true in the Third World, but it is increasingly a new and vital force within the group. And herein lies our hope.

It is self-evident to us that we want to be the pawns neither of East nor West, economically or politically. If any Third World country is to be free of dependence on any external source of power; democratic in the complete sense of pluralism and participation; and seek to provide both a material basis for prosperity and a system ensuring that it is equitably shared, it can only pursue this third path which we attempted in Jamaica.

We will continue to pursue it.

APPENDIX
DESTABILISATION DIARY

Events which occurred in Jamaica between 1976 and 1980 have raised what is still a controversy as to whether the Central Intelligence Agency of the United States government played an active role in destabilising Jamaica under the Manley administration. The events include unprecedented levels of violence, terrorism, organised public protest and a propaganda campaign locally and overseas. At times the events were strikingly reminiscent of the period leading up to the military coup which toppled the Allende government in Chile. But throughout the period US officialdom strongly denied responsibility for any such destabilisation attempt.

Henry Kissinger, Secretary of State: '... not aware of any action by the US government designed to weaken the Government of Prime Minister Manley ... US being blamed for things that are indigenous to Jamaica ... I remain a firm friend to Jamaica.' (Conversations with Foreign Affairs Minister Dudley Thompson during 6th General Assembly of the OAS in Santiago, Chile, June 1976).

William Luers, Deputy Assistant Secretary of State: 'I speak for all agencies of the United States government ... I wish categorically to deny that the US Government is doing anything to undermine or destabilise the legitimate Government of Jamaica.' (Speaking before the House Committee on International Political and Military Affairs, June 14, 1976).

Sumner Gerard, US Ambassador to Jamaica: 'Allegations of US destabilisation are scurrilous and false.' (Address to businessmen in Kingston, June 30, 1976).

Bearing in mind the experience of Chile can one believe this? In response to repeated charges of US-CIA interference in the constitutionally elected government of President Salvador Allende, US officialdom gave equally firm denials.

Henry Kissinger, Secretary of State: 'The CIA had nothing to do with the coup, to the best of my knowledge and belief, and I only put in that qualification in case some madman appears down there who without instruction talked to somebody.' (Testimony before Senate Foreign Relations Committee repeated in *New York Times,* September 8, 1974).

Jack Kubisch, Assistant Secretary of State for Inter-American Affairs: 'I wish to state as flatly and as categorically as I possibly can that we did not have advance knowledge of the coup that took place on September 11 ... there was no contact whatsoever by the organizers and leaders of the coup directly with us and we did not have definite knowledge of it in advance ... As official spokesmen of the US government have stated repeatedly, we were not involved in the coup in any way.' (Testimony given at hearings before the Subcommittee on Inter-American Affairs, September 20, 1973).

Edward M. Kory, US Ambassador to Chile from October 1967-October 1971: 'The United States did not seek to pressure, subvert, influence a single member of the Chilean Congress at any time in the entire four years of my stay.' (Testimony before Senate Committee reported in *New York Times,* September 16, 1974).

WHAT WAS THE TRUTH?

The New York Times (September 8, 1974): 'The Director of the Central Intelligence Agency has told Congress that the Nixon Administration authorized more than $8 million for covert activities by the agency in Chile between 1970 and 1973 in an effort to make it impossible for Salvador Allende ... to govern. The goal ... was to "destabilize" the Marxist government ... The testimony of Mr. Colby indicated that high officials in the State Department and White House repeatedly and deliberately misled the public and the Congress about the extent of United States involvement in the internal affairs of Chile ... '

The New York Times (September 15, 1974): 'Secretary of State Kissinger personally directed a far-reaching Nixon Administration program designed to curtail economic aid and credits to Chile after the election of Salvador Allende ... well informed government sources said today ... After the election of Dr.Allende, Mr. Kissinger ... took charge of a series of weekly interagency meetings at which administration officials worked out a policy of economic sanctions ... against Chile ... The sources emphasized that Mr. Kissinger's economic activities against the Allende Government were distinct from his involvement in clandestine CIA operations, although both programs were controlled by him with great secrecy ... '

The Senate Intelligence Committee: On September 15, 1970, 'the CIA was instructed by President Nixon to play a direct role in organizing a military coup d'état in Chile to prevent Allende's accession to the Presidency.' (Ambassador Kory was separately instructed to encourage the Chilean military to make a coup).

'The 40 Committee authorized nearly $4 million for opposition political parties in Chile. Most of this money went to the Christian Democratic Party (PDC), but a substantial portion was earmarked for the National Party (PN).'

The CIA spent $1.5 million in support of *El Mercurio*; its 'propaganda project' produced magazines, books, and special studies, and developed material for placement in newspapers and on radio stations and television shows; it financed, supported an opposition research organization.

'Throughout the Allende years, the United States maintained close contact with the Chilean armed forces, both through the CIA and through US military attachés.' The CIA engaged in a 'deception operation' to arouse the military against 'Allende's involvement with the Cubans; and in a shortlived effort to subsidize a small anti-government news pamphlet directed at the armed services ... '

In October 1971 the 'group which might mount a successful coup' came to the CIA station's attention, and 'by January 1972 the station had successfully penetrated it and was in contact through an intermediary with its leader ... It is clear that the CIA received intelligence reports on the coup planning of the group which carried out the successful September 11 coup throughout the months of July, August, and September 1973 ... '

DIARY OF EVENTS — 1976

It is against this background that we now place on record a diary of events in Jamaica as they unfolded in 1976, as an example of what occurred.

January 2: The election year begins ominously, when on January 2 the *Daily Gleaner* publishes an editorial replete with lies, half-truths and malicious speculation, titled 'If he fails ... '
'Analysis of Jamaica in 1975 requires new terms, compels new philosophical concepts, new fears, recognizes new repositories of power in the land. No longer is Parliament supreme, no longer is Parliament the place where national policy is publicly pondered and dissected, no longer are the majority party MPs (who technically choose the Prime Minister) truly influential.

Indeed a great many of them are running scared, they are bullied openly and covertly by the activists who make party policy without standing for election . . . '

This 'national' newspaper finds it possible to lay the gravest charges of usurpation of constitutional authority and subordination of parliament and parliamentarians by a handful of party activists, without one shred of supporting evidence.

It might be useful to note that the Editor of the Daily Gleaner is Mr. Hector Wynter, a former chairman of and candidate for the Jamaica Labour Party. Under the previous JLP Government he also served as a Cabinet Minister and a Diplomat.

Incidentally, the editorial is later repeated *verbatim*.

January 4: The then United States Secretary of State, Henry Kissinger, leaves Jamaica, unsuccessful in his mission to dissuade Manley from supporting the presence of Cuban troops in Angola. Despite his failure to secure support on the Angola question, Kissinger assures Manley that there is no CIA interference in Jamaica.

It is therefore interesting to note that later in the month Kissinger tells the House Finance Committee that he has instructed US Missions abroad to warn Third World governments that their relations with the United States would be judged by their 'statements and votes on that fairly limited number of issues we indicated are of importance to us in international fora'.

What he does not say to Manley or the House is that just before his visit the CIA station in Jamaica had been strengthened with the arrival of the new Chief of Station, Norman Descoteaux. His formal title is Attaché. Descoteaux had previously been assigned to Headquarters (1962-65), Ecuador (1965-68), Buenos Aires (1968-70), Headquarters (1970-73), and Guayaquil, Ecuador (1973-75).

January 5: Officials of the International Monetary Fund and World Bank hold preparatory meetings for the conference of the IMF and World Bank set to open in Kingston, September 7. Simultaneously, violence erupts in the western section of the city. The violence continues and on the eve of the opening of the conference, culminates in the burning of sections of Jones Town and Trench Town, by terrorists armed with sophisticated weapons. The attack leaves hundreds homeless, and over a million dollars of damage, and provides material for a number of sensational articles filed by the large corps of foreign journalists who are in Kingston for the IMF meeting.

January 6: The then Minister of National Security, Keble Munn, announces that the security forces have arrested 19 members of a group known as the Yap fighters, who operated from Yap Sam Lands. The area is a stronghold of prospective JLP candidate Ferdie Yap Sam who was to figure prominently in events later in the year. Munn says those arrested are believed to be connected with the storage of guns and ammunition and were being trained for operations against the government.

January 7 (am): Six armed men invade a construction site on Marcus Garvey Drive in Kingston. They attack and shoot to death police constables Garfield Brown and Arthur Campbell, who are on duty at the site. A third policeman, Carl Thomas, is injured in the attack. The incident sparks a work stoppage at the Mobile Reserves Harman Barracks where the two policemen are from. Normalcy returns only after the policemen are addressed by the Prime Minister who promises firmer action against the gunmen and more equipment and vehicles for the force.

January 7 (pm): Two more policemen are shot while on duty at the US Embassy.

The repercussions of the two events and how they are reported abroad are a spate of tourist cancellations from the United States and Canada.

January 8: The nature of the reports on the violence appearing in the overseas press prompts Deputy Prime Minister David Coore and the National Security Minister to call a press conference primarily for the foreign journalists. They make clear the fact that the violence is restricted to a small area of Kingston and not the entire country as the reports suggest. But the damage is already done. Tourist cancellations continue to pour in.

January 9: As the violence continues, Manley announces new legislation to revitalise the Gun Court: mandatory life imprisonment for illegal possession of a firearm. In addition, a ban is placed on marches and demonstrations. By this time, the security forces state they are satisfied that the violence is the work of hired, 'well paid' gunmen.

January 11: Against the background of the continuing violence, primarily directed against PNP communities, individuals and party meetings, as President of the PNP, Manley announces the party's proposal to establish community self-defence groups to act as an unarmed warning service. The move, however, sparks controversy. It is denounced by the JLP and the Jamaica Manufacturers' Association, and meets with much concern by the Church. Adding its piece the Association of Chambers of Commerce calls for a shutdown of business in protest against the proposal as well as the escalation of violence itself, while the Chamber of Commerce asks, 'Is the Prime Minister proposing to introduce a Mongoose Squad, Black Shirts or Ton Ton Macoutes to Jamaica?'

January 12: Wall Street Journal ... title, 'Dismantling an Island Paradise', '... Prime Minister Michael Manley's People's National Party is the most inept of all the Western governments that fancies itself democratic ... whatever the reason for the public unrest, it certainly hasn't been smoothed over by the government's economic policies ... As a result of the IMF-World Bank meeting here, the United States will through these international institutions be increasing its financial aid to Mr. Manley's Jamaica and other Third World governments. Americans, upset about this, should take heart at Mr. Manley's comments. Jamaica is not going Communist. It is merely going bananas ...'

January 14:   Revere Copper and Brass Incorporated announces that its Jamaican subsidiary Revere Ja. Ltd., is suing the Manley government over its bauxite production levy.

Daily Gleaner publishes front page story headlined '280 Cubans coming to build school', in a context of its publication of hostile response to the PNP proposal of community self-defence groups. The Cuban government had offered to build a secondary school in Jamaica as a gift utilising Cuban labour and raw materials. Since Cuba has no excess of foreign exchange this is the only practical form that such assistance programmes can take. At the same time the present inability of the Jamaican government to provide educational facilities for all makes the gift a very important one. The article immediately prompts a series of attacks, among them the Joint Industrial Council for the Building Industry which claims that Jamaican labour is being by-passed, and the Jamaica Chamber of Commerce sees the arrival of Cuban workers as 'letting in a wooden horse of Troy'.

Of course there is no question of by-passing Jamaican labour since the school is not available on those terms in the first place.

January 15:   The local Soroptimist Club passes a resolution calling on women to withdraw their services from their employers and communities as well as their husbands and families to protest against political violence. They call for action on February 2, but a meeting to discuss the matter with representatives of 20 women's organisations ends abruptly and in disorder as the representatives of the PNP Women's Arm and the majority of women's groups present disagree vociferously with the Soroptimists' proposed course of action and question the motives of this traditionally dormant and small middle class grouping. The proposal is indeed reminiscent of the activities of middle class women in Chile before the coup.

January 16: Allan Isaacs, Minister of Mining and Natural Resources, is dismissed from the Cabinet for alleged leaking of Cabinet documents to the opposition. A week later he resigns from the PNP styling himself as an independent MP. However, he later officially joins the JLP and eventually becomes a candidate for that party in the 1980 elections. It is interesting to note that on the morning of the 16th before the Prime Minister makes the announcement, the *Gleaner* carries a story headlined "PM demands resignation from cabinet ... Isaacs quitting as minister ... refuses to give up Parliamentary seat.'

January 22: Isaacs issues statement charging 'rising ascendancy of party over constitutional government, including parliament itself ... unelected members have greater voice in government today ... they do not stop at democratic socialism, to them it is only a step to establishing the Cuban model of socialism-communism.' Note, the statement echoes the line taken by the *Gleaner* editorial of January 2 and is equally without foundation.

January 24: The focus on violence and the Allan Isaacs affair overshadowed a brewing crisis in the eastern parish of St. Thomas, a crisis which took centre stage on Saturday 24, when 13 people died from flour poisoning, bringing to 17 the number killed after eating meals which included counter flour. The first death was recorded on December 30, and between then and January 2, 4 people died. The cause of the deaths is finally pinpointed on January 25. The then Health Minister Ken McNeil announces that the deadly poison parathion is responsible. It appears that a shipment of counter flour was contaminated with the poison en route to Jamaica although parathion had been banned from Jamaica for many years.

February 2: Violence again erupts in the western section of the city, (policeman and civilian killed, 2 policemen wounded, public transportation withdrawn from the area, and 6 schools close).

February 10: Violence continues in the city, arson and bombings in Jones Town and Trench Town, and the seventh policeman killed. By mid-May, 16 would fall as the death toll reaches 90.

February 11: Gang of terrorists on motorcycles invade Alcoa's plant in Clarendon. They damage equipment and injure a number of workers. The plant is immediately closed. The attack follows an announcement by Alcoa that it intends to lay-off workers as a consequence of the effects on its operations of a strike of railway workers. Alcoa's management says the plant won't reopen until a guarantee of safety is received. The closure follows recent industrial action which brought the plant to a standstill.

February 12: *Miami Herald's* Don Bohning writes article titled, 'Jamaica building up to a political showdown', '... rightly or wrongly, much of Jamaica's influential private sector openly expresses the fear that Manley is leading the country down the path of Cuban-styled leftist totalitarianism.'

February 13: Pan American Airways announces that it is suspending services in Jamaica, after 47 years of operations here, in a 'cost reduction' move. It cites the loss of 8 million dollars on the route the previous year.

Carl Rowan writes, 'Deeper troubles for Jamaica: ... Jamaica perhaps as much as any nation symbolises the struggle between the world's rich nations and its poor ... The grim irony is that Michael Manley could discover that the burdens of the past are too many for his party to cast off and that little black Jamaica is too poor even to afford a social revolution ... '

February 14: Tourist Board reports massive visitor cancellations.

February 15: JLP Deputy Leader Pearnel Charles tells meeting: 'Cubans versed in espionage are infiltrating the Jamaican society.' Totally baseless.

February 17: Terrorist gunmen set up ambush in the Olympic Gardens area, 7 people are shot.

February 22-23: Weekend violence results in 5 killed and 8 wounded. 3 are shot by gunmen who attack a youth club dance in Duhaney Park. The following weekend another dance at Barbican is attacked and 2 more youths killed.

February 28-29: Weekend violence in Olympic Gardens, and violence also hits Central Village in St. Catherine.

March 11: The island's leading business organisations set up a united front in the form of the Private Sector Organisation of Jamaica — PSOJ. Two trends were to emerge in the organisation, one which sought to defend the free enterprise system in Jamaica and portray it in a favourable light to the public; and another, which sought to use the organisation as an instrument to defeat the PNP government. Carlton Alexander, its president, is a patriotic businessman and represents the first trend. He attempts to keep the organisation on a non-partisan footing. But he would be outnumbered by the trend represented by Winston Mahfood of the JMA, who is rabidly anti-government, and the two executive directors who serve the organisation in the next few years, Anthony Abrahams and Anthony Johnson. Both would become ministers when the JLP came to power.

March 11: Seaga is forced to warn his constituents, after they mob a party of policemen, hurling bottles, stones and other missiles at them as they try to recover a car in which gunmen had been travelling.

March 17: New York Times, James Reston writes: 'Fidel Castro's Cuban government according to high officials of the Ford administration has entered into an agreement to train the police forces of Jamaica, and is also increasing its political contacts with black power elements.' Totally false.

March 27: Christian Science Monitor, Benjamin Wells writes: 'Mr. Manley's decision to send his personal police squad to be trained by Cubans is disturbing, not only to highly placed Jamaicans but to US and other Hemispheric officials. They regard it as another muted, ominous step in Fidel Castro's growing influence, not only with Mr. Manley, but with the extreme Marxist and black power elements that are surrounding Mr. Manley.'

The facts are that Jamaican security forces are often trained in the United Kingdom and Canada. A small number of the Prime Minister's security group are offered a short specialised course in Cuba. The course deals specifically with keeping a VIP alive, a field in which the Cubans have unrivalled experience. The offer is accepted and 8 are trained.

April 4: Leading businessman Oliver Clarke becomes Managing Director of the *Gleaner*. A month later he would be elected to the executive of the Inter-American Press Association — IAPA — whose connections with the CIA had become public knowledge since 1963. The Board of IAPA includes four executives from the notorious Chilean newspaper *El Mercurio* — Augustin Edwards, Herman Cubillos, Rene Silva Espejo and Fernando Leniz. Cubillos has since served as Foreign Minister of the Chilean Junta.

April 5: The Aircraft Owners and Pilots Association, based in Washington, writes to its members to 'stay away from Jamaica until it is clear that we are welcome, and will not be abused by your Bureaucracy'. This letter was written in the wake of an article by Ralph Blumenthal of the *New York Times* News Service entitled 'Caribbean Challenge' published by the *Gleaner* 1 April.

April 11:   Miami Herald ... 'They (Jamaicans) fear that Michael Manley is leading Jamaica towards Castro-style socialism ... '

April 16: Violence continues, 2 killed and 5 injured in the Corporate Area.

April 21: More violence, 3 dead, and 5 injured.

April 22: 4 more killed — curfew in Olympic Gardens.

May 9: Prime Minister Manley holds top level meeting at Jamaica House with the heads of the army, police and the National Security Minister, to discuss new approaches to the continuing violence. The meeting results in a decision to establish a Joint Police/Military Command Centre, which brings together the intelligence units of both wings of the security forces.

May 11: Health Minister Ken McNeill advises the Medical Council of Jamaica that under the Cuba-Jamaica Co-operation Agreement, 15 Cuban doctors are to arrive in Jamaica to assist the country's health care system. Although the island's medical services are badly in need of medical personnel, the proposal and, in time, the doctors when they arrive, become the target of sustained abuse from the JLP, the *Daily Gleaner* and right-wing elements in the medical profession. But time and popular response are to prove the yeoman service and value of these doctors to the Jamaican health care system, a service which the JLP unashamedly retains when it finally secures State power in 1980.

May 19: The wave of violence takes an unprecedented and dastardly turn as terrorists set fire to a tenement block in Central Kingston killing 11 people, most of them children, and leaving some 500 homeless.

May 22:   The Toronto Globe, Earl Copeland writes: 'Like Castro, he (Manley), has so far used his knowledge of economics to destroy the existing system. The next step is to put the new system in place ... elections are scheduled for 1977, if the winds of protest do not reach hurricane force before then.'

June 1: Violence flares in Spanish Town leaving 3 dead.

June 5-6: Weekend of violence, 2 killed, 5 wounded in the City's west end necessitating a 24-hour curfew.
     Discovery of a small hospital used by terrorists in Tivoli Gardens, the constituency of the leader of the opposition.

Security forces confirm the existence of 2 prison cells used by terrorists in Rema, opposition stronghold. The cells are discovered after 2 citizens are abducted, beaten and held captive for 9 hours. They manage to escape and report the incident to the police.

June 7:   Women's Crisis Centre, recently formed by reactionary middle class women, stage walk for peace dressed in black carrying a symbolic coffin. Again note the parallel with the activities of reactionary middle class women in Chile.

June 7:   Dudley Thompson, Minister of Foreign Affairs, while attending the Sixth General Assembly of the Organisation of American States held in Chile, complains to Kissinger about 'suspicious harmony of hostility emanating from various sections of the US Press'.

June 7:   2 more people shot dead in the Corporate Area.

June 10:   Manley and his three regional counterparts, Forbes Burnham, Errol Barrow and Eric Williams, meet in Port-of-Spain, Trinidad. They discuss charges of destabilisation of Jamaica, Guyana and Barbados and affirm that the paramount objective of Caribbean policy was the stabilisation of the region. Particular note was taken of the critical economic problems facing Jamaica. This resulted in a joint loan of $80 million to Jamaica by the three CARICOM partners.

June 15:   For the first time in Jamaica's history, a foreign diplomat, Peruvian Ambassador, Fernando Rodriques is brutally stabbed to death ushering in yet another dimension in terrorist violence.

June 18:   Herb Rose, political organiser of the JLP, resigns and states: 'From my inner knowledge of the JLP I am now satisfied that its whole strategy is based upon violence, and the use of violence as a means of obtaining victory at the polls.' He reveals a plan by the JLP for increased terrorist violence which specifically implicates the Deputy Leader of the JLP, Pearnel Charles.
   Police find arms cache in Trench Town clock tower area. The find includes a submachine gun stolen from the Army Headquarters, 5 revolvers, 431 rounds of ammunition, 1 detonator, cleaning equipment for firearms and 2 walkie-talkies.

June 19:   In the face of escalating violence and intelligence reports Prime Minister Manley acts on the recommendation of the security forces and declares a State of Emergency, the second in the history of the country. In the first week, 13 people are detained, including the

Deputy Leader of the JLP, Pearnel Charles, 2 other JLP candidates — ex-army officer Peter Whittingham and Ferdie Yap Sam — and a PNP candidate Edwin Singh.

June 29: Reporting to parliament the following week, Manley discloses the discovery of a document which speaks of a conspiracy code-named 'Operation Werewolf', written by the same Peter Whittingham and aimed at overthrowing the Government. One of the documents discovered, headed 'St. Ann Area', lists 22 trained men, 100 submachine guns, 2 barrels of gunpowder and 50,000 anti-government pamphlets. The documents are in Whittingham's own handwriting. Manley also advises that tapes of police and military radio transmissions were found in Charles' possession, and further discloses the find of 257 sticks of dynamite and 25 rolls of fuse wire near the western capital, Montego Bay.

July 2: John Hearne returns as a *Gleaner* columnist. Hearne is joined on November 8 by Wilmot Perkins who along with David Da Costa and a collection of pseudonyms and 'letters to the editor' constitute a formidable team in the unwavering and orchestrated media campaign directed against the PNP and its leadership over the next 4 years. Hearne would eventually take open credit for their 'adversary' journalistic role in the eventual defeat of the PNP in 1980.

July 3: 4 are killed and 6 injured, 3 killed by the police. And 2 bombs explode in the Olympic Gardens area.

July 4: The Bar Association of Jamaica supports the State of Emergency.

July 6: Explosion at Alcoa results in millions of dollars of damage, closure of the plant, and 11 workers being injured.

July 9: P.J. Patterson announces that within the first 2 days of the Emergency there were 125 tourist cancellations.
   A bomb placed in a suitcase to be loaded on a Cubana aircraft explodes at Norman Manley Airport. 3 months later a bomb explodes on a Cubana aircraft off the coast of Barbados killing 73 people. Cuban exiles claim responsibility for the bombing.

July 14: State of Emergency extended by parliament for a further 100 days. The JLP opposition declines to vote. An opinion poll finds over 80% of population in favour of the State of Emergency.

July 16: Finance Minister David Coore indicates to the US travel industry media, 'There's enough indication that violence is foreign assisted.'

July 17: Daily Express, Paul Dacre writing on the State of Emergency states: 'This has resulted in virtual press censorship, and many of Mr. Manley's political opponents are jailed without trial.' Demonstrably false.

July 18: Statistics show marked decrease in crime: between May 19 and June 18 — 385 cases of violent crimes, including 69 shootings; and between June 18 and July 18 — 198 cases of violent crimes including 33 shootings.

July 24: Gleaner publishes US *News and World Report* article, 'Jamaica's Prime Minister Manley has moved closer to communist Cuba.'

August 19: The security forces report a sharp, almost 50% decrease in the crime rate in the first 2 months under the State of Emergency. After 2 months a total of 173 people have been detained. 9 are released.

August 23: The JLP refuses to field candidates for the Parish Council by-elections for Islington, St. Mary, and Bensonton, St. Ann. Seaga scoffs at the election saying the people want general elections to decide the future of the country and he demands that Manley call elections.

August 24: The *Gleaner* reprints an article published in Manchester, England, on August 6 stating: 'Increasing numbers of Cubans are arriving in Jamaica to help the left-wing government ... and are arousing concern from the opposition and middle class residents ... It is not clear how many Cubans are in Jamaica. The American magazine *Newsweek* puts the figure at 300, but unconfirmed reports in Kingston say 3,000 or more.' There were never more than 500 Cubans in Jamaica of which some 400 were construction workers on the school building programme and a maximum of 30 doctors and dentists in the medical programme. All were in Jamaica as a result of formal and public government to government agreements.

September 9: Saul Landau, American writer and film-maker, writes in the *Washington Post* of August 25 republished in the *Gleaner,* 'I returned from a 5-week stay in Jamaica with the sinking feeling that our government, or a part of it, may be intervening in Jamaican affairs as it did in Chile.'

September 12: Former CIA agent Philip Agee, on a 2-week visit to Jamaica, speaks on the work of the CIA station here and names 12 CIA operatives.

October 1: The first indication of organised anti-Jamaican activities surfaces in the United States. One Anthony McKenzie organises an anti-Jamaican meeting in Chicago to coincide with an official visit to the State by Jamaican Ambassador Alfred Rattray. McKenzie was later to form the Jamaican International Anti-Communist Movement, which gave way to the formation of the Friends for a Free Jamaica, headed by officials of the American Conservative Union, the Council for Inter-American Security and the American Council for World Freedom.

The anti-Jamaican campaign in the US escalates with a series of anti-Jamaica broadcasts by one M. Stanton-Evans, on the CBS programme *Spectrum* which is widely syndicated and also carried by the American Armed Forces Radio Services.

October 19: Marketing Minister Vivian Blake reports to parliament that a shipment of 168 tons of rice has had to be destroyed as it is found contaminated with the deadly poison parathion which claimed 20 lives at the start of the year. The rice came here from Costa Rica on board the ship City of Bochum and in the company of a shipment of parathion apparently destined for another port.

October 15: The report of the Inter-American Press Association on Press Freedom states: 'Despite the existence of a State of Emergency, declared in June this year, which conferred special powers to the security forces, the latter have not abused the powers and freedom of the press is not currently threatened'.

November 1: 10 people are shot and a building complex set ablaze during a JLP motorcade in York Town. JLP supporters on foot and in a large convoy of cars proceed to a rally in the vicinity of the PNP constituency office. An advance party led by JLP candidate Mike Henry arrives at the PNP office and starts ripping posters from the walls. PNP supporters attempt to stop them and in the fracas that follows Rowan Skyers, campaign manager of PNP candidate Hugh Small, is shot and seriously wounded. Henry is also shot in the incident. By the time the cars bearing Seaga and Shearer arrive, the skirmish is over. However, a Reuter-CANA dispatch filed by English stringer Winsome Lang, and reprinted in London and the United States, states, Opposition Leader Edward Seaga and former Prime Minister Hugh Shearer were attacked and 'narrowly' escaped death when gunmen from Small's campaign headquarters fired on their motorcade injuring 10 people. The report goes on to state that

Seaga was in a state of shock and required sedation. Lang later claimed that her story was changed at the cable office in Barbados through which the story is filed.

November 21: In spite of the violence, hysteria and the written and verbal battering the PNP has met with up to this point, the party is able to stage what is so far the largest political gathering in the history of Jamaica: 140,000 turn out to Sam Sharpe Square, Montego Bay, where Manley announces that the election will take place on December 15. The massive show of popular support leaves the government's critics dumbfounded.

December 1: At a PNP meeting in Old Harbour, Party Secretary D.K. Duncan is punched down by Army Officer Donald Grant of the Third Jamaica Regiment. Prime Minister Manley arrives on the scene and attempts to question Grant who walks away. Manley is immediately surrounded by a group of soldiers who point their rifles at him. He walks through them and they back down.

December 3: Reggae superstar Bob Marley and his manager Don Taylor are shot at Marley's home as they rehearse for a benefit concert at National Heroes Park sponsored jointly by the Office of the Prime Minister and Marley's organisation.

December 13: PNP candidate Ferdie Neita is shot by gunmen and critically wounded. He survives only after a 3-hour operation.
JDF helicopter taking Manley from Port Maria, St. Mary, to Bogwalk, St. Catherine, gets out of control. Chief pilot loses control but co-pilot Lt. Darby grabs controls, puts helicopter in dive and is able to pull it out a few feet above ground. It is stated afterwards that the chief pilot developed vertigo.

December 15: Election Day. PNP sweeps the polls taking 47 of the 60 seats.

The sequence of events outlined above establishes a pattern of disruption new to Jamaica and a level of terrorist violence and murder unprecedented in Jamaica's history. After 1976 indiscriminate terrorist violence seems to yield to more direct sabotage of national economy until the announcement of the general elections, when a new wave of terrorist violence claims the lives of some 750 people.

Does all this amount to destabilisation? There have been no Senate Committee hearings into the case of Jamaica and consequently no disclosures at that level. We do know that when the news of the PNP's defeat in the elections of 1980 reached Washington champagne corks popped. The hawks were celebrating.

NOTES

CHAPTER 1

1. N.W. Manley: Valedictory Address to PNP Annual Conference, 1969. Reproduced in R. Nettleford, *Manley & The New Jamaica*, Longman Caribbean, 1971, pp 368-384.
2. *cf* C.L.R. James, *The Black Jacobins*, Vintage Books, New York, 1963.
3. R. Nettleford, *Manley & The New Jamaica*, especially pp xi-xiii.
4. Sir John Mordecai, *The West Indies: Federal Negotiations*, George Allen & Unwin, London, 1968.
5. For a contemporary analysis of Bustamante's life and politics, see George E. Eaton, *Alexander Bustamante and Modern Jamaica*, Kingston Publishers Limited, 1975.
6. N.W. Manley, *op. cit.*
7. Whatever their initial political perspectives the political leaders of Commonwealth Africa and the Caribbean unfailingly came to see constitutional decolonisation as quite a separate process from economic decolonisation. See R.J. Barret & R.E. Muller, *Global Reach! The Power of the M.N.Cs*, Touchstone, New York, 1974; Pierre Jalee, *The Pillage of the Third World*, Modern Reader, London, 1968; also Charles K. Wilber (Ed), *The Political Economy of Development and Underdevelopment*, Random House, New York, 1973.
8. Edward Boorstein, *Allende's Chile*, International Publishers, New York, 1977.
9. See also Hugh Thomas, *Cuba: Or the Pursuit of Freedom*, Eyre & Spottiswoode, London, 1971.
10. See Orlando Patterson, *The Sociology of Slavery*, Fairleigh Dickinson University Press, Rutherford N.J., 1969; also Richard Hart, *Slaves who Abolished Slavery* (Vol. 1), Institute of Social & Economic Research, UWI, 1980.

CHAPTER 2

1. For a biographical profile of the Jamaican National Heroes, see A.P.I. Publications, Kingston, September 1969.
2. *Slaves Who Abolished Slavery* & A.P.I., *op.cit.*
3. See A.P.I. Publications, *op.cit.*
4. For an unorthodox view of this aspect of colonial constitutionalism see Trevor Monroe, *The Politics of Constitutional Decolonization: Jamaica 1944-62*, ISER, UWI, 1972, especially Chap. 1.
5. The life and work of Marcus Garvey has become one of the most researched topics especially by the international Black intelligentsia. The core of his ideas is embodied in such works as E. David Cronon, *Marcus Garvey*, University of Wisconsin Press, 1972; also Amy Jacques Garvey, *Garvey & Garveyism* Collier Books, London, 1968.
6. George Eaton, *Alexander Bustamante and Modern Jamaica*, Kingston Publishers Limited, Kingston, 1975.
7. Ann Spackman, *Constitutional Development of the West Indies*, Caribbean University Press, Essex, 1975.
8. Sir John Mordecai, *The West Indies: The Federal Negotiations*, Allen & Unwin, London, 1968.

CHAPTER 3

1. See for example Lord Moyne, *West India Royal Commission (1938-39) Reports, Recommendations and Statement of Action Taken*, HM Stationery Office, London, Card 6607, 1945.
2. Owen Jefferson, *The Post-War Economic Development of Jamaica*, Institute of Social & Economic Research, UWI, 1971; Norman Girvan, *Foreign Capital and Economic Underdevelopment in Jamaica*, ISER, UWI, 1971.
   W. Arthur Lewis, 'Jamaica's Economic Problems' a series of articles in *The Daily Gleaner*, Kingston, 1964.
3. W. Arthur Lewis, *op. cit.*
4. See Hugh Thomas, *Cuba: Or the Pursuit of Freedom*, Eyre & Spottiswoode, London, 1971, especially Chap. 9; Ramon E. Ruiz, *The Making of a Revolution*, W.W. Norton & Co., New York, 1968, Chap. 4.
5. See Hugh Thomas, *op. cit.*
6. Owen Jefferson, *op. cit.*
7. See *Economic & Social Survey of Jamaica: 1960-80*, Dept. of Statistics, Jamaica. Also *Year Book of Jamaica, 1960-80*, Dept. of Statistics, Kingston.
8. Dept of Statistics — *op. cit.*
9. Dept of Statistics — *op. cit.*

10. Terry Lacey, *Violence & Politics in Jamaica, 1960-70,* Manchester University Press, 1977.
(a) The 'Chinese Riots' as this affair came to be known involved an industrial dispute between a Chinese employer and a female worker which was to spark rioting targeted at persons of light complexion.
(b) In this case Dr. Rodney, a UWI Professor and a consistent critic of the JLP regime and its 'development' policy, was banned from returning to Jamaica having left for a visit abroad. UWI students demonstrated on campus and then on the streets of downtown Kingston. Students were joined by a vast army of unemployed youths and adults in a spontaneous confrontation with the authorities.
11. These basic analytical and descriptive points are well documented in a rich post-revolutionary literature by social scientists, journalists and historians. A direct source is Fidel Castro, *Speech to First Congress of the Cuban Communist Party,* Grove Press, New York, 1969.
12. M. Kenner & J.Petras, *Fidel Castro Speaks,* Allan Lane/Penguin Press, London.

CHAPTER 4

1. M. Manley, *The Politics of Change,* André Deutsch, London, 1974, especially p 102.
2. For a discussion of conditions under which workers offered their labour power, see *A Voice at the Work Place,* André Deutsch, London, 1975.
3. For a discussion of tax measures, see The Jamaica Information Service publication *The Budget 1973-74,* pp 9-13.
4. For an appreciation of some of the specific circumstances and conditions leading up to the formation of CBM and WF in 1964, see *Voice at the Work Place,* Chap. 6.
5. The International Bauxite Association was established in Conakry, Guinea, in 1974, see *Voice at the Work Place,* Chap. 6.
6. Rex Nettleford, *Manley and the New Jamaica,* Longman Caribbean, 1971, especially pp 59-98; also *Budget Speeches to Parliament 1973-80.*

CHAPTER 5

1. A. W. Singham (Ed), *The Non-Aligned Movement in World Politics,* Lawrence Hill & Co, Connecticut, 1977, presents sequence of the movement in terms of membership, philosophy and the conduct and refinement of policy position in a changing international context.

2. On the basis of extensive research undertaken in preparation for my Budget Speech to parliament in 1980, I was struck by this growing 'gap' and reported, in part, that: 'In 1970, 21 tons of sugar ... could buy a seventy-five horse power Ford model tractor; by 1979 it took 59 tons of Jamaican exported sugar to bring the same tractor to Jamaica.'

3. *Assessment of the Progress Made in the Establishment of the New International Economic Order and Appropriate Action for the Promotion of the Development of Developing Countries and International Economic Co-operation,* United Nations General Assembly (document) A/S-11/5, August 7, 1980, page 27, paragraphs 60, 61.

4. In *The Politics of Change,* I began to sketch the outlines of a personal philosophy of the kind of structural change relevant to the Jamaican context.

5. See my *The Search for Solutions,* Maple House, 1976, especially pp 178-210; 'Third World Under Challenge', *Third World Quarterly,* Vol. 11, No. 1, January 1980, p 28.

6. ACP Group of countries embrace African, Pacific and Caribbean states that have had structured linkages and colonial relationships with Europe over many years. Specifically they negotiate commodity prices and other arrangements under the Lome Convention with the European Economic Community.

7. The 'Commonwealth' embraces Britain, the former Dominions of Canada, Australia and New Zealand and the former British ex-colonies scattered across Africa, Asia, Latin America and the Caribbean. South Africa, of course, is not now a member of this group.

8. A discussion of this and similar themes is reported in a three-volume collection of some of his most important speeches. See J. Nyerere, *Freedom and Development,* 1973; *Freedom and Unity,* 1967, and *Freedom and Socialism,* 1968, all published by the Oxford University Press, London.

9. See my *Voice at the Work Place,* and *Search for Solution ...* especially pp 211-270

10. For greater detail, see *PNP Principles and Objectives,* Kingston, 1979.

CHAPTER 6

1. *1972-1980: A Record of Achievement,* API, Kingston, 1981, p 13.

2. For an analysis of the sociology of colonial-type society, see M.G. Smith, *The Plural Society in the British West Indies,* University of California Press, Berkeley, 1965.

3. In the sphere of media consumption for instance, prime time on

certain Caribbean Television Networks in 1975 was dominated by programmes imported from the USA as follows:

Prime Time – Without News Programmes

Jamaica	82%	Imported
St. Kitts-Nevis	100%	"
Barbados	97%	"
Trinidad & Tobago	81%	"

Source: *Caribbean Quarterly* Vol. 22, No. 4, December, 1976. There has been no significant change in Caribbean television programming since these findings.

CHAPTER 7

1. The ACP-EEC Convention of Lome and related documents, signed February, 1975, has been published by the Secretariat-General, Council of European Communities, 1975.
2. For text of my Algerian Speech, see Michael Manley, *The Search for Solutions,* Maple House Publishing Co., Canada, 1976, pp 202-204.
3. See Richard Gibson, *African Liberation Movements,* Oxford University Press, 1972, especially Part 5. Gibson's treatment of the Angolan struggle is admittedly somewhat uneven.
4. R. Gibson, *op. cit.*
5. See also footnote 4, Chap. 12.

CHAPTER 8

1. *The Book* as this 67-page document is popularly referred to in Party circles deals with: The Party and its fundamental tasks: ideological policy, including a discussion of classes in Jamaican society; economic policy — goals, objectives, the mixed economy, the state sector, co-operatives, private enterprises; social policy — education, mass media, women, the family, etc.; international policy — anti-imperialism, support for National Liberation Movements, the NIEO etc., and a comprehensive glossary defining terms like: class, capitalism, colonialism, communism, democracy, fascism, imperialism, democratic socialism, social democracy, social control.

CHAPTER 9

1. In virtually every major speech concerning the national economy that I made since 1974, I have both implicitly and explicitly articulated such assurances. See, for instance, my Budget Speeches to Parliament 1973, 1974, and 1975. Also, as pointed out previously, Vivian Blake, William Isaacs and Danny Williams, all persons with good business sector

credentials, were appointed to the Industry Ministry. There were other notable business sector appointments to other ministries. For example, Eli Matalon was appointed to the Ministry of National Security.
2. See appendix.
3. In addition to the references provided in the appendix which demonstrate clear CIA involvement in Chile, the reader is invited to read *The International Telephone and Telegraph Company & Chile, 1970-71,* Report to the Committee on Foreign Relations, United States Senate, by the Subcommittee on Multinational Corporations, June 21, 1973. Printed for the use of the Committee on Foreign Relations, US Government Printing Office.
4. The overwhelming popularity of the State of Emergency is borne out by a poll conducted by Carl Stone a couple of weeks after the announcement was made. When respondents were asked whether they supported the continuation of the State of Emergency the responses were as follows:
    Support for Continuation
    Corporate Area   81%
    Parish Towns   83%
    Rural Villages   76%
    These figures as well as a general discussion of the 1976 elections can be found in Carl Stone, The 1976 Parliamentary Election in Jamaica in the Journal of Commonwealth and Comparative Politics, November 1977, p. 261.
5. The following table sets out the comparative crime statistics for Jamaica for the period 1968-1977. As will be seen incidence of murder increased dramatically in the 1976 period.
    CRIMES OF VIOLENCE

	All Reported	% Change	Murders	% Change
1968/1969	9,981	(Base Year)	153	(Base Year)
1969/1970	5,713	- 42.7	152	- 0.6
1970/1971	4,373	- 56.2	126	- 17.6
1971/1972	11,093	+ 11.1	145	- 5.2
1972/1973	11,774	+ 17.9	188	+ 22.8
1973/1974	15,869	+ 58.9	232	+ 55.6
1974/1975	12,949	+ 29.7	207	+ 35.3
1975/1976	12,867	+ 29.7	291 (up to March)	+ 90.2
1976/1977	15,470	+ 55.0	388 (up to March)	+ 153.6

Source: *Yearbook of Jamaica,* Department of Statistics.

CHAPTER 10

1. See Carl Stone: 'The 1976 Parliamentary Elections in Jamaica' in *The Journal of Commonwealth and Comparative Politics,* November 1977.
2. In fact the PNP victory was hailed by Edward Seaga. His statement was carried on the front page of the *Daily Gleaner* of December 16, 1976. He said, 'I think the PNP scored a very clear and decisive victory ... in my long period of political campaigning I have never seen the people of Jamaica react so much to a government in power. The people have supported one Party over another and have selected one ideology over the other.'

CHAPTER 11

1. For a discussion on the general question of the sugar industry in Jamaica see my *A Voice at the Work Place.*
2. For example, see Harry Taylor, 'It'll take more than the fund to solve the LDC's problem', *Euromoney,* May 1977; Jim Morell, 'Behind the scenes at the IMF', in *The Nation,* Center for International Policy, Washington D.C., September 16, 1978; and Payer's work, *The Debt Trap,* Monthly Review Press, N.Y. and London, 1974.
3. For another treatment of this failure see Girvan *et. al.,* IMF and the Third World: The Case of Jamaica, 1974-80', pp 119-127, *Development Dialogue,* no. 2, 1980.

CHAPTER 12

1. This increasing 'dominance' is also reflected in the voting statistics. The JLP vote which was 49.6% in 1959 moved to 51.5% in 1962, 79.2% in 1972, 77.7% in 1976 and 94.2% in 1980. In 1976 the Chief Electoral Officer even found it necessary in his report on that election to point out that this was one of three constituencies in the country where 'a very high percentage of over-voting took place'.
2. This is borne out by the *Report of the Director of Elections, General Elections, 1980.* The director of elections, Noel Lee, reporting to the independent Electoral Committee, identifies problems of: training of electoral personnel, violence, late opening of polling stations, stealing of ballot boxes, tampering with ballot papers after polls were closed and over-voting as problems which affected the 1980 election. Despite the problems we do not question the basic legitimacy of the 1980 election.

3. To the extent that any election in Jamaica may have been *decisively* affected by fraud it would be the 1967 election which was won by the JLP. Despite flagrant violations of principle the JLP only won the election narrowly — 50.7% to 49.3% for the PNP.

    A dual system of voter registration was instituted for this election. This meant that persons in urban areas had to subject themselves to a different process of registration (including being photographed at a registration centre) from rural voters. The idea of dual standards for registration was wrong in principle, but if it had been fairly implemented no real harm would have been done. In fact, the system was viciously manipulated. Thousands of photographs were 'spoilt' and thousands of prospective voters could not even locate the (mobile) registration centres to have themselves photographed. In addition, many who went through the tedious process found that their names just simply failed to appear on the voters' list.

    This was a feature right across the country. It is estimated that about 250,000 voters were disenfranchised. Needless to say, the bulk of the disenfranchisement was to be found in our strong areas.

    We went to court. In the now famous case, Gladys Harrison *vs* Regina, the courts held that this supporter of ours was illegally and unconstitutionally disenfranchised.

    The election could not have been overturned at that stage but the decision gave us some useful ammunition.

    In the case of the 1972 election, the JLP Government had so seriously gerrymandered the constituency boundaries that we needed a minimum of 53% of the vote to be able to win. In addition, they attempted to offset our massive lead among youth voters by holding elections on lists so outdated that very few young voters could exercise their franchise. Very few persons, if any at all, voted in the 1972 elections who were younger than 25 years! Despite all this the PNP polled 56% of the vote.

4. For example, Edward Seaga during an interview in Florida (October 26, 1979) was quoted as follows: '... by virtue of the very close relationship that exists between the Manley Government and the Cuban regime ... Cubans ... go through Immigration and Customs without the normal arrangements ... there is a flow of 5,000 Cubans ...'

    'Manley, however, has used the State of Emergency in the past to take the same powers that Fidel Castro has in Cuba'.

    Columnist Georgie Ann Geyer, *The Advocate* (Chicago), Friday, May 23, 1980: 'Edward Seaga ... head of the Jamaican Opposition has one recurrent nightmare. He fears ..., that people within the *Marxist* (italics mine) government of Prime Minister Manley are going ... to stop the desperately needed elections of this year.' Later in the article she continued: 'Many, indeed, believe Manley ran the country down to get rid of the entire middle class and start from nothing, a last Caribbean Khmer Rouge ... '

The *Reporter Dispatch*, White Plains, N.Y., June 5, 1980, reports Winston Spaulding current Minister of National Security as follows: 'He charged Manley with secretly promising Libya to set up a 'PLO-type base' in Jamaica in exchange for a loan of $150 million. There is an 'obvious conspiracy between the international Communist Movement and the PNP, Manley's People's National Party, he charged.'

5. The following data indicate some of the factors, sometimes completely out of our control, sometimes errors in calculation by both the IMF and ourselves, which led us to believe that the IMF may have looked favourably on a waiver. The Net International Reserves of the Bank of Jamaica test had been 'failed' by US$130 million.

The Table below indicates why.

NET INTERNATIONAL RESERVES OF BANK OF JAMAICA

FACTORS AFFECTING PERFORMANCE	AMOUNTS BY WHICH PROJECTIONS WERE MISSED IN US $ MILLION
A) Increase in the oil bill (OPEC-related)	- 33
B) Increased foreign debt payment due to higher international interest rates and additional amortisation	- 31
C) It was not possible to draw down resources from the Export Development Fund and as such the transfer of payments from the cash budget to the Export Development Fund did not take place	- 25
D) Higher international inflation and interest rates led to increased payments for imports on licences which were issued for payment in 1979. The programme assumed international rates of inflation of 8.5% but the actual rate for 1979 was around 14.5%. The increases in international interest rates were of the same magnitude.	18

FACTORS AFFECTING PERFORMANCE	AMOUNTS BY WHICH PROJECTIONS WERE MISSED IN US $ MILLION
E) Underestimation of 1978 payments overhang. The programme estimate was US$80 M. The actual amount was around US$110 M.	- 30
F) Decline in export earnings as a result of floods	- 20
TOTAL SHORTFALL	- 157
LESS improved tourist earnings	+ 10
	- 147
G) Adjustment factor	+ 17
FINANCING	- 130

FINANCING

A) Running down of reserves	- 53
B) Compensatory financing and buffer stock facilities	- 42
C) Arrears	- 52
	- 147
D) Adjustment factor	+ 17
	-130

CHAPTER 14

1. Seaga's charge in Parliament that I had warned the Party privately that rejecting the IMF was suicidal and would lead to collapse of the economy was devastating. The allegation was made in a bold and convincing manner. Frankly, some of the words and phrases he used were familiar. They were based on a 'pirated' tape of the NEC proceedings. Luckily an official one existed.

    Our homework done, I reported our findings to Parliament when my turn in the Budget Debate came. The following are extracts from that section of my presentation:

    The Leader of the Opposition, for instance, boasted of the fact that he was able to get a tape recording of a meeting ... Let me be lavish in my praise of his skills in the organisation of espionage ... that he would quote it honestly ... is ... perhaps a naive assumption ... it put words into my mouth that are tantamount to a prophecy, that decisions could only lead to collapse ...

He picks up a few words at the $11\frac{1}{2}$ minute of the speech, like say three words; he then skips like say two minutes of the speech, and he picks up a single word like at the 13th minute and he puts it together as if it were a single sentence ... there is another period where 3 minutes and 6 seconds of the speech are contracted, words changed to alter meaning.'

Voice: Oh dear! ...

'There is the brilliant feat that the final words ... about economic and political suicide are pulled from the 67th minute of the speech, the context is removed, they are tied to something said more than half an hour before to create a continuous sentence ...

... I congratulate the Leader of the Opposition for feeling that the nation's business demands that he spends the hours that must have been spent in picking out single words that truly were in my voice, single sentences that truly were in my voice, lifting out whole passages that explained what the sentence meant, to create a manufactured lie!'

Voices: Shame! Shame!

Some *Gleaner* columnists tied themselves into knots trying to argue away Seaga's shame. From the majority there was deafening silence. Seaga's own silence was the most revealing.

INDEX